Speedy, a data transfer system

A SQL exercise

Stefan Ardeleanu

Stefan Ardeleanu

**The joy comes from the code,
not the word ...
in the world of programmers!**

Table of Contents

1 Introduction

Another SQL book?

Here is another SQL book! Probably this would be the reaction of any common sense reader, seeing the topic addressed. Indeed, no one can deny that this subject of querying relational databases is widespread and is much-analyzed on all sides. However, I dare to hope that the widely used query language, the famous SQL, is still of interest. If we take a quick look at the IT market and notice so much SQL code, it would be enough to give a chance to a new book! So let's see some reasons for a new book of SQL.

Consequently, there are specific themes that the reader can execute if he/she wishes. I consider my book as an opening if we consider a game of chess. The reader can continue the game, i.e., the proposed exercise, and has the power to complete and improve what I describe further here. I want this exercise to offer the reader, no matter what category he/she belongs to, both the pleasure of using SQL and the understanding of the power of this language so old but still so current.

Are we facing a new SQL?

The main thing anyone can say when they see this book entry is: "Another SQL book? Come on, don't think it's too much! What else would you be able to say about SQL? Isn't SQL the same for a very long time, almost fifty years?"

I don't want to promise a **new SQL**, that's for sure! On the contrary, there have been many attempts to replace SQL with something else in these fifty years, for different reasons, most of them somehow subjective, as I would see it. For instance, decades ago, as object-oriented programming grew and became more popular, there were countless dreams and hopes of object-oriented theorists to find an object-oriented database to replace the traditional relational database. Consequently, these specialists hoped to substitute SQL, as some programmers consider it a primitive language.

Don't get me wrong! I have so much respect for object-oriented programming! I love logic, and I have my vision in a way justified by my various points of interest. I admire and respect object-oriented programming, and for sure, this is an excellent approximation of reality. It is amazing! The concept of class, object, entity, etc. These are unique concepts coming from the history of logic and

6

philosophy. They inherit a venerable tradition of thousands of years, and they brought a real revolution in programming. However, like any discovery in the world, it has a limited area. Although humanity has always hoped for this, it has not yet reached that panacea that would cover absolutely anything!

With these trivial rows and columns, the relational database model and that natural, direct SQL language have proven to be a hard-to-break nut even for object-oriented programming. Despite the theorists' dreams of creating that object-oriented database to replace the traditional relational database, surprise! Here, the relational database has resisted heroically and is still present on the world's IT scene, more vital than ever!

NoSQL showed up later, and a few people thought it was the new SQL. A part of the world of application developers has been so eager to find this miracle that will make their lives easier! For some reason, the row and column paradigm and the SQL language are counter-intuitive and difficult to understand, despite their apparent simplicity. I recognized this strangeness when I taught several SQL courses to application programmers familiar with C # or Java. It was clear that they didn't like the row-column model and the SQL language! For them, another hope appears on the horizon of IT knowledge, the NoSQL database. Is this the new SQL? As a relief for them, here is a possible solution on the horizon of databases! Perhaps, finally, this column-line paradigm will be replaced by something more appropriate, closer to the application programming mindset. After some time, they realize that the two will learn to live together in peace and harmony, as separate and yet interconnected worlds. SQL and NoSQL indeed do the same thing: store data. However, here is a big disappointment, NoSQL is not a replacement for SQL - it is alternative and complementary.

Hence, I can't promise you a new SQL; it's the same old SQL you've known for such countless years! I cannot say that my book is a kind of revolution, and I invented a new SQL overnight, or I found some spectacular news in approaching this venerable language! I am not Gandalf, you know!

The old SQL: the past, the present. The future?

As someone who has been doing SQL for over twenty years, I am happy for SQL's resilience in the face of so many trials like the ones mentioned above. I think that the persistence and stability of this language prove, in fact, a unique quality! The area of relational databases, to which we can include the SQL language, has proven to be one of the most conservative IT world areas. This feature does not mean that this zone is static. On the contrary, there are continuous improvements from one version to another, any database system you may choose to analyze. Periodically, you will find new syntaxes and performance improvements. However, the basics are more or less unchanged.

Therefore, we continue to utilize the old SQL. All database systems, be they Oracle, SQL Server, PostgreSQL, MySQL, etc., are quite satisfied with SQL and do not seem to have change plans! They incorporate other things into their engines, other technologies maybe, but SQL remains the core. When it comes to storage and data systems, one of the primary sources remains the relational database, and SQL is like English, the universal language! What a coincidence, because SQL is perhaps the most English language at any point developed!

If it is still the old SQL, what else can be said? How could anyone be original with such venerable technology? Well, there is a challenge for one trying to say something about SQL! This test includes me too! Another good question is: do we need another book about the old SQL?

My answer is: why not? Of course, I do not hide my degree of subjectivity because I am an SQL developer. Thus, I have every interest in promoting my preferred technology! However, apart from the inherent subjectivity, I genuinely believe that there are objective reasons for even more information on this matter. First, the number of projects that require SQL is still very high, given that a large percentage of our data is still in relational databases. Secondly, most people doing software development are application programmers, like Java, C#, Python, etc. They are taking care of their job, and, in addition to other things, they handle the SQL code at whatever point essential. Sometimes there are just peanuts, simple things, depending on their software projects. However, suppose there is a large amount of data manipulation in relational databases, despite the facilities offered by platforms such as Visual Studio. In that case, SQL code's quality can be relatively low. Very often, our software products show performance issues in the back-end, the relational database layer. And these situations are not rare. From this point of view, an improvement in the SQL code's quality is necessary, even for the large mass of application developers using Java, Python, or anything else.

I am a (relational) database programmer, and I can find my projects and do mainly database development. I don't depend too much on anything else. I am mostly interested in data in the relational format. There are many projects in which this is the goal; keep playing with the surrounding data! I play with rows and columns and find my ways to handle them as better as I can! I fight for my projects, and I choose them carefully. I am a data programmer, so I do what I like. In a certain way, for me is simpler. I have some experience with application development technologies like Delphi or C#. In any case, I generally preferred the back-end and the relational database, so I spent significant time in them over the long run!

Again, many software engineers do many things simultaneously, Java with SQL or possibly Python or C # with SQL. For them, life is not such an extravagance; they can't keep away from SQL no matter if a lot of them might want nothing more than to avoid it. For example, let's take a web programmer! If the SQL part of his/her project is trivial, he/she does not even notice the SQL behind/inside. Nevertheless, if the complexity of data manipulation in a relational database reaches a certain level, things can become more difficult for them. Therefore, improving their SQL skills can be a reasonable goal for some developers and help them get better quality in what they deliver.

In any case, SQL isn't only the past, yet it keeps on being what's to come. I think a well-explained set of exercises can be valuable for many categories of people like application programmers, computer science students, eventually high school IT students, or only adults who want to convert from various other professions into programming. This language is a paradox, but it is a relatively simple language. Despite this, not too many software engineers write SQL optimal code.

I hope to bring something new in this book and describes a type of SQL- based system, like a relevant example. At this event, I need to show that occasionally one can assemble a total module utilizing this straightforward language, rather than essentially using all the other things, just because it would keep up with fashion!

Set-based approach - the desired SQL model

As maybe some of you may know, I published a book: "*Relational Database Programming.*" The ideas in this book came after long periods of SQL programming. Years of development accompanied by various reflections on my work led to this book's publication. The initial title of the book was "*Two styles of database development.*" In a way, the original name was more suggestive but still less effective in terms of marketing.

My past SQL book shows the importance of the **set-based approach** in database development. Over the years of work, especially after gaining enough relational database programming experience, I struggled with one thing, perhaps more than others: the lack of performance due to inappropriate programming style. I called this development style **atomic,** and I find this inefficient, similar to the development method specific to application programmers like Java or C #, etc. I will shortly review a bit.

Speedy, a data transfer system. A SQL Exercise

Surprisingly, but most developers are not necessarily intimately familiar with the relational model. Or maybe they are, but because of its apparent simplicity, they don't take it seriously. Rather, they do not fully understand the need for a specific programming methodology, which I call the *holistic* style by the opposition with atomic. This **holistic** is the *set-based* programming style.

Therefore, I think the original title was more suitable because it describes two different programming styles in a relational database. There is a clear contrast between the two. Most application developers, who come from Java or C #, write SQL code in a somewhat wrong and non-optimal way because they do not differentiate between the two modes. My objective was to clarify that some switching is required. The application developers should think in a different paradigm and write their code lines holistically when writing in the relational database. For example, classes are an excellent concept in OOP but are not suitable for a relational database; it has practically nothing to do with it.

Like many of us who work in software development, I spent time rewriting code snippets and continuing others' work. On this occasion, among other things, I had performance issues, such as excessive times for various executions or even blocking problems. It happens to many of us. These types of problems are not a secret but one of the ongoing challenges for programmers worldwide. Regarding the relational database, I realized after a few years of work that one reason for poor performance is the inappropriate development style. Developers tend to forget that they have to think in terms of datasets in a relational database. They need to think holistically and not atomically. As a result, they open cursors very easily, move data quickly to variables or structures of a particular type, and divide the work atomically.

In my previous book, I described many situations. I explained how one could do the same work in two ways, the atomic path, specific to application developers, and the holistic way, based on sets, specific to database developers. I imagined various exercises and offered dual solutions in both ways. Naturally and coherently, application developers ought to adjust their work in the relational database. They should do that if they want better performance and even improved readability. Apart from the database's health, the holistic style is simpler and readable if you compare the two approaches. I don't want to say it's easier to understand because it is relative to everyone's experience. I was surprised to talk to application developers who quickly understand code written in twenty lines with two cursors but have trouble understanding a simple SQL statement in five lines! It is easier for them to open a cursor, transfer one thousand columns or expressions from the cursor into some variables, manipulate those variables, etc., instead of driving a simple SQL statement that will handle the one thousand lines in one instance. Unbelievable but true, everything is relative to one's own work experience.

These considerations are relevant enough if the amount of data to be processed and the logic's complexity are not trivial. Of course, if you have a simple system that handles a bit of information and has a low degree of simplicity, the problems will not become visible. Performance issues will show up in more complex situations, not in trivial scenarios. But this is a well-known principle of performance in any software structure; problems arise as the complexity increases.

I have a good friend, Mark. He is a great programmer dealing a lot with customers, and he has a nice poster in his office. Later, I found out that the motto in the banner is quite famous. A funny guy, dressed very officially, looks at you with a bottle of beer next to him. You can see the statement at the top of the sign: "*I don't always test my code.*" Of course, being under the pressure of immediate results, we are often unable to test everything as we should. This reality is so every day in programming; there is no need to insist. At the bottom of the poster, you can see the sequel and hear what's funny: "*But when I do it, I do it in production.*"

I laughed with crocodile tears when I saw this famous remark. I remembered numerous days in my programming activity when I went to a customer site or another and discovered many things I couldn't find at the office. I learned so much from users that no business analyst could teach me! Contact with the production environment is so valuable for us programmers! Unfortunately, nowadays, there are so many layers involved! With such a vast infrastructure of positions, we rarely learn anything because users are no longer accessible. However, of course, no one should do testing in the production environment. This joke is famous and funny, but so true, even after so many years of experience!

Production will continue to remain a valuable test environment, whether we like it or not. The first meaning of the above saying is that, quite often, we cannot test everything using the dev, test, or QA environment, despite our desire to have perfect testing. Sometimes there are mysteries revealed only in production. Besides, in terms of performance, the production context is even more valuable. When we talk about database development, the real problems will often end up mainly due to the complexity of the production environment's data. The distinction between the two programming styles is much more visible using a complex environment, such as production. If there is little data, any logic is perfect, especially in database programming! You can open ten cursors and loop with immense pleasure; you can work in a relational database, being in Java or C #. You can even try to simulate some OOP models in a standard relational environment. There will be no performance issues at all! "*La Vie En Rose,*" as Edith Piaf would say!

Please analyze the last paragraphs partially seriously, but also jokingly. Of course, I do not promote testing in the production environment! However, having a domain with a complexity close to production is beneficial for any software developer. Especially for a database programmer! Possessing enough **quantity** and **variety** of data to test our code is critical for detecting the problems, mainly performance ones.

I consider this new book a continuation of the previous one, as I still plan to promote the set-based approach as much as I can. That does not mean this book will be a replica of my last one. Although given the importance of the topic in relational databases development, even an unlimited number of paperbacks would not be enough. Fortunately, more and more database specialists are promoting the set-based approach, big names in the industry. On the other hand, all database systems such as Oracle, SQL Server, etc., contain numerous features for the set-based approach. In my opinion, the only problem is that programmers should be aware of the need to use this holistic way when moving from their environment to the relational database.

The set-based methodology will continue to be present until the end of relational databases. They are closely related. Even in this book, in most of my exercises, I will always solve the problems holistically.

Now it is time to move on and continue my introduction with another opposition. Let's see what it's all about, with this new distinction! When speaking about differences and antagonisms, I can also see the complementarity. For example, during a convoluted logic, one can combine the holistic approach with the atomic style, simply because sometimes we cannot solve problems holistically entirely. Then, we have to compromise. The developer will create a mixed logic in such a case! Part of the process will be holistic and part of it atomic. Sometimes, this is the only option.

Programmer versus product specialist

Among other lessons, there is one we should learn to recognize: there is a place for each of us in the world! I want to say a few words about myself. I started programming in the 2000s, quite late, after the age of 30, and I was a little overwhelmed, at first, by the variety of languages, tools, and technologies. How difficult it must be now for young programmers, when the number of technologies has grown exponentially, it is hard to imagine! On the other hand, some of us see a single world, as I see my SQL world, while others deal with countless technologies and manage to accommodate them easier or harder. Every software engineer's destiny is unique throughout everyday life, even if we can establish similarities quite often, and there are specific patterns and standard highlights.

When I started my career a little late, at 32 more precisely, I liked the databases from the very beginning. My first projects were with SQL Server and Delphi. I remember how I devoured the SQL Server materials and books I found and the pleasure of SQL! It was love at first sight! After some years with various technologies, I decided to look mainly for database development projects, mostly SQL-related. Hence, I became an honorable SQL specialist and did my best to perform in this field!

Most of us, software engineers of all kinds, are practical persons and not scientists. Pushed by the ones who pay us, companies with their businesses, we need to solve problems and, in general, quickly. The difficulties in front of us are practical and humans, mostly economic, but not necessarily. We learn to use our technologies and apply them to the real world.

Alternatively, nowadays, the number of readers is declining everywhere. In the face of the video and social media attack, the book world is trying to resist heroically! In the world of IT, we may not be the most profound readers because we can quickly google and find the solution to almost any problem we try to solve. We don't have that much patience to read books from A to Z, even technical or maybe mostly technical. Programmers are no exception: reading activity has been in decline for many years, and this tragedy continues to grow unaffected by anything. At least that's how I think it's a tragedy, being a person who got used to the book since childhood!

As for the world of IT books, there are so many! And not just books, but documentation, specifications, forums, blogs, and so much information. It is a miracle if someone fails to find what they are looking for on the internet! Speaking of my favorite topics, such as the Oracle database, SQL Server, PostgreSQL, etc., new books appear every month, year.

What can I say? How dare I say that I am adding something new to this world invaded by information-related topics? Well, I'm a simple database programmer. However, I do have my vision. I don't pretend to be unique or invent wheels. I don't know if most of the books, but many of them are **product** books. These are books written by product specialists. I am not that kind of person!

To better understand, I want to give you an example of what I mean by this. I was at a SQL Server Saturday event and met a guy. He was a SQL Server specialist knowing so much about the product that I was amazed! He knew all that was new! Like a guru! He was also a trainer, an MVP; he had his presentations at the conference. Here he described some very interesting syntaxes of the Transact SQL language and at the same time showed some new features. After the demonstrations, we were on a coffee break and discussed one or the other, mainly SQL Server topics. Suddenly, while we were talking, he mentioned that he had never been a programmer!

Speedy, a data transfer system. A SQL Exercise

I was a bit shocked at first! Being naive and unaware of the distinction, I imagined that if someone presented such programming techniques in a specific language, one should have at least a few years of programming experience. This assumption proved to be false. I went home and reflected on the discussion and the meanings. I realized that product specialists, like my colleague in the conversation, may never know what programming is, like Transact SQL programming, let's say. Still, they know the features, see the product, do exercises, illustrate characteristics, etc. I realized the difference between a SQL Server **programmer**, as I am, and a SQL Server product specialist like him. Some are both! Many product specialists are coming from programming. Some not! In any case, the distinction exists, and it was interesting to become aware of it. Similar considerations apply to IT trainers. Some trainers are delivering some courses, like programming, for example. Some may have direct experience with the language, but others not. Many trainers are more like product trainers, and they play with tools and languages, learn features, etc.

To continue the parallelism, let's move on to books, especially IT books. Similarly, you can find product books or other types of books, for example. Let's think of prominent vendors like Oracle or Microsoft. Large computer products, such as Oracle or SQL Server database systems, regularly release new versions. These involve new syntaxes, various improvements of all kinds, new features, etc. As a result, a continuous series of product books describe these changes, which are very useful in the IT market. These are product books, and the focus is on explaining and, why not, promoting the technology or tool. And we need these publications, of course. They clarify the qualities of the products. We, the IT subject matter experts, either software engineers or whatever else like DBA, and so forth, should stay aware of the new highlights however much as could be expected. This book type is maybe the most common one in the IT market!

I would like to know everything! Lamentably, I have only 24 hours, and I need to rest as well. I have to stay with my children; I have to do some sports. I have always loved sports and secondly because I have to support myself. I stay at the computer for so many hours, so I have to compensate, and for me, the method is to practice regular sports. I love racquet sports, for example. So, like all of us, we must give priority. In conclusion, I can't know everything! Pretty simple!

Thus, I am a database programmer and not a product specialist. I try to keep up with the new techniques and characteristics as long as I need them in my projects, although I would like to dedicate more time and learn more about new features. But the priority is given to my projects and, if a particular detail is useful, I immediately make an effort to understand it and use it properly. I made these comparisons because I want to clarify from the beginning that this will be a book written by a database programmer and not by a database product specialist.

Hence, please do not expect to find features of one product or another, specific characteristics of Oracle or SQL Server, technologies that I love while spending so many years using them. The components and techniques in Oracle and SQL Server are inherent, and they are part of my book, but not as a goal in itself, but as a consequence. The purpose is somewhat similar to that indicated in my previous book. I want to share my programming experience and not reveal any features you may find in product books or documentation. To clarify this point and avoid misunderstandings, I am not saying that they are not useful. On the contrary, they are! But this is another type of book.

In short, the primary source of my books is my direct experience. Therefore, please do not expect to find any new Oracle or SQL Server features unless by coincidence. These can happen accidentally, of course. But that is not the purpose of this paperwork.

The need for refactoring

One of the most common tasks I have had in recent years has been to rebuild various processes. There is a constant need to fix the code for several reasons. New technologies are everywhere, new techniques and new concepts, the most promising miracles if we look at the market. Nevertheless, realistically, some companies may have the finances to change their systems in such a radical way, but many do not! Most companies have to live with what they have. They continue to develop existing systems, improve things, add new business lines to their current products, improve performance wherever there are serious issues, etc. On the other hand, the quality of being something new is not always a guarantee of improvement!

The complexity of any site is high, and it isn't easy to see the whole image. I'm not mainly an architect, after all! I am more like a database developer, and I hardly see the grass in my yard. And here, in this particular field, there is a constant need for refactoring, which I can undoubtedly say, at least from my personal experience! Of course, there are exceptions, and I do not intend to generalize.

I am a real database developer specialized in manipulating data in different relational databases. I often improved various SQL logics. In general, ameliorating these SQL processes means finding better ways to code in other parts of the system, generally related to data processing.

One of the first reasons for refactoring is the need for better database performance. When we mention this, we can understand so many things! Refactoring is one of them, and this is generally the final solution. The DBA is trying to tune the system and, eventually, try to add all kinds of features available for the database system. DBA tries to tweak the design and finally tries to add all sorts of features available to the database system. DBA sets new parameters in the environment, but he/she can rarely intervene in logic. Sometimes the results are excellent and sometimes not. However, DBA intervention is only part of the equation and not always the most important.

The architect tries to find the best structure for one system or another. The design and architecture component is critical, which is the foundation for any software product. It all starts with a good design! However, the development time will come. Even though it is a new system, programming's style is a critical component. So, even for a new system, it matters how we develop things.

How about an existing system that has been in operation for years and the people working there have gone? This system is experiencing severe performance issues and needs improvement. Maybe even a new approach is necessary to replace the old system, which is often the best solution. But this is not always possible for the software company or the client that manages its systems. Occasionally, projects need to be adjusted, and logic needs to be improved because it cannot completely change the software. In conclusion, refactoring parts of enterprise software is sometimes a practical and affordable way!

When building a new product is not a valid option, refactoring a system is a challenge and requires patience and trust, a lot of work, and concentration. The programmer responsible for rewriting the code needs to understand the existing logic at a reasonable level. He/she needs to understand pieces of code written many years ago and rewrite them better, in a modern and optimal way. Very often, the reason for refactoring is **performance**, but not only. Other reasons might come into the game, like **portability** and **maintainability**. After many years of usage, some systems are almost impossible to read and understood by newcomers, becoming almost unintelligible and incomprehensible. Consequently, maintainability is one other primary reason for refactoring. Moreover, a system is not merely maintainable anymore and requires significant adjustments.

Portability is also a common reason for refactoring. For example, for software companies that need to maintain the same system in various databases, they need to consider the portability and keep the SQL code to function correctly in multiple database systems with a reasonable amount of work.

These concepts, performance, portability, or maintenance, apply to the entire infrastructure or another. My concern is the relational database and, of course, SQL. My goal is to show how the SQL code can be more readable, more portable, and better. I would consider the third component as central! From this point of view, refactoring or rewriting the SQL code is one solution that can bring huge improvements for all three.

A simple design model

So what is the purpose of this book? Is there a guideline for this written work? What do I want to reveal from my experience that it is worth spending a few hours of your life reading this paper? Simple questions, I hope, and I wish for inspired answers!

I want to describe some general features of a specific type of product. I want to illustrate an overly simplified version of such a system. It is a **data transfer** structure. I will introduce a design model for this kind of system that uses relational databases, such as Oracle or SQL Server. Suppose that in my previous books, the emphasis was on relational databases programming and the set-based approach. This time, I want to describe a specific design and development model, something similar to a data migration process or data replication. Nevertheless, the set-based approach is the primary technique for the development process.

For some people, the idea of a data transfer/migration may seem trivial or uninteresting. I consider the opposite! First, I believe there is a lot of such work everywhere, and I intend to demonstrate this in the following chapters. Regarding the terminology, it isn't easy to frame the terms and clearly define the concepts. Data transfer is the process of moving data. One particular scenario is when you transfer data from one system to another. One other word for that is data migration. Maybe this has a special meaning. Specialized tools and utilities are trying to help companies achieve this goal of data migration, an option. Nevertheless, some concepts are very slippery and support numerous interpretations. The idea of data migration is one of such notions.

There is so much variety in this concept, and I don't pretend to be a strong theorist of the subject, which I am not. But I have practical experience in the field. After some years working on such projects, I can say that this is one right place for a database developer like me! Given that the relational database is still on the list, the data migration system often aims to migrate the data to a relational database from a software structure that may or may not be a relational database. The migration can be purely SQL-based or not! The project can be challenging and exciting. I had the chance to spend some time working on these types of projects, and I had the opportunity to design systems of this type.

When I mention design, I also mean development because this book is not pure architecture! Design and development are all together, for sure. Suppose you have an excellent SQL design, say, and implement it using the traditional style of application developers using multiple cursors. In that case, the low quality breaks the design value of the code. Conversely, if database design is inadequate and not suitable for a set-based approach, trying to work on a set-based basis can be difficult.

The design and development and I refer strictly to relational databases, where I have the expertise, are interchangeable. You cannot have a good design and a bad implementation, and it is difficult to have a good performance with an imperfect structure.

Several guidelines will drive the process of describing this type of system. First of all, I want to make you understand the need for such a system. I will insist on this idea, and I want to show that this need is quite common for many sites surrounded by various applications that need to communicate together. Secondly, even though theoretically, the market is full of tools and technologies that are supposed to fulfill this task of data transfer/migration, I would say that we can acquire this task easily by using the common SQL language. The model that I propose here is explicit and suggestive.

The idea is to design and build a simple model from scratch, imagine such a product, actually two systems that coexist at a site, and show that these two software products can function as one. The means to achieve this goal is the data transfer system itself.

Initially, I thought of using the term "data migration." However, after a few moments of reflection, I felt that the name "data transfer" is much more appropriate. Although, in the end, I would like you to remember that I want to offer an exercise in using the SQL technique. The practice is, after all, a transfer of data between two systems.

A continuous process

Another thing I want to reveal in the following pages is the continuity of such a process. Imagine a site using many IT software products, each of which manages a part of the business. Each application is accurate and does its job. However, they can share things, for example, processes and data. Of course, the manager may one day decide to change everything. The big boss can say: "*that's enough*!" One may choose to give up all existing computer systems. The manager has just discovered a computer application that does everything! This wonder application processes all business segments. Things happen as if Gandalf sneaks into the company and arranges everything perfectly. Now there is only one software system, one and only one! The precious application, the unique design to master them all! "*The ring that rules them all!*"

Sometimes these dreams come true, and some companies can achieve this goal of having a system that manages everything. But sometimes not! First of all, the cost of replacing all of them is very high. Second, the new magic structure is not always as magical as it claims to be. Very often, circumstances force companies to stick with what they have. And what they have is a chain of software applications that manage different segments of a larger business.

For these types of situations, quite common, there should be some ways in which the software products collaborate in one way or another. These interactions between different systems are not always necessary. Some products are entirely independent and do not require communication with others. But some software products are interconnected, and some form of cooperation is beneficial, if not mandatory. This storyline is the one that I have in mind. Try to imagine many software applications need to work together and act as one, at least in some parts. The data transfer system is like a connector between various software structures, and the connection can be continuous or discrete. The process of data transfer/migration from one place to another, in a constant manner, will allow a variety of systems to act, more or less, as one unified system.

Of course, the product above is not a wonder system, like the manager's dream one. It has its limitations and does not replace a completely new design that could solve everything. Nevertheless, this is an affordable solution and can mimic a single application to some extent. Data transfer is continuous and incremental, allowing updates and deletions to simulate a unit from a diversity. Creating such a utility has a minimal cost compared to the individual reconstruction of the component systems or replacing the software chain with a new one.

Let's say you have two software systems, such as A and B, that work separately, but interact to some degree, share some data, and so on. There is always the option of a new system, called C. This will replace both A and B applications. Like the magic programming language (C), perhaps the best of all time, this is an entirely new system that does the job of both A and B and maybe even more. Nevertheless, some companies cannot afford C, or perhaps C is not an option for various reasons. In this case, the enterprise must survive, A and B operating separately. However, A and B must speak, finally, communicate and transfer data. Sometimes this cooperation needs to be continuous, and there needs to be a way to simulate even C itself to some degree. I want to explain how such a system that uses the SQL language can mimic the C system.

In conclusion, my goal is to show that we can build a compromise and create a (fake) new C system. It will unite the two software systems, A and B, into one. The new C system is A and B linked to a D, and this D is the data transfer itself. This D is like a long line connecting two bridges.

We will imagine a site; we will visualize the two software structures and build the data transfer. We will try to give life to computer applications, accompanying software products by their users. Despite technology, humanity comes first!

2 Speedy: initial design

From Data and Star Trek to database programming!

If there is any constant in our lives today, we can say with sureness that one of them is related to data and, consequently, to databases. We are all affected by information, and it is not easy to imagine ourselves without the data that surrounds us everywhere.

I want to make a parenthesis and prepare an analogy. I have many passions in the field of fiction and science fiction. Among other things, I am a Star Trek fan. I think of our dear "Data" android when he processes almost any topic to reveal the necessary information and, finally, to help gain knowledge about the desired subject. Do you remember? Captain Picard asked him to analyze a particular situation. "Data" turned his eyes upside down and, relatively quickly, managed to find out almost everything he could get about this problem. Now, you can consider this approach as having excellent performance, right? Imagine that Mister "Data" accesses a vast database and quickly processes what he needs, and returns the desired information that helps aster Picard and his team solve their dilemma.

Going back to the present and leaving Data and Picard away, we can imagine that Mister Data's processing capabilities ultimately rely on the same source as today, a database. Of course, the power of today's databases is limited. However, a visionary can imagine tomorrow's databases, as in Star Trek. What we will have in a few centuries, we owe to those of today, and yesterday and tomorrow, right? Aside from the tremendous amount of information stored in Star Trek storage systems, we are impressed with the incredible speed that allows Mister "Data" to process this database. Thus, to move back into our world from Star Trek's imaginary one, I would say that it is our duty, programmers, among other categories involved in this task, to do everything possible to achieve better performance whenever possible.

Okay, enough is enough! Let's get back to the present, for real! It is time to return from the imaginary world of the future to our subject. I can tell you for sure; this is not a science fiction work! Although, it certainly would have been a much more exciting book! My goal is limited to relational databases, as they exist today. Nobody knows how long they will last on the market! There are other options now, and things seem to change with the speed of light in IT's dynamic universe. However, at least so far, the relational database remains a constant and valuable asset, as well as the SQL language. Whether we like it or not, SQL is

20

still there on the list, and many companies store their data in relational databases. Thus, all the technical considerations in this book are related to SQL, with examples given from the world of Oracle and SQL Server. However, most of them are very similar in any other system, such as PostgreSQL or MySQL or any other database management system you prefer.

Now, I want to continue my journey and try to simulate one activity. First of all, the inspiration for my exercises is the real world, which means my projects. On the other hand, being passionate about philosophy and being a former teacher and trainer, I tend to explain and, why not, even to philosophize sometimes! The source and inspiration for this book's ideas is my experience. I like to reveal and explain simple exercises that will help other developers use various similar techniques. I'm not saying I have full originality. If some of my SQL scripts seem too simple for John (Joanna) Doe, that means he/she has enough experience or maybe even quite similar experiences. The world is large enough, and there is sufficient space for everyone. What I want to do is try to explain certain things as best I can.

Data transfer or data migration?

So what happens? In most of this paper, I would like to describe an example of a **data transfer** system. This type of module corresponds to a common type of project and is sometimes specific to database developers. Despite this particularity, this exercise is not necessarily specific to database programming. Anyone else can do this work! And quite often, the work is done by any kind of programmer, in any other technique. Moreover, I am sure you all know that the relational databases are flooded with code written by application programmers, Java, C #, or anything else, who do not always write correctly, being obviously influenced by their specific style of programming.

However, I can say that this volume is mainly for people using SQL, either database programmers, or not. Design and development ideas that could derive from it may be useful in other similar projects. Please take this as what it is, an example.

There is a similar term in the specific terminology, which brings a lot to what I want to present. Nevertheless, I avoid using this concept, although I could do so. I will consider them quite close in meaning!

I want to talk a little about the classic idea of **data migration**. But, before anything else, let's see some statements from Wikipedia about the concept of data migration. I want to make sure that I respect the agreed definition because there are so many meanings of this notion. Hence, I will start the discussion with Wikipedia to make sure the subject is correctly set.

Speedy, a data transfer system. A SQL Exercise

"Data migration is the process of selecting, preparing, extracting, and transforming data and permanently transferring it from one computer storage system to another. Additionally, the validation of migrated data for completeness and the decommissioning of legacy data storage are considered part of the entire data migration process.

There is a difference between data migration and data integration activities. Data migration is a project through which data will be moved or copied from one environment to another and removed or decommissioned in the source. During the migration (which can take place over months or even years), data can flow in multiple directions, and there may be various migrations taking place simultaneously. The ETL (extract, transform, load) actions will be necessary, although the means of achieving these may not be those traditionally associated with the ETL acronym.

By contrast, data integration is a permanent part of the IT architecture. It is responsible for the way data flows between the various applications and data stores—and is a process rather than a project activity. Standard ETL technologies designed to supply data from operational systems to data warehouses would fit within the latter category."

I initially wanted to avoid confusing terminology, so I preferred to take a few statements from the Wikipedia definition. The data migration process aims to transfer data from one environment to another; in my case, I consider relational databases. However, the concept is more general and does not strictly involve relational databases. To continue, I suppose a source environment and a target one, at least. A staging area can be defined, an intermediate layer between the source and the target.

Moreover, this staging zone may be persistent or not or may not be present at all! There can be many sources and many targets in a more complex scenario. In this case, of multiple sources, we may need to integrate them, and here comes the concept of data integration, as described above. The complexity may vary, from a reasonable or even simpler to a sophisticated and complex system of such type.

But the need for such a process? There could be many reasons for data migration. It also depends on where we are. One is to be in a classic OLTP environment, and another to be in a multi-source data warehouse. In this second case, we are not talking about a simple data migration process but about an ETL that requires a more complex architecture than a simple data migration system.

For example, there may be two or more software applications running in parallel, even in a data warehouse. The two are separated, but they have to communicate somehow. It is common for any customer to use these software products to find a way to communicate. A typical scenario is to build a data migration process between the two databases behind the IT products.

During these chapters, some ideas will come back and will be re-explained and re-evaluated. Despite my efforts for strictness and order, writing is not an exact science and not even programming. I intend to share my experience in database design and development and build a different book type. I'm sorry I might disappoint some of my readers who will be eager to see lines of SQL code right away! I plan to explain from time to time, and I am aware that I am at risk. I believe that programming is real life! This activity's biggest challenge is not the programming language itself but the business behind any IT solution. As programmers, our ultimate goal is to understand the world and reveal it through our information systems.

The reason for a data migration system might starts with a single application. However, when talking about migration, there are always two points of interest: the right segment's geometric concept. There are two points, A and B, and we draw a line between the two points, called ends. There must be two points; otherwise, there is no segment, right?

We consider A as the source and B as the target by dragging the segment from A to B. If we have A in mind, we want to draw the part to B. Vice versa. If we have B in mind, we need to look back at A and extract the sector from A to B. A is the beginning, and B is the end. If we assimilate A and B with two information systems, A is the source, and B is the destination. If we think from perspective A, we can consider an export from A to B. If we analyze from perspective B, we will find an import from A to B. In my scenario, I consider a target system like B, and I start from here.

I will soon start the example that will lead most of my book. Before I do that, I want to say a few more words about my understanding of a data migration process because each reader will have their preconceptions based on their past projects, if any similar. For example, we can see various meanings regarding job descriptions checking Monster, Job Serve, or LinkedIn! Currently, there are many opportunities in the market for projects involving data migration. So I ask the reader; try to recognize a specific significance of data migration, and if you find a better word for it, please use it freely in your mind. I know it can be vague.

Hence, in this book, data migration is a process that involves transferring data from one source to one destination. I see data migration as an *ongoing process*. There is a **first-time** execution when the first data transfer occurs. Later, this is followed by others, maybe in an **incremental** fashion. Various actions can occur against the elements involved. In this paper, I do not understand data migration as a single process; although there is this meaning, this is not the one I have in mind. Data migration could only be an initialization process! If we think of a data migration process in this way, we initialize a database, and then we're done! Well, that's an acceptable meaning, but it's not what I'm talking about!

Data migration can also be like a simpler ETL. In general, ETL is an ongoing process with an initialization phase that begins with a historical data transfer. After that, the data is periodically moved from different sources and integrated. Data migration is not necessarily a process that involves historical databases. But we can see it as a continuous process of data transfer between two databases, and, for example, it can have a massive initial data transfer followed by incremental ones.

Data migration may require database development when referring to relational databases, and the best means for this development, in such a scenario, is the SQL language. Now, I hope it's clear what I mean when it comes to data migration, and I can start with the real-life example that will drive most of the book. Don't forget to see this as an exercise that will illustrate what SQL can do!

In terms of terminology, throughout this book, even if it's probably not precisely the same thing, I'll use the words "data migration" and "data transfer" alternately.

The Yellow Shoe Factory

Now is the time for my example! This book is not a classic technical book, and it is a little different because of my writing style. Of course, it is a SQL book that presents a specific system, data transfer. In addition to the predominant technical aspects, the book contains a social and fictional component. I will introduce a series of fictional characters in an imaginary enterprise that will give human and social significance to the chain of software systems. I will present a fictitious social framework that will intertwine with the concepts and ideas of design and development that I would like to share.

I consider a site, a factory called "*Yellow Shoe.*" This plant produces shoes and has a strong IT department. The size of the company is small to average. It has many IT applications that work in parallel; many information systems perform various tasks and manage multiple processes. Each of these software products covers specific segments of the company's business.

Moreover, imagine a software product, "*Shoes are everywhere.*" This module covers a specific activity, such as shoe manufacturing! What a coincidence, right? This application runs on different customers who deal with that line of business, shoe assembling. Clothing is something we all need, so there is enough space for these systems! Among others, this software runs on "*Yellow Shoe*" and works quite well. Any resemblance to reality is pure coincidence.

What about other pieces of software running on "*Yellow Shoe*?" There might be multiple systems in addition to "*Shoes are everywhere!*" And this is quite common because the complexity of a business is not always easy to accommodate.

The desire for integration, what a beautiful dream? You can read about it from all major vendors like Oracle, Microsoft, and others. Buy the entire chain, and your enterprise is completely covered; you don't need anything else, even the word integration is out of range! This ad looks so appealing, and, surprisingly, many customers don't buy the whole chain right away! Well, first of all, there is a small problem here! The price for this complete enterprise-wide system is not always affordable, and not many enterprises can pay the fee. Even leaving aside any price considerations, integration itself is a very demanding and challenging task to accomplish. Some individual companies' specifics make it almost impossible to be entirely covered by a single software application!

Very often, the complexity of human life, economically, socially, is still beyond the power of our software systems, I would dare to say. Any reasonable software engineer knows that every little detail that may seem trivial can cause severe headaches! If I wanted to make a categorical statement, as an experienced developer, this is: *"nothing is easy in programming!"* Now, some people might say I'm mixing things up, but it's not entirely true. After all, the micro-universe of the developer reflects in the macro-universe of the IT business. Starting from a small problem that a software engineer encounters and moving to its entire infrastructure with the chain of IT software applications, somewhat similar rules apply! There will be tons of water flowing in the Atlantic until we will have our master "Data" and his processing capabilities!

Otherwise, the concept of "*integration*" into a customer site to configure its system chain is not easy to achieve. Very often, any enterprise is a mixture of software applications living together. These software products cover as many of the required lines of business as possible. The next question is: how do these software applications coexist? Some of them can work independently, while others not! If not, the enterprise must try at least a partial integration of its IT products!

Thus, this shoe factory is a plant called "*Yellow Shoe.*" You can visualize, as an exercise of imagination, the Yellow submarine! Like in the famous Beatles song, where many of them live next door, similarly, the *"Yellow Shoe"* factory workers live in a small, lively, mythical town and build footwear! Not just yellow, as you can imagine! All the colors in the world! Inside the company, many employees use a variety of IT products. Some of them use the *"Shoes are everywhere"* software for manufacturing activity, while others deal with another application for accounting purposes. The second system is called "*Yellow Panther,*" almost like the famous Panther that delighted my childhood! Only that this time, my panther is yellow and not pink! It seems that this is the policy in this company; any name must contain the color yellow in it! Don't worry; shoes can have all the world colors, and, after all, that's what matters! It would have been a severe limitation, and the factory would probably have gone bankrupt a long time ago. Thus, they are at least two modules at our site, one for **manufacturing** and the second for **accounting**. The manufacturing falls to the module *"Shoes are everywhere"* and the accountancy for *"Yellow Panther."*

What about the users?

Like any reputable enterprise, users achieve their goals using these computer systems. Several characters use this software and will participate in the story of this book. These are all employees of the enterprise! Some users! For example, one of them uses the product *"Shoes are everywhere."* She is Angelique, a manufacturing specialist. She generally introduces new items in this system, new shoes. Regularly, she may need to get a list of footwear from Joanna. Who is Joanna? She is another user, an accountant, and she is working in the other module. Joanna is one of the users of *"Yellow Panther."* They are not the only ones, but they will be the actors in our fantastic story that will give color, I hope, to the system's technical specifications described in this book.

The software applications are entirely independent, and Angelique carries out the manufacturing while Joanna is in charge of accounting. Each of them is more or less ignorant about the other's job and the associated computer applications. And the systems themselves are not accessible to each other. Thus, Angelique has to communicate with Joanna using Excel lists!

Let's describe the process: Joanna adds the shoes to the *"Yellow Panther"* system for the first time, in most cases. After a while, she goes through excel lists because both Joanna and Angelique love excels, like any respectable and honorable business user! Angelique will add the products (second time) to the manufacturing system. Later, she can add the bill of materials or generate the stocks, for example. Nevertheless, sometimes, Angelique adds the items herself to the manufacturing software. In this way, it happens from time to time that the same footwear pair appears as a duplicate in *"Shoes are everywhere!"*

I forgot to mention one more character, Johnny Babanus! To be more specific, he is the main one! He is the database architect and specialist working in the IT department for *"Shoes are everywhere."* He knows better than anyone the database and the manufacturing system insides. He was always so proud of his Latin roots, considering his surname, a bit unusual.

It is part of our lives, programmers, to live with our systems; they are part of our families and, whether we like it or not, we sometimes spend even more time with them than with our wives and children! Consequently, Johnny Babanus knows the program because he spent many years with the database and the objects inside. He knows almost everything, is familiar with shoes, suppliers, and vendors, sees any field, be it natural or artificial. Paradoxically, suppose a Guru is someone with extensive knowledge of something. In this case, software engineers who have spent many years in their IT products become Guru in these systems, at least in the areas directly involved!

The work with two systems in such a manner cannot continue like this! The big head of the *"Yellow Shoe"* finally asked someone from the *"Shoes are everywhere"* team to do something and try to help them solve these problems. Johnny was glad to hear this because he was aware that these issues are real. I will later clarify better the difficulties encountered with the completely distinct operation of these two computer applications.

To complete this presentation and the fictional part of the book, you should know that there is a reliable IT division with good programmers at the *"Yellow Shoe"* site. Systems like *"Yellow Panther"* and *"Shoes are everywhere"* require local maintenance and administration, sometimes a lot of additional development. The last character is Jean-Luc. He is the developer working for the *"Yellow Panther"* who handles any necessary customization that may be required. Jean-Luc works with Joanna, his favorite colleague. He's the IT guy, and Joanna is the accounting specialist, the lady of accounting, the best *"Yellow Panther"* business user! Jean-Luc is not a typical guy! It looks more like the Jean-Luc Picard style, always elegant and polite, with excellent taste; he has class! Anyway, to conclude, once Jean-Luc is in the dilemma of any business problems, he asks Joanna. Once Joanna has a technical issue with Panther, she calls Jean-Luc. Sometimes, after years of teamwork, a very close relationship can arise between a business user and a programmer. After such a long time, they are almost best friends!

Before continuing, I want to emphasize that this imaginary part tries to give a human character to the technical book. There is also a satirical component through which I want to make the book enjoyable. Finally, the fact that the business users are women and the two programmers are men has no significance. I have worked with many ladies in teams of programmers and, I don't think there is any difference. The value of a programmer or a business user has nothing to do with gender. Statistically, the number of men in programming is still much higher than the number of women, but the proportions are changing, and the reasons are more historical. By tradition, let's say! Take these four characters as what they are, some funny users and programmers trying to give a human and funny face to a technical book. Don't think more, is not the case! Try to imagine some likable characters and let them make your reading more enjoyable. Technical books lack this charm of life, and these characters are trying to fix this gap.

Here is a diagram showing the actors and the two systems that work at the *"Yellow Shoe"* site.

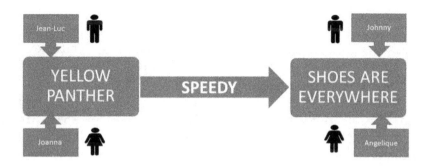

Figure 2-1 Yellow Shoe Site

"Shoes are everywhere": the target system

As mentioned earlier, the big boss at "*Yellow Shoe*" asked Johnny to start building a continuous data transfer process. This way, users like Joanna and Angelique will avoid doing the same thing in two distinct software modules. Moreover, they will no longer define the same product twice in both systems. But the most important consequence will be the elimination of inconsistencies that may occur. Besides, final reports requesting data from both systems, such as Excel files that arrive at the manager's office in critical situations, will no longer be incorrect.

Even if it seems absurd, there are so many similar cases in various locations around the world! This paradigm is not the Dadaists' surrealist art but the cruel reality of the different companies' IT services that host them. And, of course, I do not generalize!

As for what is needed, there are many alternatives to these types of problems. I am not saying that the proposed choice with the data transfer software is the best or always the right choice. As an alternative, the enterprise management can decide to buy a dedicated data migration tool and integrate the two or even many systems using such a specialized utility. Such options exist and, if necessary, can be tested and used. Another solution could be to buy a third system to do the job of the two. Some options are more expensive than others, may require more resources, etc. I would say that this solution imagined by Johnny is the most convenient if we look at the value for money. I can say this solution is suitable quite often.

Master Babanus received the green light from the big boss to start the job. The first task, a name. What should he call this new system? Johnny was a big fan of cartoons. Even today, as an adult, he sometimes watches, and most love the old comics from the golden age of Walt Disney. One of his favorite characters was Speedy Gonzales, known as the fastest mouse!

On the other hand, because Johnny is the kind of programmer oriented towards performance, he always valued the SQL code's execution speed. Thus, his combined reflections and the close connections between SQL logic's rate and the brave mouse's speed determined him to decide on the name of the new software product. The system's name will be **Speedy**. If he manages to make an application as fast as Gonzales's speed, Johnny will be satisfied. "*Speedy is his name,*" said rhetorically, Johnny! Johnny is very proud of his name. Let's hope this system will perform according to the expectations, relatively high!

What is the location of the new software system? Honestly, it can be anywhere. The new module can be separate. Alternatively, it can be part of the target product itself, the manufacturing system, and Johnny can build it as an extension. It is less probable to be inside the Panther, but it is not impossible. There is no categorical option; anything is possible. It depends, of course, on the situation. What is important is that the type of system I have in mind is entirely SQL-based, straightforward, and set-based as much as possible. We can use any possible environments such as Oracle, SQL Server, or PostgreSQL, where the differences between different database management systems play a minimal role. Of course, other options or technologies are available.

Now, these two software applications work in parallel. Management approves Johhny's solution and decides it's time to design and build this new system to connect the existing two. Johnny was pleased when he heard his leaders' decision and began to think about the best way to do it.

Master Babanus and his team are preparing for this task. First of all, Johnny knows his system better than anyone. He quickly paints the "*Shoes Are Everywhere*" database schema, the **target** database, to use the data migration terminology. "*Here it is, as seen below, and here we begin our work, dear readers!*" Your task is to build this transfer system with Johnny! Please be my quest to create the target in any database management system you want. It should work almost everywhere.

From now on, the real technical part begins. There will be a lot of SQL scripts that you will execute. As databases, I will use SQL Server and Oracle. Of course, you are free to use any database system you want.

Listing 2-1 The target design for the "Shoes are everywhere" database

```
-- Same script for Oracle and SQL Server.
CREATE TABLE Countries
(
    Country_Id          INT NOT NULL,
    Country_Name        VARCHAR(255) NOT NULL
);
ALTER TABLE Countries
ADD CONSTRAINT Pk_Countries_Country_Id PRIMARY KEY
(Country_Id);
CREATE TABLE Languages
(
    Language_Code       VARCHAR(20) NOT NULL,
    Language_Name       VARCHAR(255) NOT NULL
);
ALTER TABLE Languages
ADD CONSTRAINT Pk_Languages_Code PRIMARY KEY (Language_Code);
CREATE TABLE Product_Types
(
    Type_Id             INT NOT NULL,
    Type_Code           VARCHAR(20) NOT NULL,
    Type_Name           VARCHAR(255) NOT NULL
);
ALTER TABLE Product_Types
ADD CONSTRAINT Pk_Types_Id PRIMARY KEY (Type_Id);
CREATE TABLE Suppliers
(
    Supplier_Id         INT NOT NULL,
    Supplier_Code       VARCHAR(20) NOT NULL,
    Supplier_Name       VARCHAR(255) NOT NULL,
    Country_Id          INT NOT NULL,
    City                VARCHAR(255) NOT NULL,
    Address             VARCHAR(255)
);
ALTER TABLE Suppliers
```

```
ADD CONSTRAINT Pk_Suppliers_Id PRIMARY KEY (Supplier_Id);
ALTER TABLE Suppliers ADD CONSTRAINT Fk_Suppliers_Countries
FOREIGN KEY (Country_Id) REFERENCES Countries (Country_Id);
CREATE TABLE Manufacturers
(
    Manufacturer_Code          VARCHAR(20) NOT NULL,
    Manufacturer_Name          VARCHAR(255) NOT NULL,
    Country_Id                 INT NOT NULL,
    City                       VARCHAR(255) NOT NULL,
    Address                    VARCHAR(255)
);
ALTER TABLE Manufacturers
ADD CONSTRAINT Pk_Man_Code PRIMARY KEY (Manufacturer_Code);
ALTER TABLE Manufacturers
ADD CONSTRAINT Fk_Man_Countries FOREIGN KEY (Country_Id)
REFERENCES Countries (Country_Id);
CREATE TABLE Products
(
    Product_Id                 INT NOT NULL,
    Code                       VARCHAR(20) NOT NULL,
    Name                       VARCHAR(255) NOT NULL,
    Type_Id                    INT,
    Supplier_Id                INT,
    Manufacturer_Code          VARCHAR(20),
    Color                      VARCHAR(100),
    Gender                     VARCHAR(10),
    Measure                    INT
);
ALTER TABLE Products
ADD CONSTRAINT Pk_Products_Id PRIMARY KEY (Product_Id);
ALTER TABLE Products
ADD CONSTRAINT Uq_Products_Code UNIQUE (Code);
ALTER TABLE Products ADD CONSTRAINT Fk_Products_Types
FOREIGN KEY (Type_Id) REFERENCES Product_Types (Type_Id);
ALTER TABLE Products ADD CONSTRAINT Fk_Products_Suppliers
FOREIGN KEY (Supplier_Id) REFERENCES Suppliers (Supplier_Id);
```

```
ALTER TABLE Products ADD CONSTRAINT Fk_Products_Man_Code
FOREIGN KEY (Manufacturer_Code)
REFERENCES Manufacturers (Manufacturer_Code);
CREATE TABLE Commercial_Names
(
        Commercial_Code              VARCHAR(20) NOT NULL,
        Product_Id                   INT NOT NULL,
        Commercial_Name              VARCHAR(255) NOT NULL,
        Manufacturer_Code            VARCHAR(20),
        Language_Code                VARCHAR(20)
);
```

ALTER TABLE Commercial_Names ADD CONSTRAINT
Pk_Commercial_Names_Code PRIMARY KEY (Commercial_Code);

ALTER TABLE Commercial_Names ADD CONSTRAINT
Fk_Commercial_Products FOREIGN KEY (Product_Id) REFERENCES
Products (Product_Id);

ALTER TABLE Commercial_Names ADD CONSTRAINT Fk_Commercial_Man
FOREIGN KEY (Manufacturer_Code)

REFERENCES Manufacturers (Manufacturer_Code);

ALTER TABLE Commercial_Names ADD CONSTRAINT
Fk_Commercial_Languages FOREIGN KEY (Language_Code) REFERENCES
Languages (Language_Code) ;

As you can see above, the *"Shoes are everywhere"* manufacturing database contains the followings:

♣ A central table that defines the products, mainly footwear! This table is called Products. The main features of the product, friendly and comfortable footwear, are described here! You can see the shoe code, name, color, gender, size, type, supplier, manufacturer, etc.

♣ Some of the attributes are visible in the lookup tables, such as product type, supplier, and manufacturer. There is another language lookup table

♣ Finally, there is a table with commercial names for the products in various languages and manufacturers. Please see that one product may have a set of trade names depending on the chosen language and manufacturer. There is a classic one to any relationship between the Products table and Commercial_Names.

Looking at the database and the system model, Johnny realizes that his first goal is to identify the *entities* required to process the two modules. Speaking of entities and attributes, he quickly recognizes that he needs to define and classify them. Secondly, he needs to identify the information for the data transfer. What do we need to transfer? Of course, not everything, but only what is necessary for the destination system. Angelique and her team lead the process and know what is needed.

Therefore, a classification of the *entities* and their *attributes* is required. Thus, and so, Johnny rolls up his sleeves and starts the work. Let's see what is needed, and let's start classifying!

Before we go any further, perhaps a diagram will give the reader a better idea of the *"Shoes are everywhere"* manufacturing system.

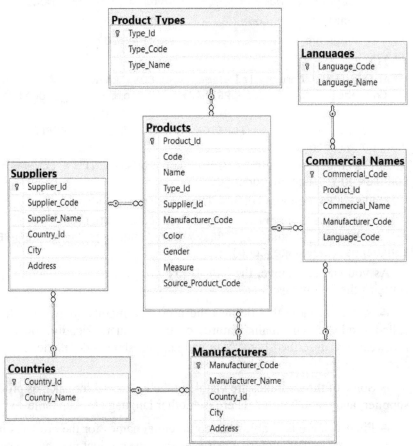

Figure 2-2 Shoes are everywhere manufacturing system diagram

Dear reader, please remember to run everything in the database, no matter what you use and not necessarily Oracle or SQL Server. The purpose of all these considerations is strictly related to the SQL code, and you should not lose touch with it. If you get bored and don't like to read so much and especially don't like some of my non-technical style paragraphs, don't worry, I understand. You can jump directly and access the code! Even better, run the code, run the SQL statements, and come back to my notes. Your understanding will improve as you move back and forth. Our goal now is to classify, re-classify, and prepare entities, attributes, and relations.

Let's continue! I briefly described the target software; *"Shoes are everywhere,"* the ultimate goal. Two systems should work together, and we need to try to imagine the flow between them. One of the first things to look for is the list of articles for data transfer between systems.

If we use standard terminology in programming, one of the first inquiries would be: who are the entities involved? Any information system of any kind aims to implement one or more lines of activity. According to object-oriented programming terminology and relational databases, the **entity** is New York's Central Park; the whole world revolves around it!

For example, take a university and its information system. Several main entities define the university's activity, such as instructors, students, courses, etc. In our footwear factory, it is quite clear that there is at least one central entity in question: the shoe itself, the product. And, like Michael Jackson's latest show, *"This is it!"* We can imagine more, but for simplicity, we are content with what we have. One entity is enough to illustrate the purpose.

The above diagram describes the list of tables required for the process, such as associated products and lookup tables. Johnny needs to get things ready and start analyzing the business. He talked to Angelique and other users; he gathered their opinions and thoughts. After several stormy sessions and detailed analysis, he summarized his database's needs for the new module.

After a few days of work, Master Babanus built the scheme and isolated the necessary objects, i.e., required at the destination. He made his specifications, especially after discussing everything with Angelique. Moreover, his interest in her was becoming more than professional! She was indeed the user working with his application, and she knows a bit about her sister software, the Panther. Well, to tell you a secret, in addition to the satisfaction of a developer who has completed the first part, the right specification, he began to dream in secret, being impressed by Angelique. Maybe, who knows, if they continue to work closely together, something will come! Johnny was quite excited after the analysis phase. Perhaps it's too early to say he was already in love, or maybe not! Was it just an ordinary business relationship or the beginning of a new romance? They were in separate, completely independent departments, as in two different institutions, they just met, but there was some chemistry between them. Let's wait and see!

The metadata layer

Johnny is now sure of his needs for the new process. He got the target requirements chart, thanks to Angelique. The next step should be a double-check with the source system, the accounting module, as far as it is accessible, and see if the entities and attributes needed for data transfer are available. The job of a business analyst is not easy and requires patience and insistence. It must ensure that it extracts information correctly from users. Like a data warehouse process, in which the theory says that it is better to start from what is needed and not from what is available, in data migration, Johnny followed the same approach and initially checked the target, which means Angelique! First, he questions Angelique what her needs are. Immediately after the discussions with Angelique, Johnny changed his interest to the other side and went to the " *Yellow Panther*" team. He spoke to Jean-Luc and Joanna and tried to understand if Angelique's requirements are available in the Panther software. He finds a perfect match, and he moves to the next step, attribute classification.

These elements are the attributes of footwear, in general, because it is the central entity for the transfer process. A simple table is sufficient for this purpose, and, for simplicity, there is a small number of attributes. In a real system, the number of properties to be transferred can be relatively large and dynamic, as the list can expand depending on the evolution in time. Let's see below!

Listing 2-2 The definition of attributes

```
-- Same script for Oracle and SQL Server.
CREATE TABLE M_Attributes
(
    Attribute_Name          VARCHAR(30) NOT NULL,
    Target_Object           VARCHAR(30) NOT NULL,
    Attribute_Type          VARCHAR(30) NOT NULL,
    Attribute_Usage         VARCHAR(30) NOT NULL,
    Attribute_Length        INT,
    Attribute_Data_Type     VARCHAR(30) NOT NULL
);
```

This table marks the beginning of a new layer, a separate set of objects between the two systems, the **metadata** structure. This layer is essential for such a process. In general, whenever there is a mechanism involving multiple systems, there is a need for a separate metadata layer to describe the functionalities between the modules involved in the process. Of course, each software system has its metadata structure, but a common and standard layer of metadata is missing when many systems are involved. This table is the first one in this new level!

Looking at the target's design and analyzing the necessary fields, the attributes use a simple structure. This table starts with M_, and the reason is simple. This table is a metadata table and expresses a definition and a transition from the source application, "*Yellow Panther*," to the target system, "*Shoes are everywhere.*" Before looking further, let's define a few attributes using the simple design above. For our scenario, what we have is enough.

Johnny uses the pretext to meet Angelique again for new discussions and analyze what is available at Panther and not. So, after all these debates at the customer site, Johnny can finally prepare his excel! The famous Excel, generally database programmers, do not like it so much, but users idolize it. Let's see what is needed; the file used wisely!

As the brain of the data transfer team, Johnny Babanus leads the process. Consequently, Johnny will prepare the list of attributes required from the target. Variations may occur, and this list might suffer changes in time. Some properties might not even be available. According to the discussion at the "*Yellow Shoe*" factory, these are the required attributes.

Looking at target design and trusting Angelique as a responsible and competent user of the manufacturing system, Johnny completed the list of necessary attributes. Here it is, as seen below:

Table 2-1 List of required attributes

Attribute Name	Attribute Type	Attribute Length	No per product
Product Name	String	255	one to one
Product Type Code	String	20	one to one
Supplier Code	String	20	one to one
Manufacturer Code	String	20	one to one
Color	String	100	one to one
Gender	String	10	one to one
Measure	Integer	5	one to one
Commercial Code	String	20	many to one
Commercial Name	String	255	many to one

Manufacturer Code	String	20	many to one
Language	String	20	many to one

This list of properties is finally here in this Excel file and is waiting to become a SQL script! An invitation to dinner with Angelique is the grand prize for the project's first phase as a happy ending. Life is beautiful, and work can sometimes be enjoyable! For the moment, in his dreams! The project has not started yet; it's just the BA phase, just the beginning. Johnny has to wait, but no one can stop him from dreaming, right?

So now Johnny has received his script, and the first set of attributes is defined. Remember to run this on your system so you can see what's going on. Get the joy out of the code, remember!

Listing 2-3 The values for the attributes

```
-- Same script for Oracle and SQL Server. Don't forget to
commit if running on Oracle.
INSERT INTO M_Attributes (Attribute_Name, Attribute_Type,
Target_Object, Attribute_Usage, Attribute_Length,
Attribute_Data_Type)
VALUES ('TYPE_CODE', 'SIMPLE', 'PRODUCTS', 'IMPORT', '20',
'STRING');
INSERT INTO M_Attributes (Attribute_Name, Attribute_Type,
Target_Object, Attribute_Usage, Attribute_Length,
Attribute_Data_Type)
VALUES ('SUPPLIER_CODE', 'SIMPLE', 'PRODUCTS', 'IMPORT', '20',
'STRING');
INSERT INTO M_Attributes (Attribute_Name, Attribute_Type,
Target_Object, Attribute_Usage, Attribute_Length,
Attribute_Data_Type)
VALUES ('MANUFACTURER_CODE', 'SIMPLE', 'PRODUCTS', 'IMPORT',
'20', 'STRING');
INSERT INTO M_Attributes (Attribute_Name, Attribute_Type,
Target_Object, Attribute_Usage, Attribute_Length,
Attribute_Data_Type)
VALUES ('PRODUCT_NAME', 'SIMPLE', 'PRODUCTS', 'IMPORT', '255',
'STRING');
INSERT INTO M_Attributes (Attribute_Name, Attribute_Type,
Target_Object, Attribute_Usage, Attribute_Length,
Attribute_Data_Type)
```

```
    VALUES ('COLOR', 'SIMPLE', 'PRODUCTS', 'IMPORT', '100',
'STRING');
    INSERT INTO M_Attributes (Attribute_Name, Attribute_Type,
Target_Object, Attribute_Usage, Attribute_Length,
Attribute_Data_Type)
    VALUES ('GENDER', 'SIMPLE', 'PRODUCTS', 'IMPORT', '10',
'STRING');
    INSERT INTO M_Attributes (Attribute_Name, Attribute_Type,
Target_Object, Attribute_Usage, Attribute_Length,
Attribute_Data_Type)
    VALUES ('MEASURE', 'SIMPLE', 'PRODUCTS', 'IMPORT', NULL,
'NUMERIC');
    INSERT INTO M_Attributes (Attribute_Name, Attribute_Type,
Target_Object, Attribute_Usage, Attribute_Length,
Attribute_Data_Type)
    VALUES ('COMMERCIAL_CODE', 'MULTIPLE', 'COMMERCIAL_NAMES',
'IMPORT', '20', 'STRING');
    INSERT INTO M_Attributes (Attribute_Name, Attribute_Type,
Target_Object, Attribute_Usage, Attribute_Length,
Attribute_Data_Type)
    VALUES ('COMMERCIAL_NAME', 'MULTIPLE', 'COMMERCIAL_NAMES',
'IMPORT', '255', 'STRING');
    INSERT INTO M_Attributes (Attribute_Name, Attribute_Type,
Target_Object, Attribute_Usage, Attribute_Length,
Attribute_Data_Type)
    VALUES ('COMMERCIAL_MANUFACTURER', 'MULTIPLE',
'COMMERCIAL_NAMES', 'IMPORT', '20', 'STRING');
    INSERT INTO M_Attributes (Attribute_Name, Attribute_Type,
Target_Object, Attribute_Usage, Attribute_Length,
Attribute_Data_Type)
    VALUES ('LANGUAGE_CODE', 'MULTIPLE', 'COMMERCIAL_NAMES',
'IMPORT', '20', 'STRING');
```

Okay, we're moving forward. Let's make some distinctions! So far, there are two types of tables, two layers. There is the target system with the first set of tables, the manufacturing system that works at *"Yellow Shoe,"* as you can see in Listing 2-1. You can also see the source system, the *"Yellow Panther"* accountancy software. The assumption is that this is unknown to the target, but everything is possible! There are many choices here, at least two: either the two systems are accessible to each other so that a certain logic can allow direct access. In my opinion, this is an optimistic scenario. The second choice is that the source

38

is unknown and cannot be accessed directly. My situation is the latter, but I will present more details soon.

Whether known or unknown, the source and target objects are on the same layer. These objects should communicate using one way or another, and these objects store data. There is another table that stores the definition of attributes prefixed with M_. This table is an excellent example of a metadata object and has a different nature. You can see that this table describes the target elements, see the correspondence between column names in the target tables, the "*Shoes are everywhere*" system tables, and the values in the M_table. You can also anticipate defining processes in this metadata table, such as transferring from one location to another. It is traditional to talk about a metadata table in a data warehouse system. The best example is an ETL in which there is a specific metadata schema or even a database. A metadata table may describe both data and processes. Moreover, in a metadata-driven ETL, the development itself can derive from the metadata. Even in a simple data migration system like this one, there is a metadata layer, and the first object in it is the M_Attributes table.

You can see that this table is different from the rest. The set of target tables, such as products, trade names, are the tables that define the shoe factory's current manufacturing system. Apart from this system, the accountancy system manages another line of business. The tables there are unknown; only Jean-Luc knows them. These tables store data, and M_Attributes stores metadata; that is a big difference!

Regarding the attributes, you can see the following necessary information that defines a property:

♣ Attribute name. Specify the target attribute name and, if necessary, the source attribute name. The source specification depends on whether the source is directly accessible or not! We assume only the first for simplicity, and we do not care about the source's attribute name.

♣ Attribute type. Attributes can be of different types. For simplicity, I choose two types: SIMPLE and MULTIPLE. The value is simple when it is one for every detail, such as color. The property is multiple when there are many commercial names because there can be many such names for each product. A variety of classification could be imagined here, depending on the characteristics of the attributes

♣ The target object. This object is the name of the target table, or maybe view, etc. We may not be interested in source object identifications; we should not necessarily store this information. However, if anyone can consider it, this information could also exist. If the source and target are directly accessible, somehow, this information could be useful.

♣ Attribute usage. Looking from A to B, we consider the direction. The type is import, which means that data migration is an *import* utility, from the accounting system to the manufacturing system. The *export* option may exist if the intention is to export to a third system, managing a new business line. Or, maybe Angelique wants to export some of her manufacturing information to the "*Yellow Panther!*"

♣ The length of the attribute, such as the size of a string, for example.

♣ The data type of the attribute can be string or numeric.

This scenario is quite simple, and this should be the minimum information required in such a metadata table.

In conclusion, this was the first thing Johnny did. He defined the set of attributes required for the new process. The variety of scenarios is quite large, and I try to simplify to build a good plot, but simple enough to explain it in these few pages of this book.

The target lookup data

What about the lookup data? This type of data corresponds, in the terminology of the data warehouse, dictionary, or dimensional data. See manufacturers or suppliers! With two systems running on one site, most manufacturers or suppliers are the same because the location is the same. However, the lines of activity are different. According to this, some of them may exist in one module or another. Thus, sometimes, we might need common lookup data for transmission through the software applications. For example, one supplier may exist in the accounting system and not in manufacturing. What to do in such a case? When the supplier goes through *Speedy*, should it be created in the destination system? Or not, and in this case, users need to make sure that this one exists. Hence, Angelique should first manually create the missing suppliers at the destination.

The target system already contains some search data, like material types, the suppliers or manufacturers, and the languages. To complete this part, let's add some values (see below).

Listing 2-4 The values for the lookup data

```
-- Same script for Oracle and SQL Server. Don't forget to
commit if running on Oracle.
INSERT INTO Countries (Country_Id, Country_Name)
VALUES (22, 'US');
INSERT INTO Countries (Country_Id, Country_Name)
VALUES (11, 'France');
```

```
INSERT INTO Countries (Country_Id, Country_Name)
VALUES (17, 'Mexic');
INSERT INTO Languages (Language_Code, Language_Name)
VALUES ('EN', 'English US');
INSERT INTO Languages (Language_Code, Language_Name)
VALUES ('FR', 'French');
INSERT INTO Languages (Language_Code, Language_Name)
VALUES ('ES', 'Spanish');
INSERT INTO Product_Types (Type_Id, Type_Code, Type_Name)
VALUES (1, 'AB', 'ankle boot');
INSERT INTO Product_Types (Type_Id, Type_Code, Type_Name)
VALUES (2, 'AS', 'athletic shoes');
INSERT INTO Product_Types (Type_Id, Type_Code, Type_Name)
VALUES (3, 'CS', 'cycling shoes');
INSERT INTO Product_Types (Type_Id, Type_Code, Type_Name)
VALUES (4, 'HB', 'hiking boots');
INSERT INTO Suppliers (Supplier_Id, Supplier_Code,
Supplier_Name, Country_Id, City, Address)
VALUES (1, 'EN', 'Eagle Nice', 22, 'New York', '554 W 45th St,
Chelsea');
INSERT INTO Suppliers (Supplier_Id, Supplier_Code,
Supplier_Name, Country_Id, City, Address)
VALUES (2, 'LS', 'Lala Shoes', 11, 'Paris', '93300
Aubervilliers');
INSERT INTO Suppliers (Supplier_Id, Supplier_Code,
Supplier_Name, Country_Id, City, Address)
VALUES (3, 'SM', 'Shoes From Mexico', 17, 'Mexico', 'Blvd.
Adolfo López Mateos 3401');
INSERT INTO Manufacturers (Manufacturer_Code,
Manufacturer_Name, Country_Id, City, Address)
VALUES ('MLS', 'Mar Lu Shoes', 22, 'Cleveland', '22, Mayfield
Road');
INSERT INTO Manufacturers (Manufacturer_Code,
Manufacturer_Name, Country_Id, City, Address)
VALUES ('MA', 'Malerba', 11, 'Bordeaux', '445 Treville ');
INSERT INTO Manufacturers (Manufacturer_Code,
Manufacturer_Name, Country_Id, City, Address)
```

```
VALUES ('FFM', 'FOOTWEAR FACTORY MEXICO', 17, 'Mexico', 'León,
Guanajuato');
```

Now, let's review what is here! The target; the manufacturer system "*Shoes are everywhere*" working at the "*Yellow Shoe*" enterprise. Inside, there is some static information like the lookup data. These are the manufacturers, suppliers, languages, and shoe types. Another relatively common option is to initialize the lookup data in the target system from the beginning. If, on the other hand, the lookup data is not so static and comes from any external or alternative module, such as an ERP or any other source, the generation of lookup data can also be part of the data migration system. There is no problem with this, but only that the complexity of logic increases.

The set of dynamic target tables updated frequently is the set of products and commercial names. The purpose of this simple data transfer system that I am trying to simulate here is to complete these two dynamic target tables.

A process of this type can have many meanings, as discussed earlier. If we think of a classic data migrations system, such an approach can be a unique migration, a kind of initialization of a target from a source. This type of data migration can also involve a lot of work and may require a lot of investigation until we grasp the source's characteristics and match the target.

However, the data transfer process I have in mind is continuous and incremental. The progressive data migration system relies on a staging area, such as a place to detect the changes. Updates in the target will occur depending on the results in the staging area.

In conclusion, we defined the target; we populate some lookup data in it. We also describe a metadata table for attributes.

My purpose is to illustrate a simple data transfer process. I imagine an enterprise, a footwear company named "*Yellow Shoe*." This company has its manufacturing system: "*Shoes are everywhere*." Secondly, another application works on the site, which is not accessible. Let's say this is an accountancy application called "*Yellow Panther*." The first module should be feed from the second one. The manufacturing software is the target system, while the accountancy is the source one.

Hence, now everything is ready to start building our little data transfer process, *Speedy*. There is the destination software that needs data. There is a list of attributes already defined in a metadata table. Of course, this classification was made by Johnny based on the requirements, considering users like Angelique! And here we are, the first step in the process. These are the premises. We described the main components, source, and target and designed the metadata table that explains the attributes in question.

3 Where there is a gate, there is a way out!

The black entry of Mordor

I love Tolkien and have seen "*The Lord of the Rings*" countless times. I still remember when Frodo, Sam, and Gollum arrived for the first at the *Black Gate* in Mordor. It was terrible and scary! But these were not the most frightening things for the brave hobbits, but the gate that made Mordor inaccessible. I imagine similar feelings and thoughts for a programmer who has no knowledge of SAP and sits in front of such a system trying to extract data from it! Or, to generalize, in front of any unfamiliar IT structure! I choose SAP as an example because I know how difficult it is to extract data if you do not have an acceptable level of understanding! Frodo and his team took the pass of "*Cirith Ungol*" and chose to face Shelob. For Johnny Babanus, the migration team leader, in his first attempt at the "*Yellow Shoe*" factory, the facts are clear. He doesn't know the sourcing ERP system, the "*Yellow Panther,*" and needs to find a way to access this software and get the required information. He needs an entry; let's hope easier to obtain than the black gate of Mordor! With the same characteristics, like impenetrability, resistance so the portal will be inaccessible to anyone else!

The concept of a **gateway** to a system, very simple and easy to use, is not something extraordinary or unusual. Moreover, I would even say that this is quite common to some extent. But first, let's see how to build this entry!

One of the first notions that students learn in universities in relational database courses is the master-detail model. From a technical point of view, the source area's image will be precisely the illustration of this banal model, so there is no need to ask yourself and see here unusual or exotic techniques! However, this simple design can still be very robust and powerful, and we must not forget simple and good things just because times change. Over time, some rocks remain standing, right?

Now, let's go back just a bit to some non-SQL concepts, taken from classical object-oriented programming, and looking a bit closer to the entities involved in a system, such as a product or an invoice. Nowadays, when the world is dominated by IT applications, implementing various businesses, we encounter entities everywhere! The model is so practical and so adequate! In our example, imagine a kind of plant or factory where the goal is to create products, shoe items: we first see the product itself. The product is the primary entity. Or, check a website like booking.com; we might see objects like the hotel or pension or whatever, or maybe another one like the customer, etc. In almost any classical system, the entities are involved, and this is one of the standard IT concepts that reflects the realities defined by any line of business.

The notion of entity is part of the model that maps to one business's realities or another. It does not matter what language or framework you are using to implement that reality. I imagine a team of professionals dealing with Java or C# or anything else! These guys handle entities of all kinds and continuously think in this paradigm of entities, classes, etc. When designing and simulating various realities and phenomenons, they see the associated objects belonging to whatever classes, define their attributes and properties, etc. Of course, they think object-oriented, which is part of the most common mindset.

What about the raw data itself, the trivial paradigm of rows and columns? The simple data, you can assume it relational, for my sake! What is the primary purpose for this variety of software applications, if not the data behind? Data exists and lives in many ways, and there are new approaches to data storage and data manipulations. Despite the dynamism in IT, some areas are more liberal and others more conservative. Although their end seemed predictable so often, the relational databases are still very alive on the market! Compromises between new models and the classic, relational model are present quite often!

To conclude the idea and move on, the business context described here is elementary. Let's assume one software product for manufacturing shoes. There might be various factories and plants that are using this application. The life at these sites is similar and different. Moreover, very often, many structures coexist and communicate within the *"Yellow Shoe"* site. The software company that builds the manufacturing system does not know about the other software products at customers' sites. Thus, it decides to implement this gate at the external network and ask: please fill this gate whenever you want to send something to me!

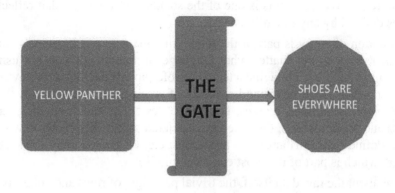

Figure 3-1 The gate mirroring the source area

The entrance to Speedy

If the source is not accessible directly, you can build a portal in the shape of a set of tables. I call this the gateway to the source system. Before doing that, I want to take a closer look at the target design once more. This structure is simplified and familiar.

Assuming there is no direct contact with the accountancy system, an access gate must map the source (the accountancy software). This gate will be like a mirror of this product for the manufacturing system, the data transfer application's target.

I need to clarify one matter. The entry is an output gateway from the data source. On the other hand, the gate's specifications come from Angelique because she has defined what is necessary. Angelique and Johnny define the gate specs, and Jean-Luc and Joanna confirm/infirm the validity of requests made by their partners.

What do you notice first analyzing the target's design? And this observation is quite typical. You can see a **leading entity**: the product, the shoe item, either yellow or not! In this kind of paradigm, there is one prominent presence, and almost everything else is an attribute of that one. This scenario is not rare, and I would say that this is quite typical to many similar enterprises. There is a specific object or set of items in the center of the universe for that business.

Speedy, a data transfer system. A SQL Exercise

The complexity can be higher, and there may exist three or four main parallel entities, each with its own set of attributes. If that is the case, the process can be extended and similarly cover these more real-life scenarios.

Therefore, I can imagine an entry to the process that simulates the data source. I call this the gateway to the source area or vice versa and consider the source area as a portal. The access gate is, from the target's perspective, the entire source area itself. According to the destination, it is not only the whole source area but its necessary segments. In other words, the gate or source coincides with what the destination needs. For example, in the Products table, there might be 100 columns. From these 100, only 15 are necessary attributes according to the destination requirements. Speaking of this table, we can say that the gate may use these 15, and the source area means only these 15, and the rest of 85 are not part of it.

Finally, let's see the gate design. I imagine this portal as composed of two tables, in the classical master-detail architecture, with the master identifying the product and the details are the shoe item attributes. In this way, Johnny can potentially cover almost everything, as demonstrated in the following chapters.

Let's see the gate structure below.

Listing 3-1 The gate, the source area

```sql
-- Same script for Oracle and SQL Server.
CREATE TABLE Gate_Header
(
    Product_Identifier  VARCHAR(20) NOT NULL,
    Business_Code       VARCHAR(20) NOT NULL,
    To_Delete           INT
);
ALTER TABLE Gate_Header
ADD CONSTRAINT Pk_Gate_Header PRIMARY KEY
(Product_Identifier);
CREATE TABLE Gate_Details
(
    Gate_Detail_Id      INT NOT NULL,
    Product_Identifier  VARCHAR(20) NOT NULL,
    Attribute_Name      VARCHAR(255) NOT NULL,
    Attribute_Value     VARCHAR(4000) NOT NULL,
    Attribute_Link      INT DEFAULT (1) NOT NULL,
    To_Delete           INT
);
ALTER TABLE Gate_Details
```

```
ADD CONSTRAINT Pk_Gate_Details PRIMARY KEY (Gate_Detail_Id);
ALTER TABLE Gate_Details ADD CONSTRAINT
Fk_Gate_Details_Gate_Header FOREIGN KEY (Product_Identifier)
REFERENCES Gate_Header (Product_Identifier);
```

Elementary, my dear Watson, Sherlock would say! As in the profession of a private investigator, simplicity is the watchword in a programmer world! There are two tables, the first one is the mirror of the central entity (in our case, the footwear), and the second one is the set of attributes for each object. In our case, there is the product itself in the first table, the shoe item, correct? Please go back and check the first table, Products. This table has the columns code and name that are the ones that uniquely identify the product. Fortunately, in the *"Shoes are everywhere"* database, there is a **unique** constraint for the product code. We have luck, and this is a favorable scenario because it simplifies things from the beginning. In the absence of it, as seen later, things can get more complicated.

The uniqueness of the central entity

One of the essential characteristics of a system is the **uniqueness** of the leading entities. In our case, the fact that there is a unique business key for the product is a consistent design! It is not always like this, sometimes this is not happening, and there is no way to identify the primary entity uniquely. There are almost always some attributes that could locate the principal objects but not in an exclusive manner. It may be possible to identify the product, in our case, by two or three fields, which could be the desired solution. For example, a concatenation of the two or three columns or expressions into one can goes into the product identifier.

Sometimes the unique identification by using meaningful fields is not possible. We can manipulate artificial identifiers instead. Anyway, these are not reliable. But, with care and effort, this substitute is viable. There is still a solution! Some easier than others; every project is different; there is no generic recipe!

Now, coming back to the portal, the source area mirror, if this might be accessible directly from the origin system, well, in this case, I am not sure how much there is a need for this gate! We can build a direct logic to fill the target structure. It depends; there are so many aspects involved in this equation! Sometimes, even in this scenario, using a gate as an intermediate between the source and the target can be the best solution.

Anyway, quite often, direct access is not possible for various reasons. In this case, we need to imagine this gateway at the source system entrance and populate it. As we already understood from the previous chapter, there are many teams. One team that implements and handles the data transfer system work with the users at the *"Yellow Shoe"* site. There is the popular guy from the IT crowd,

Speedy, a data transfer system. A SQL Exercise

Johnny Babanus! But there is also the second team, dealing with the "*Yellow Panther.*" In general, their knowledge does not intersect. The guys working at "*Shoes are everywhere,*" lead by Johnny, possess specific manufacturing product expertise. Johnny and his programmers, analysts, testers, and business users are completely unknowledgeable regarding the accountancy product and vice versa.

What is the conclusion? The data transfer system of this kind has a remainder and is not entirely free and independent. Jean-Luc has his role; this is what I want to say. Johnny invented the portal; he assumed this portal was filled with information and started from here. What about the task of filling the entrance?

There should be such a task; it is mandatory. Johnny Babanus does not know everything! When he has been to the "*Yellow Shoe,*" he talked to Angelique, but not only. He also had a lot of meeting with Jean-Luc. Not with the same flavor, but with the same business relevance and efficiency! As two excellent professionals, Johnny and Jean-Luc analyzed, discussed, and agreed on their collaboration. Johnny drove the discussion, as he was the requester. He described the gate to Jean-Luc and explained the restrictions he must meet when filling the portal.

One of the first responsibilities of the "*Yellow Panther*" team is to identify the product uniquely. The shoe item is distinct in the manufacturing system (lucky). But that is not a reason to have the same unique constraint in the other application, the panther. If a similar restriction exists in the "*Yellow Panther,*" then we are covered! However, this is an optimistic scenario! If not, Jean-Luc's team needs to find a way to build such a unique identifier and pass it to the portal.

Let's take a look for a while in the other garden; let's take a look at the accounting team. The sourcing team is lead by Jean-Luc, who else but someone with such an impressive name as the Enterprise's captain can be so handy to acknowledge such a complicated system like the accountancy one. Joanna and Jean-Luc are working together in the parallel team at "*Yellow Panther.*" Their task is to extract the data and fill the gateway!

Among the first responsibilities of any simple system like this one is the central entity's unique identification. This property, of uniqueness, needs to be available in both applications. We know it exists in the manufacturing system. The question is if this code exists in the accountancy system too? Johnny doesn't know, and he asks Jean-Luc. There is a collective effort in the beginning. Therefore, let's ask the Hamletian question: Is the product unique in the source or only at the destination?

In any case, Jean-Luc and his team need to find a way and extract the unique code and product name from their database. They have their separate logic responsible for this extraction. This operation needs to be consistent; the programming logic should transfer the same code every time for the same pair of shoes. Even here, the logic's complexity may vary, but it usually should not be too difficult due to the target simplicity.

After this problem is solved and the product is correctly and uniquely identified, the *"Yellow Panther"* team needs to dig into the source tables and gather the attributes and details.

What are the required attributes? Usually, this is a question-driven from the target system. For sure, all the mandatory fields in the destination are necessary, in one way or another. Either these should exist in the Panther or, if not, supplied somehow with some default values or generated during the transfer process. Anyway, the required attributes are a decision driven by the target; they know what they need from the source. The Jean-Luc team will build their logic to supply these attributes in the detail table (see the above gate details table).

Once Jean-Luc finishes this task, periodically, he fills the gate representing the source, and *Speedy* will receive the input and start its execution. After this logic ends, things are going smoothly. The advantage of this approach is that the data transfer system is entirely independent of the source. There can be any 10, 20, or 30 source systems, but the gate is the same. Of course, the cost is that, for every case, the sourcing team needs to fill the entrance. But the two groups coexist independently. *"Speedy"* system is built once and maintained with new attributes, for example. At every site, the sourcing team will also develop the logic to fill the two tables once, and then things go without too much effort. So, in a normal situation, there is an initial effort, and that's it. Lean-Luc is back to his usual old tasks regarding the maintenance of the *"Yellow Panther."*

Any enterprise like *"Yellow Shoe"* can buy a software system that covers everything, the dream software! But, quite often, this is not possible. Despite the efforts made by the big software companies, the customers using the various systems are forced to survive and manage with many applications handling multiple and diverse segments of their business. Sometimes, I would quite say often; the IT products need to coexists, integrate somehow, even to act almost like one. For these kinds of situations, a data migration product like *"Speedy"* is precious.

Thus, having this gate ready to go, presenting it to the customers' technicians, there is only one task for them. Fill in the entry! What does that mean? We will see the design soon! Just a bit of patience, please!

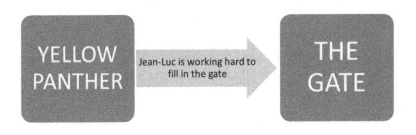

Figure 3-2 The logic to fill the gate

Jean-Luc, please, fill the portal!

When imagining Johnny at the *"Yellow Shoe"* company site speaking to the colleagues working at the accountancy system, it functions there for ages. Johnny and Jean-Luc face to face, that's quite a challenge for Johnny! But, like his courageous ancestors from the Roman empire, you should know he is not afraid of any enemy, and Jean-Luc is proven to be his valuable partner and not an enemy. That does not mean that, sometimes, in other similar enterprises, other Jean-Luc may act as enemies. Sometimes, new systems or changes, in general, are not welcomed, and the hosts do everything they can to prevent these. Fortunately, this was not the case now. Even if this Panther system exists for ages, there was no resistance and opposition against Johnny. Jean-Luc understood that the manufacturing application, *"Shoes are everywhere,"* needs to take energy from the *"Yellow Panther"* accountancy system. He understood the need for a connection.

This gate is a simplified model. But how much information do you think you can cover with such a simple model? More than expected, I would say. You will be amazed when you try in a real system!

For the core system representing the source, the target is now extraordinarily accessible and straightforward in a simple design. How difficult is it for the specialists in the core software to fill this source? Well, this is another question. How difficult is it to fill a master-detail structure from a complex system? Typically, if the team working at the core application are the right professionals and knows their product well enough, the task should be relatively accessible.

50

However, depending on it, this task might be simple, averagely available, but it can also be challenging or demanding. So, I am not saying this is always a possible or an easy option.

Alternatively, the customer can buy a data migration tool to ensure this communication! But I can hardly believe it will be easier! However, there is no panacea in IT like anywhere else in life. I present a solution, that's all.

And I start with the cost of the solution first. It is well-known that every problem and result has costs and benefits. I offer a solution, the use of a gate as an entry to a source system. The advantage is that this provides independence. The cost is an assumption: the assumption that someone will fill the entrance. There needs to be a sourcing program team to build a logic that needs to populate this entrance. The structure of the gate is trivial. Hence, in most cases, this logic should not be very hard.

In my example, users like Joanna define the products in her application for accountancy purposes. Accountancy is always the first in line! These shoes are here first. I do not want to go to Angelique and say to her: please add the products a second time in the manufacturing system. They did that many years, but this has to stop!

I imagine the entrance to the *"Yellow Panther,"* and I conceive the core specialists fill this gate at the customer site, by Jean-Luc himself, with Joanna's help! And I need to accept that this is the cost of the data migration system. A logic should exist in the accountancy system!

My kingdom for a code! A unique code!

If there is something to say that is critical is a unique code to identify the central entity, the product code, in this case. This Product_Identifier field can be anything, but the meaning is always the same. If such a data migration system is to function correctly, there needs to be a way to solely identify the primary entity (entities), in our case, the product. It is like you are looking into a crowd and you want to find whatever person. What is implied in this search is that, once you determine the person in question, this result is undoubted, and there is no possibility of confusion!

Therefore, the first and perhaps most critical task for colleagues in the parallel team, for Jean-Luc and Joanna, is that they should start and dig into their system and see if there is any single field or field combination of the product. And here there are so many options that we need another book to describe them all! But, in general, in any well-designed system, there is such a field (fields). We may call this the **unique business constraint** of the system. It can be, for example, a real unique product code. In factories, sometimes, products are identified in meaningful ways. Occasionally, a combination of significant values can determine the shoe item. Of course, there are maybe many principal entities in a more complex system, so many business constraints.

What is this business constraint? It may be a product code with a product type or a name associated with a department! In my opinion, first, the specialist will check to see if there is any meaningful way to (uniquely) identify the footwear item business-wise. It can be a field or many fields that might have true business meaning and uniquely identifies the product. These are the best because they are stable, reliable, and significant. Both IT teams and business teams can participate in the identification process; validation is natural. If Jean-Luc can find the match key in this way and is sure that this path is out of any confusion, which means this way is univocal and assure uniqueness, half of the problem is solved. Whatever happened to the product, anything that crosses to the target through the data transfer system is reliable, in the sense that, even if something went wrong, the topic of discussion is stable, the products that are involved are safe.

It is like in a dialogue when two or many participants are debating a specific topic. What makes the difference between a real conversation, based on reasoning and logic versus a fake dialog, where persuasion and personal interests might prevail, for example. To be able to have a coherent dialogue, one of the first rules is to be able to sustain the idea in the discussion, to be able to fix the topic of a debate, and not to deviate from it. Identifying the subject of an argument is the first and successful rule of a dialogue. Otherwise, what is happening? The conversation participants change the subject, but they do not admit this and state that they keep the discussion thread. The conclusion is evident to all of us, no need to insist.

Now, what is the relevance of this analogy? The uniqueness of the object, the singularity is necessary to do things consistently. The persistence of any data transfer system relies on the unequivocal identification of the entities in the process.

We finish the first step: to identify the product uniquely. This identifier can be natural or artificial. Even if it's a surrogate, mathematically and logically speaking, it is the right candidate for identifying the entity. However, not the preferred one, in my opinion. A surrogate identifier can be passed from the sourcing system to the target system but generated in a one-to-one match with a business-wise id whenever possible.

After Jean-Luc can indisputably touch the product, he needs to pass this information to the gate. He needs to fill the product_identifier with something (see Listing 3-1). As mentioned earlier, Jean-Luc will generate, during the logic in the source, an artificial identifier to pass it through the interface. If that is the way, the development should be reliable enough so that the logic can always reconstruct, again and in a categoric and precise manner, the artificial identifier (product_identifier) from the meaningful source identifier.

If you check the header, you can see the field business_code. This field is a product code that may have strong relevance from the business point of view. It can be the same as the product_identifier. If such product code exists in the manufacturer system and identifies from the business point of view the shoe, and if this is unique and not secret somehow, we are happy! Diversely, if this code exists and is non-unique or cannot be revealed or secret or has a higher length, Johnny can generate a parallel code and send it to the gate. This code will be artificial in most cases.

Thus, the source area's first step is a logic entirely unknown for the system's target owners. The gate's header is filled and seems reliable! By reliable, I understand that every time Lean-Luc fills the source's entrance and receives a product identifier like MammaMia, he is sure that it is the same and not something else. So, either MammaMia is a unique code for a product, like a shoe product code, let's say, or that MammaMia is a generated code. There is either an artificial source identifier like 100 or a real product code like whatever actual code behind him.

The effect of this first logic is the first set of materials ready for transfer to the target. Let's see the example, first gate header:

Listing 3-2 The first set of products available

```
-- Same script for Oracle and SQL Server. Don't forget to
commit if running on Oracle.
INSERT INTO Gate_Header (Product_Identifier, Business_Code)
VALUES ('AT12_TS_098', 'AT12_TS_098');
INSERT INTO Gate_Header (Product_Identifier, Business_Code)
VALUES ('NM94_AX_121', 'NKS_LRM_093');
INSERT INTO Gate_Header (Product_Identifier, Business_Code)
VALUES ('AT12_RE_106', 'AT12_RE_106');
INSERT INTO Gate_Header (Product_Identifier, Business_Code)
VALUES ('NM92_DD_191', 'NKS_BKM_135');
```

This set of insert statements is the result of the logic developed by the accountancy team. As such, I just added here to be easy for the reader to generate the data required for the following exercises. There are, in the first entry, four materials. Let's see the data quickly! I don't need to remind you to run this on your system.

Table 3-1 Gate header (first execution)

Product Identifier	Business Code
AT12_TS_098	AT12_TS_098
NM94_AX_121	NKS_LRM_093
AT12_RE_106	AT12_RE_106
NM92_DD_191	NKS_BKM_135

Even if this seems to be the simple part, the source's logic might not be so easy. Anyway, if uniqueness is not fully acquired, the entire data transfer system will not be reliable, which might happen. All kinds of workarounds will probably come into effect to solve this problem. In the absence of uniqueness for the entities in question that will exchange data during the data transfer process between a source and a target, the entire application will be challenging to maintain. This first step is essential, and I encourage everyone to set up such a system to channel all their energies to solve this crucial problem. You can see that two products have a different product code and two not. The product code is a business field, and the product identifier is a unique key. Sometimes it is the same; otherwise, not, as in the example above.

What next, of course? Well, not difficult to guess! Let's see what the next task for the source IT team is.

Jean-Luc is searching for details

Now that he identified the product and the gate header is ready, Jean-Luc can move to the details. Here comes the second part, getting the properties of the product, the shoe item. This task will once more validate his abilities and knowledge of the accountancy system. He is living with the Panther for many years! Although the gate is extremely accessible, the core system might be very complicated. Still, in most cases, the extraction and the logic required to fill the entry should not be very hard. Anyway, it depends on the accessibility of the Panther, and there might be significant differences. For example, extracting information from a system like an SAP system is quite challenging and requires a lot of knowledge, both business and technical.

Looking at the gateway details design table (see Listing 3-1), we see that Jean-Luc need to fill, for every attribute to be imported into the target and make Johnny happy, the following information in a normalized fashion:

♣ He needs to supply an artificial identifier either from a sequence or identity-based etc. Of course, this is maybe not mandatory, but it is always good to be sure you have uniqueness, even in this case. You never know when you might need it! The column name is Gate_Detail_Id; it is just the artificial identifier for a detail.

♣ He needs to specify the product identifier. This field is the foreign key to the header and represents the product itself. All the attributes specified here are product attributes! He should not accept orphans! Any detail belongs to a shoe; there is nothing but shoes here.

♣ Jean-Luc needs to fill in the attribute's name from the list of characteristics, the field Attribute_name (see Listing 2-3). The attribute name could have been enforced by a foreign key constraint referencing the lookup table M_Attributes (see Listing 2-2). Nevertheless, this is not a must and not even always possible if the metadata schema is not in the same database as the source or target. Usually, the table that defines the attributes should be more complex and should allow more variety. In our case, for simplicity, he considers one attribute name and sets it as unique. The richness of attributes is vital, and different types of properties might have the same name, for example!.

♣ He needs to specify the value for the attribute, the field Attribute_Value. Again, for simplicity, he considers just a string, but, of course, more variety may be present here, various data types, etc.

♣ If you check the gate design (see Listing 3-1), you will see the column To_Delete. What is the meaning of this field? What is happening if Joanna removes a product or even an attribute from the *"Yellow Panther?"* Jean-Luc should set the value one (1) for this column, and Johnny will know that he needs to do something. He may delete the product entirely in the *"Shoes are everywhere"* or flag it somehow etc.

♣ Last but not least, there is the Attribute_Link column. I want to explain more about this column's meaning later when I show it its usefulness. Keep in mind, for now, that this column becomes necessary in situations where we have many fields for a particular attribute. Moreover, these attributes should be multiple for an entity. As you will see later, this will be the case for commercial names. Until then, see the default value as one and ignore this column for now. We'll get back to it later.

Now, Johnny and Jean-Luc are looking at this database table and laughs happily! This portal, this mirror of the source, is too simple, seems quite a piece of cake! If you only see the whole side of the glass, it is. How hard it's to extract the information from the source, this is something that is beyond his powers, but it seems that Jean-Luc manages to do it quite well!

On the other hand, Johnny starts and prepares the information for Jean-Luc, having a clear goal in his mind. He needs to extract the required attributes from his systems and send them to the source area team to utilize them and fill the gateway appropriately.

First of all, as the data transfer team leader, Johnny is driving the process. Consequently, he prepares the list of attributes required from the target. From one side to another, some properties might always show up, while others not.

Looking at the target design, Johnny makes a list of required attributes and sends it to Jean-Luc. Let's see the list and add it in an excel file:

Table 3-2 List of required attributes

Attribute Name	Attribute Type	Attribute Length
Product Code	String	20
Product Name	String	255
Product Type Code	String	20
Supplier Code	String	20
Manufacturer Code	String	20
Color	String	100
Gender	String	10
Measure	Integer	5
Commercial Code	String	20
Commercial Name	String	255
Manufacturer Code	String	20
Language	String	20

Johnny and Jean-Luc live in different worlds. Johnny is part of the destination team, and he may lead the data transfer process, while Jean-Luc is responsible for the accountancy system, the source. Both applications play at the same customer site, the "*Yellow Shoe,*" and they need to live together in peace and prosperity! Like in the Vulcan world, "*Live long and prosper,*" as Spock would say! Being both Star Trekkers, this is how the two engineers greeted each other when they met and started work!

Some of the attributes prepared by Johnny are easy to obtain from the "*Yellow Panther.*" Other properties may not be so accessible and require a lot of effort. Further details might not even be available in the source system, and Jean-Luc may not possess them at all. Johnny and Angelique are preparing this excel with caution, and they deliver it to Jean-Luc. He is now completely aware of Johnnys' needs. The next step is clear. Jean-Luc will start the work and investigate his Panther system and see what he can deliver. He sees what he has and not, and he prepares the list of answers for Johnny. For example, maybe the Panther does not store commercial names for the products; they might be stored in a third system or never stored elsewhere.

Consequently, these will never fill the gate. The necessities of a target are not always satisfied by the source. Therefore, the options are limitless.

After a careful investigation of his system, Jean-Luc and Joanna will update the excel with what is available. Their communication will continue until the list is ready. Afterward, Jean-Luc will start digging into his database using whatever means he wants. I mean, he can extract his data using SQL, or maybe using Java or C#, or what means he has at his disposal. It does not matter. Jean-Luc must build his logic to fill the gate's second side, the source detail table named Gate_Details.

Finally, he wrote his program from the source area and filled the data transfer system entrance to serve the destination. Let's assume this SQL code after some research and work. The result of his effort will be the fact that the gateway is now full, and the data transfer interface is ready to receive the first meal!

Now we assume this logic exists due to Jean-Luc efforts. Let's picture the result of his work in a set of insert statements. For easy access and the option to do everything yourself, I prefer to list many insert statements. Please run this in your system and see what you got! The most important thing here in this work is for the readers to reproduce my example. Please be my guest!

Listing 3-3 The first set of materials ready to go (detail)

```
-- Same script for Oracle and SQL Server. Don't forget to
commit if running on Oracle.
INSERT INTO Gate_Details (Gate_Detail_Id, Product_Identifier,
Attribute_Name, Attribute_Value)
VALUES (1, 'AT12_TS_098', 'PRODUCT_NAME', 'Black Adidas
Torsion original ZX flux');
INSERT INTO Gate_Details (Gate_Detail_Id, Product_Identifier,
Attribute_Name, Attribute_Value)
```

```
    VALUES (2, 'AT12_TS_098', 'GENDER', 'Male');
    INSERT INTO Gate_Details (Gate_Detail_Id, Product_Identifier,
Attribute_Name, Attribute_Value)
    VALUES (3, 'AT12_TS_098', 'COLOR', 'Black');
    INSERT INTO Gate_Details (Gate_Detail_Id, Product_Identifier,
Attribute_Name, Attribute_Value)
    VALUES (4, 'AT12_TS_098', 'TYPE_CODE', 'AS');
    INSERT INTO Gate_Details (Gate_Detail_Id, Product_Identifier,
Attribute_Name, Attribute_Value)
    VALUES (5, 'NM94_AX_121', 'PRODUCT_NAME', 'Nike Zoom Pegasus
Turbo 2');
    INSERT INTO Gate_Details (Gate_Detail_Id, Product_Identifier,
Attribute_Name, Attribute_Value)
    VALUES (6, 'NM94_AX_121', 'GENDER', 'Female');
    INSERT INTO Gate_Details (Gate_Detail_Id, Product_Identifier,
Attribute_Name, Attribute_Value)
    VALUES (7, 'NM94_AX_121', 'COLOR', 'Pink');
    INSERT INTO Gate_Details (Gate_Detail_Id, Product_Identifier,
Attribute_Name, Attribute_Value)
    VALUES (8, 'NM94_AX_121', 'TYPE_CODE', 'AS');
    INSERT INTO Gate_Details (Gate_Detail_Id, Product_Identifier,
Attribute_Name, Attribute_Value)
    VALUES (9, 'NM94_AX_121', 'SUPPLIER_CODE', 'LS');
    INSERT INTO Gate_Details (Gate_Detail_Id, Product_Identifier,
Attribute_Name, Attribute_Value)
    VALUES (10, 'AT12_RE_106', 'PRODUCT_NAME', 'Adidas Samba Rose
Core Black');
    INSERT INTO Gate_Details (Gate_Detail_Id, Product_Identifier,
Attribute_Name, Attribute_Value)
    VALUES (11, 'AT12_RE_106', 'GENDER', 'Unisex');
    INSERT INTO Gate_Details (Gate_Detail_Id, Product_Identifier,
Attribute_Name, Attribute_Value)
    VALUES (12, 'AT12_RE_106', 'COLOR', 'Black');
    INSERT INTO Gate_Details (Gate_Detail_Id, Product_Identifier,
Attribute_Name, Attribute_Value)
    VALUES (13, 'AT12_RE_106', 'TYPE_CODE', 'AS');
    INSERT INTO Gate_Details (Gate_Detail_Id, Product_Identifier,
Attribute_Name, Attribute_Value)
    VALUES (14, 'AT12_RE_106', 'SUPPLIER_CODE', 'EN');
```

```
INSERT INTO Gate_Details (Gate_Detail_Id, Product_Identifier,
Attribute_Name, Attribute_Value)
    VALUES (15, 'AT12_RE_106', 'MANUFACTURER_CODE', 'MLS');
INSERT INTO Gate_Details (Gate_Detail_Id, Product_Identifier,
Attribute_Name, Attribute_Value)
    VALUES (16, 'NM92_DD_191', 'PRODUCT_NAME', 'Nike Lance Cycling
Shoes Men 41');
INSERT INTO Gate_Details (Gate_Detail_Id, Product_Identifier,
Attribute_Name, Attribute_Value)
    VALUES (17, 'NM92_DD_191', 'GENDER', 'Male');
INSERT INTO Gate_Details (Gate_Detail_Id, Product_Identifier,
Attribute_Name, Attribute_Value)
    VALUES (18, 'NM92_DD_191', 'COLOR', 'Silver');
INSERT INTO Gate_Details (Gate_Detail_Id, Product_Identifier,
Attribute_Name, Attribute_Value)
    VALUES (19, 'NM92_DD_191', 'TYPE_CODE', 'CS');
INSERT INTO Gate_Details (Gate_Detail_Id, Product_Identifier,
Attribute_Name, Attribute_Value)
    VALUES (20, 'NM92_DD_191', 'SUPPLIER_CODE', 'EN');
INSERT INTO Gate_Details (Gate_Detail_Id, Product_Identifier,
Attribute_Name, Attribute_Value)
    VALUES (21, 'NM92_DD_191', 'MANUFACTURER_CODE', 'FFM');
INSERT INTO Gate_Details (Gate_Detail_Id, Product_Identifier,
Attribute_Name, Attribute_Value)
    VALUES (22, 'NM92_DD_191', 'MEASURE', '41');
```

The first part of the project is ready! Jean-Luc completes his task; he delivered *"Speedy"* input and filled the gate with the required information. He was able to fill the header and send a unique identifier for the product. Then, get the details, the product's attributes, and reload the gate's second side, the detail table. He writes a set of procedures and functions in his way and using his means, and from now on, executing his code, he will be able to fill the gate whenever necessary.

Now, let's quickly look at the gate details in a tabular format and analyze the first wave of data knocking at the target's doors! Let's see the proof of concept of Jean-Luc's work. And, with this, for now, Jean-Luc can rest. We will not call him soon! He can work on the Panther, for now, leaving *"Speedy"* aside!

Table 3-3 The gate details (source area details)

Product Identifier	Attribute Name	Attribute Value
AT12_TS_098	PRODUCT_NAME	Black Adidas Torsion original ZX flux
AT12_TS_098	GENDER	Male
AT12_TS_098	COLOR	Black
AT12_TS_098	TYPE_CODE	AS
NM94_AX_121	PRODUCT_NAME	Nike Zoom Pegasus Turbo 2
NM94_AX_121	GENDER	Female
NM94_AX_121	COLOR	Pink
NM94_AX_121	TYPE_CODE	AS
NM94_AX_121	SUPPLIER_CODE	LS
AT12_RE_106	PRODUCT_NAME	Adidas Samba Rose Core Black
AT12_RE_106	GENDER	Unisex
AT12_RE_106	COLOR	Black
AT12_RE_106	TYPE_CODE	AS
AT12_RE_106	SUPPLIER_CODE	EN
AT12_RE_106	MANUFACTURER_CODE	MLS
NM92_DD_191	PRODUCT_NAME	Nike Lance Cycling Shoes Men 41
NM92_DD_191	GENDER	Male
NM92_DD_191	COLOR	Silver
NM92_DD_191	TYPE_CODE	CS
NM92_DD_191	SUPPLIER_CODE	EN
NM92_DD_191	MANUFACTURER_CODE	FFM
NM92_DD_191	MEASURE	41

Is the gate ready? What about some homework!

Now Jean-Luc can go back to his regular duties and continue his routine activities in the Panther doing whatever he needs to do: maintenance, support, maybe development! He completed his task and, if the results are correct, he will come back to his program and update whenever new attributes will be necessary, for example. Because this is always possible, the sets of features are dynamic, and more and more information may be required for the target in the future, which means that Lean-Luc's code may require some maintenance. But for now, he finishes his work.

Let's analyze this first input to the data migration system:

♣　You can see the unique identifiers in both Table 3-1 and Table 3-3. The data is coming from the *"Yellow Panther."* It can be artificial; it can be a simple integer or a string or even have a business meaning in the source. The only matter that is highly critical is the identifier's uniqueness. Being unique in the accountancy module will be transported to the target and have the desired consistency. The entire communication relies on this feature. Otherwise, any transmission is an illusion!

♣　You can also see in the header the business code. This necessary information is coming from the source. Usually, this could be unique if it is a real product code. However, there is no strict requirement of this type. It can be unique in combination with other fields. You can see (Table 3-1) that Nike shoes have such codes. These go directly to the gate. For instance, Adidas shoes do not have such product codes. In this case, you can see how Jean-Luc is passing the same product identifier for Adidas shoes as product codes too.

♣　In the detailed source table (Table 3-3), you can see the attributes. Material Name is always transmitted. The name is mandatory in the target (see Products' design in Listing 2-1, second chapter). Both product name and product code are compulsory in the destination. Typically, the portal must contain the attribute material name. During the processing logic, there are various ways to handle a potential missing name. For example, if the source does not pass a name for the product (less probable but not impossible), Jean-Luc can transmit the product identifier instead. However, a product with a meaningless name is a bit absurd. If you check the central table's design, you can see that the table Products has only two mandatory fields: code and name. And this will correspond to the column PRODUCT_CODE in the header and the attribute PRODUCT_NAME.

Speedy, a data transfer system. A SQL Exercise

♣   See how gender, color, and product type code are always part of all the products. See the correspondence between the attributes in the gate and their corresponding columns in the target. Some of these will come via the lookup tables. But this is part of the data transfer system itself, so that I will come back later at this. These attributes are all simple, which means a one-to-one relationship with the central entity, the product. They can, however, miss.

♣   Note that the supplier code and manufacturer code are not always present. For various reasons, the source cannot send everything, and maybe some products miss some information. That is why these products have some attributes, while others do not. These two, supplier and manufacturer, are also simple, which means somehow directly to the shoe item, one per product. One product can have one supplier or one manufacturer, not many.

Before finalizing this part, filling the so-called gateway, the Panther's image, or the input, I would like to add some more notes regarding Jean-Luc and his team and their communication.

As mentioned earlier, Johnny and Jean-Luc are not aware of what they have on each other. That is why this gate exists to fill this lack of mutual knowledge and allow proper communication.

But that does not mean communication and exchange of information do not exist between the two sides. In particular, Jean-Luc periodically may receive specifications from Johnny and his team, and he needs to update his logic that is filling the gate eventually. The lookup data is transmitted somehow to assure some consistent information from the beginning, as much as possible.

Let's take some attributes, for example, color. There are the colors blue and black in the target system, and Jean-Luc should be aware of the color names that are not always standard. Maybe Jean-Luc has a variety of colors, and he has light blue and dark blue instead. Or vice versa. As much as possible, they should try to work together and make things consistent, if possible.

Then there is the gender field! In the manufacturing application, gender is Male, Female, Unisex, Boys, Girls, etc. Usually, Jean-Luc should send the same naming conventions from the Panther team. Now, Jean-Luc has M and F instead of male and female. As part of his logic, Jean-Luc will try to map and send "Male" instead of M and "Female" instead of F to assure consistency and not create fake genders, as M and F are fake genders from the manufacturing point of view!

The same considerations apply to lookup data. If you review the target design, you can understand that Johnny might prepare a list of lookup names and codes, like Language and Types. Typically, the languages and types should be neutral, so Jean-Luc should adapt and try to send the same values if the source names differ. A kind of mapping will occur. We do not want to have many Swedish languages, as there is just one!

What about manufacturers and suppliers? Jean-Luc received a list with providers and tried to identify the common ones and send the same codes for these, if possible and if these are common. But maybe some suppliers or manufacturers do not exist in the target. These providers need to be part of the destination. Or not, it depends on what is required. These variations are part of the *"Speedy"* system's implementation, and we will see more in the next chapters. For example, maybe new suppliers are automatically created in the target if they do not exist. Or perhaps, the transfer process does not allow this, and any new supplier must be made manually by the users, considering this scenario is very rare. Many options are on the table!

I want to rephrase here, and with this, I finish the topic, that the sourcing team will receive some information from the destination group to ensure data consistency. To speak in a data warehouse terminology, avoid steps like consolidation or cleaning from the beginning, if possible. We all know how hard these steps are! We are not in a data warehouse system, although there are similarities with an ETL. Nevertheless, we considered one source of data and one target from the beginning, so you can name it a simplified ETL, although it was not my intention to speak about a data warehouse. But consolidation and cleaning may show up even in a simple system like this one if Johnny does not receive objective data from Jean-Luc. It is easy to allow redundancy and inconsistency in our designs; this is a lesson that we always learn!

Before concluding this chapter, I would like to suggest to my readers the first homework. This part of the book is for those readers who are really interested in practicing if there is such a thing! Imagine the Panther system, build a simple database and create a logic that will fill the gateway of the source system. On this occasion, you could see how simple or, on the contrary, difficult it can be to complete a simple structure of master-details from a standard database. Consider your first task, as others will come. As I said earlier, I am also a database trainer and I think this approach is useful to some readers who see this book as an SQL exercise/course. Therefore, this exercise includes an active component of the reader, who can complete the book and contribute. This SQL exercise can be seen as a project proposal for a student or a group of students, as a sketch whose completion is at the student's discretion. Defining a Panther structure and creating a related SQL logic that will fill the gate is a part that remains a task for a reader eager to increase their SQL efficiency.

Finally, the gate breathes. The data migration system has its input; there are already some test data for the first execution. The implementation team did the job and continuously helped the sourcing team prepare the logic to fill the gate. Is now the time to move on to the real programming logic? Is the time to see some SQL?

4 Check the entrance consistency

Are we ready for the logic?

In the previous chapter, I analyzed the concept of a gateway to a sourcing system. By definition, a data transfer program like *"Speedy"* involves a source area and a target, such as a starting point and an endpoint. The purpose is to transfer information between the two locations. I described the entrance, an input to the source system, or a mirror of the source area, according to the target requirements. As mentioned, this mirror is not a real one but an approximation because it will reveal what is required by the destination. As I said in one of my previous chapters, transferring data does not merely copy a source to a destination. It is less than that! The data transfer takes place according to the target requirements. The process is activated on-demand, and the request comes from the destination. For example, maybe only a small part of the source is needed. The data transfer process will try to accommodate that part only. Thus, the mirror's metaphor is not entirely accurate because the portal is not the source itself but the subset required by the target!

In the previous chapter, I illustrated all the teams' efforts, especially the sourcing team, to fill this portal. Consequently, we already have some data; the first four products are placed in the gate by Jean-Luc, the "*Yellow Panther*" leader of the source system.

The example describes a common scenario with two software applications working together on a single site: an accounting software and a manufacturing one. Both information systems manage different single business segments of shoe production. The accounting team has built a development process that fills the portal, and this gate will become the entrance for the manufacturing system, the target. Sometimes, the world of applications living together can be peaceful and neutral; each business line may be distinct, while software may not interfere with each other. But there is also the scenario in which applications must communicate. And this is the case within "*Yellow Shoe!*" These two systems are not distinct, but they share some data elements. Joanna creates most of the accounting products, and some of these items are necessary for various purposes in the manufacturing software.

Why do the programs need to communicate? As explained, there is the possibility to create the products twice. We can assume different users, but after

64

all, this is not so relevant. The duplicate's work idea is not compelling without mentioning that it leaves room for inconsistency. The products are the same, so they can be defined twice, even if for different purposes, they can reach situations such as one footwear can be wrongly defined as two!

What about *"Speedy"*? The data transfer system can be part of the target as an extension. Or it can be a completely separate IT application. Alternatively, there are a lot of data migration tools on the market! These are highly generic and require both source and target connectors. This approach is, of course, an alternative solution. Please do not accuse me of rejecting this alternative from the start! But what I want to offer here is a custom, purely SQL-based choice. There are no visual tools and facilities, no hidden code, no fancy and modern features, but the same old classic SQL language! This SQL-based utility is my proposal for a data transfer system!

Let's continue. Now that the gateway is ready, what's next? Can we start some logic? Can we finally get to the point of beginning the actual process of developing *"Speedy?"* Even if there is a risk of disappointing you, I must postpone this moment! We can't start work yet!

"Speedy" has to wait for a simple reason. I spent the entire previous chapter explaining the portal. We talked about Jean-Luc and the process he and his team build to fill the gate, the two simple tables that make up the entrance. Jean-Luc already delivered a data sampling that populates the portal, meaning *"Speedy"* can start. However, the answer is no. We can't begin the transfer process logic yet, and we still have to be a little patient. Why all this, what is missing? Just a bit of patience, and you will find out!

Sorry, the gateway is not ready yet

The ultimate goal of the data transfer system is to populate the destination zone. So far, the only thing we have is the so-called gateway. This entry is a simple master-detail structure that should be completed from the source area by a dedicated team led by our brave Jean-Luc, with his logic written inside the source.

Hence, the next thing that comes to mind is to start the work. To begin building logic, write SQL code, or maybe anything else like Java or Python for developers that fills more comfortably with other technologies, we could imagine a staging area and think about design. All this will come soon enough, but there is still something before that!

Let's talk a little more about the gate because this chapter is still on it, whether you believe it or not! The process written by Jean-Luc will populate the entrance periodically. Joanna will define new shoe items in the accounting system, and other business accounting users will update various information about these. From time to time, manufacturing software may require access to some of these products. Jean-Luc's process will run at the request of some users like Angelique or anyone else. Eventually, a job might periodically check for new updates from the accountancy system, etc. What kind of updates? For example, maybe a shoe changed its type or has a new commercial name, or perhaps a trading name changes its text, or a pair of shoes is out from the *"Yellow Panther*!*"* Any of the three classic actions against data, addition, update, or deletion, can be applied in whole or in part to the products by specific attributes.

One of the characteristics of the gateway is **volatility**. The entrance is transitory because the changes are coming as requested from *"Yellow Panther."* What was there before was removed entirely before each new execution. The portal will contain precisely the changes in the sourcing system since the last run. Thus, let's say I fill the gate now. The process runs and allows the product data to transfer to the target. At the next execution, the entrance is truncated and refilled with the new product information. So, this is a good thing, and we have no history to keep; we care about nothing but the present!

Thus, the gateway has no maintenance!. There is nothing to maintain at this set of simple tables; make sure someone like Jean-Luc filled them correctly whenever needed and releases them completely every time a new execution starts. In this case, what else is to be said? Why is the gate not ready yet? Why can't we continue the work and start looking at the development?

The answer is simple. I am sure that the *"Yellow Panther"* specialist, Jean-Luc, has won Johnny's trust. However, I ask you, can he and the entire data transfer team entirely rely on this subjective feeling? Can they be sure that the portal's data is accurate and will not cause any inconsistencies and errors when running *"Speedy"*? Suppose there are some sayings in software development. In this case, you can take this: *"nothing is certain in software programming,"* and there is always a place for the unexpected and, unfortunately, do not talk about pleasant things!

There is a reason for the delay in revealing the data migration process. Johnny wants to try to have a clean and safe procedure as much as possible. To do this, the staff must ensure that the portal is consistent, which means that Johnny must anticipate any possible inconsistency from the beginning.

Okay, let's see what this is about! It's not hard to guess. I am referring to execution errors that may occur. The process in the sourcing system periodically populates the gate with a simple structure. However, according to Angelique and Joanna's discussions, the data elements coming from the source through the entrance should be validated in some way by Johnny and Jean-Luc, the IT guys.

Despite the team's efforts at the source site, errors may still occur during the process. Improper data can either stop the process during its execution or slip inconsistencies into the destination, the worst-case scenario. One of the virtues of

66

a good programmer is a sense of anticipation: guessing what mistakes might occur is what he/she should do from the beginning. Johnny decides in the first instance to treat this as a separate task of the process.

Thus, to conclude this statement's explanation, the entrance is not ready, and the process cannot begin yet. The reason is that the entry must be **checked** and double-checked before being released through the data transfer system. To conclude, *"Speedy"* is not ready to start yet.

Johnny's sixth sense, the key to success

How can Johnny predict as many mistakes as possible from the beginning to ensure a clean and smooth process? What technique will allow him to have a target area free of inconsistencies, as much as possible, and make Angelique a happy user? What can fearless Johnny Babanus do to make the *"Shoes everywhere"* manufacturing system consistent and reliable, using the *"Yellow Panther"* s data? Well, there are many things, but first, a clean gate.

Any good developer knows how important it is to analyze the business and accurately describe its problems adequately. A partial understanding can cause so many disappointments and issues in the logic behind it. Therefore, in this context, a productive dialogue between teams is the basis for a clean and safe entrance that will generate adequate quality data at the destination.

But the team of programmers who write the transfer system is aware that it cannot entirely rely on this. Consequently, they try to imagine that Jean-Luc is the worse programmer ever! Of course, that's not true: he's a great one! However, it's just a game of imagination. *"Speedy's"* team tries to anticipate what might be wrong based on the target system's structure and the portal. In our scheme, data migration aims to protect the manufacturing system and ensure the best possible data quality.

Moreover, if you are trying to imagine a more complicated process, more checks need to be performed to ensure consistency and accuracy. We must try to predict as many errors as possible and be aware that some may be more severe than others and, left untreated, could block the process. Instead, others can be logical and not stop the process but lead to wrong or incorrect data in the destination system. I don't know which is worse. I would say the second!

How can the brave Johnny Babanus accomplish this task? Simply, the only thing he has to do is imagine a set of rules to control the entrance. I called these rules of coherence or **SQL consistency rules** because he will use the classic SQL language for this purpose! What other programming languages could Johnny use better to check two simple tables in a relational format?

In the last part of the chapter, I will reveal some of these rules of coherence. Again, simplicity is the keyword. The gateway is elementary, so the rules are relatively simple. However, depending on what we want to verify, creating a specific SQL rule can be quite challenging! As any database programmer knows, even if SQL is simple at first glance, the level of complexity can reach unexpectedly high levels. As I always like to say, you can do wonders with SQL!

First baby steps

The source system is a reliable application, and that means the gate should be as well. It is quite amazing to equate a complex system like *"Yellow Panther"* with a structure as simple as this portal, just two simple tables! But this is the reality! The cohesion of the Panther should be passed to the gate and kept until the end. Johnny builds a set of predefined SQL statements, acting as formulas. Depending on any customer's specific needs, he can add others, and the list can continue to grow in time.

The first thing that he needs to do is to create one table that will store these consistency standards. On this occasion, I will reveal the second metadata table after the one with the attributes. For simplicity, the table will store minimum information. These rules are simple here, but usually, things are more complicated. Nevertheless, for our purpose, this is sufficient.

Let's define it here, now.

Listing 4-1 The checking area

```
-- Same script for Oracle and SQL Server.
CREATE TABLE M_Consistency_Rules
(
    Rule_Id             INT NOT NULL,
    Rule_Name           VARCHAR(255) NOT NULL,
    Rule_SQL            VARCHAR(4000) NOT NULL
);
ALTER TABLE M_Consistency_Rules
ADD CONSTRAINT Pk_M_Consistency_Rules PRIMARY KEY (Rule_Id);
ALTER TABLE M_Consistency_Rules
ADD CONSTRAINT Uq_M_Consistency_Rules UNIQUE (Rule_Name);
```

This table contains a rule name, a rule identifier, and the rule, the SQL statement itself. Remember that we are in a relational database, so the checks are in SQL. The rules act against the gate that reflects the source area, and the purpose is simply to verify. It's amazingly effective but straightforward at the same time! The portal is such a trivial structure, but it is remarkable how much complexity it can incorporate into such a basic design! You can imagine very complex data migration systems or sophisticated tools developed by specialized companies that, after all, do almost the same thing!

I have already explained the reason for this metadata table, which contains a set of consistency standards. Johnny wants to avoid potential problems in the data transfer utility and mainly target data issues. To do that, he will try to anticipate as many of them!

Let's look at some possible inconsistencies that may arise from the source system. These are just a few examples. Based on these, you can try to generate additional consistency rules later. I advise you to add more variety to this system, add more tables in the target, and imagine more rules to check the new data elements. Let's first list some possible issues followed by the associated SQL consistency rules that should correct them.

To be able to imagine some potential inconsistencies, you need to have an understanding of the destination. The goal is to fill the target, and there you have to look if you want to detect possible data issues. Besides, you should have in mind two simple tables that identify the entire source system. I advise you to review the gateway again before you begin, as all consistency rules will be written against it (see Listing 3-1). Now let's see some simple rules executed against the entrance and view some standard rules below:

♣   The source header has the To_Delete column. This field is an indication to the target that the product is no longer part of the source system. Someone deleted a pair of shoes from the Panther! If this field's value is one, then the product should be either deleted or invalidated somehow in the target. But what if this value comes for a product that does not yet exist in the destination? For instance, it was not part of any previous *"Speedy"* execution. This scenario is not reasonable because you obviously cannot specify a target deletion for a product that has not been previously transferred! The flag should be one for products that are   already   in   the   destination.   See   the   rule   below *This_Product_Does_Not_Exists_Cannot_Be_Removed*.

♣   The gate header has a unique constraint already enforced by the field product identifier. However, you do not want to reach that point and let Oracle or SQL Server trap the error later in time. Consequently, a rule would of do that in its place. For that, Johnny will imagine the consistency rule named *The_Product_Identifier_Should_Be_Uniquely_Specified*.

♣   Now let's move on to the gate details table. The first reasonable rule is to set the attribute name according to the metadata. Maybe a foreign key constraint would have worked, but perhaps there are many attributes with the same name and different types if we continue to classify the properties. But we need to be aware that constraints, for example, are local to one system or another. This checking process is not part of any system; it is between them. So, Johnny assumed there is no such constraint here. Thus the list of attribute names should match the attributes' names in the metadata table based on a SQL consistency rule. (see Listing 2-3). The name of this rule is *The_Attribute_Name_Is_Wrong*.

♣ The following rule refers to the length of the attribute if it is a string. The attribute size is in the metadata table and is easy to detect. There is a field for the string values in the gate with a length of 4000, trying to cover all kinds of attributes (the field Attribute Value). Moreover, each property has a specific size. Let's enforce this consistency rule to ensure this is coming correctly from the source with an adequate length (less than or equal to the one in the target). The name for this rule is *The_Length_Of_The_String_Is_Exceeded*.

♣ If the attribute is numeric, we can check the string's contents accordingly, and a rule can detect and retrieve an error if the contents of the property are not numeric. This rule is called *This_Attribute_Should_Be_Numeric*. Otherwise, an Attribute_Numeric_Value of type numeric could improve the source area.

♣ Many options are available for the attributes manufacturer and supplier. Johnny can consider them present in the target and define a rule to verify manufacturers and suppliers' existence accordingly. Alternatively, Johnny may allow the creation of new manufacturers and suppliers in the target later. Johnny potentially chooses both options, which means he decides to create some settings for the data migration system to deal with these alternative situations. Many choices are possible based on the characteristics of the customer hosting the target system. Accordingly, a new metadata table needs to be defined to allow these settings. Let's see below!

Listing 4-2 The settings area

```
-- Same script for Oracle and SQL Server.
CREATE TABLE M_Settings
(
    Setting_Id              INT NOT NULL,
    Setting_Name            VARCHAR(255) NOT NULL,
    Setting_Value           VARCHAR(255) NOT NULL,
    Setting_Description     VARCHAR(4000)
);
ALTER TABLE M_Settings
ADD CONSTRAINT Pk_M_Settings PRIMARY KEY (Setting_Id);
```

```
ALTER TABLE M_Settings
ADD CONSTRAINT Uq_Setting_Name UNIQUE (Setting_Name);
```

This table is simple but can store a potentially significant range of choices, depending on the situation. What do we have here?

♣   The first field is a setting identifier, a technical column with no significance, just a key. He will use this column in the gate updates later during the verification process.

♣   The second column is the setting name. Usually, this should say what it is about, the meaning! The setting name should be unique.

♣   After that, there is a setting value. There may be a set of predefined, acceptable values, such as yes or no, or free text values. Again, it depends on the context.

♣   Finally, there is a setting description. A summary is a useful explanation of the meaning.

For now, Johnny will imagine two values for a setting called allow_new_suppliers. He uses the list of predefined values, YES or NO. Similarly, for the setting allow_new_manufacturers, he chooses the same values YES or NO. These are similar to the 1/0.

Let's create two rules: "The Manufacturer Does Not Exists" and "The Supplier Does Not Exists."

Johnny assumed that the type of code should exist in the source as it exists in the target. Consequently, he chooses not to add a setting for this. If it comes from the source system wrongly, the rule will be *"The Product Type Must Exists."*

These are just a few introductory and genuine examples that illustrate the power of SQL to manage complex systems for migrating data between a source and a destination through a transition set of tables called the gateway. One can achieve the same goals using sophisticated tools and utilities. I am sure that sometimes they are necessary due to the complexity of the different systems' logic. Nevertheless, SQL language and a simple philosophy can often solve this problem of partial integration between two software products in a very admirable way. That's why I will always promote the SQL language. I think that topics like data migration, so widespread on so many sites, can be solved much more efficiently using the SQL language. Architects and managers often prefer to choose more sophisticated means or tools, even if SQL could do the job. Like in fashion, sometimes we prefer to select specific solutions because they are new and modern.

Now, let's build the rules described above. As mentioned earlier, I encourage you to add more complexity to the target, add another table or one or two new fields, design other attributes, and build some consistency rules.

I advise you to work independently and increase this exercise's complexity in your local systems. The ultimate goal of *"Speedy"* is obviously to help you create similar structures in your environments. I would be delighted and proud if some developers follow some of my tips and use some of my ideas.

Defining the SQL consistency rules

Now it's time to work again! These consistency rules, given the simplicity of the gateway, should not be too complicated. In general, the above statement is true. However, it depends. Sometimes it can be quite difficult to impose them. Do not just look at the simplicity of the set of two tables, the gate. Sometimes, to force a consistency rule, the task can be so tricky that it can take hours or days to complete, and the length of the SQL rule can be impressive! I'm sure most readers know that SQL capabilities are potentially huge.

Before defining the set of SQL consistency rules, we need to think about how to signal the potential error. Cohesion rules aim to identify that the entrance is in a certain way. If inconsistent or even incorrect data from the source system is allowed to pass through the gate, it can interrupt the process or cause data issues to the destination. What happens if such SQL consistency rules are violated? There should be a way to report this issue. Johnny looks at it in two ways, as shown below:

♣ The first option is to try to update the portal if such a violation occurs. To do this, one could add new fields in the entrance, both the header and the details, a set of error identifiers that will indicate the broken consistency rule. Whenever there is an error violation, an update will occur, and the rule identifier will update in the error field. Lines with an error value will be the lines that signal the rule violation.

♣ The second choice is to build a separate set of tables to store errors. Logic will move the dirty lines in this set of tables. These lines will disappear from the gate; the process will be of a cut and paste type! However, it is not always possible to completely isolate the errors from the so-called good lines, and sometimes there might be interdependencies. This solution is more challenging to implement. I will try to explain more later, after seeing some action!

Let's see the two possible solutions:

Listing 4-3: Alter the gate to be ready for check

```
-- Same script for Oracle and SQL Server.
-- The first solution
ALTER TABLE Gate_Header ADD Error_Id INT;
ALTER TABLE Gate_Details ADD Error_Id INT;
```

```
-- The second solution
CREATE TABLE Gate_Header_Errors
(
    Product_Identifier        VARCHAR(20) NOT NULL,
    Error_Id                  INT NOT NULL
);
CREATE TABLE Gate_Details_Errors
(
    Gate_Detail_Id            INT NOT NULL,
    Product_Identifier        VARCHAR(20) NOT NULL,
    Attribute_Name            VARCHAR(255) NOT NULL,
    Attribute_Value           VARCHAR(4000) NOT NULL,
    To_Delete                 INT,
    Error_Id                  INT NOT NULL
);
-- SQL Server
ALTER TABLE Gate_Header_Errors
ADD Error_Date DATETIME DEFAULT (GETDATE());
-- Oracle
ALTER TABLE Gate_Header_Errors
ADD Error_Date DATE DEFAULT SYSDATE ;
```

Either solution offers advantages and, as always, disadvantages. One question is, if there are errors, what will we do? A variety of options are available.

The first question is what to do with the rest of the data if there are consistency errors. For example, in a data transfer process, the gate has a thousand lines, and 25 contain inaccuracies. Or, even better, there is a single line with an error. What to do with the remaining 975 lines? Or with the remaining 999 lines?

♣ One solution is to stop the process and, finally, ask Jean-Luc to review his logic, check the lines with the broken rules, and see why they are present. Jean-Luc and his team will review the input data or their development. If they find problems in logic, they will try to correct and reload their process. Then, they will generate the portal again and run *"Speedy."* This solution is safe and, once the error disappears, Jean-Luc's team corrects the logic, and this error should not return in general. Another reason for the error could be some erroneous data from the source.

♣ The second solution is to isolate the error-free lines and start migrating the data with the correct values. If the gate has one thousand records and two are inconsistent, what to do with the remaining ones? Should we waste so many resources for so few lines? Should we block the remaining 998 rows for these two? Alternatively, we can try to isolate the two records, eventually including the connected ones, if any, and let *"Speedy"* run for the rest of the secure rows. However, this solution involves risks, as it is not always clear how interdependencies exist between right and wrong lines. It is not very easy, and sometimes it is impossible to isolate the right rows from the wrong ones. This solution is more convenient but risky. And what happens if there are 998 errors and two correct lines? Who makes the distinction? How do we know what the right proportion is? We could consider rejecting the process if there are 998 errors out of a thousand, and we could try to isolate the mistakes if the balance is opposite, two errors out of a thousand.

♣   The third question is whether the verification process should review all gate lines under any circumstances? One idea is to stop checking after you receive the first error. Another option is to scan all input lines and detect any possible errors so that Jean-Luc's team can analyze them all and fix them, eventually. If the *"Speedy"* team chooses the solution to stop the import from the beginning after finding the first error, there may be a performance improvement. The alternative is to go through the whole gate every time, report all the mistakes, and finally send them to the support team. Performance is a cost here if Johnny chooses the second option. One is examining ten lines, assuming the first error after ten SQL statements and shutting down, and another is going through a million ones and detecting three errors. Either option is black and white, again the same balance everywhere! It depends on the size of the portal and how much data there is at a time.

Finally, let's look at these SQL consistency rules in action. We already described them earlier, so now let's take them one at a time. I hope some of you will be happy with what you can do with pure SQL, what miracles you can accomplish using this language! This language is like wine; as time goes on, it gets better and more efficient. So it's time for SQL; it is time to see the rules of magical consistency. Be aware of the same dualism; some consistency rules are Oracle-specific, and others are SQL Server-specific.

Listing 4-4 Rule 01: This product does not exist. Thus, there is nothing to delete!

```
-- SQL Server version.  Check this rule next chapter.
INSERT INTO M_Consistency_Rules (Rule_Id, Rule_Name, Rule_SQL)
VALUES (1, 'This_Product_Does_Not_Exists_Cannot_Be_Removed',
'UPDATE Gate_Header SET Error_Id = 1 FROM Gate_Header dest
```

```
    WHERE dest.To_Delete = 1 AND NOT EXISTS (SELECT 1 FROM
Staging_Products sr WHERE sr.Product_Identifier =
dest.Product_Identifier)') ;
    -- Oracle version. Don't forget to commit! Please run this
rule.
    INSERT INTO M_Consistency_Rules (Rule_Id, Rule_Name, Rule_SQL)
    VALUES (1, 'This_Product_Does_Not_Exists_Cannot_Be_Removed',
    'UPDATE Gate_Header dest SET Error_Id = 1
    WHERE dest.To_Delete = 1 AND NOT EXISTS (SELECT 1 FROM
Staging_Products sr WHERE sr.Product_Identifier =
dest.Product_Identifier)') ;
```

Speaking of Oracle and SQL Server or other similar systems, we can consider portability as a goal if we need to maintain some SQL in many database systems. For sure, SQL portability is a tremendous advantage for software companies. I like the ease with which we, database programmers, can move through different database management systems. But if I choose between portability and performance, I always prefer database performance. And sometimes we have to compromise between them. I do not necessarily intend to prove portability when describing the rules of consistency and logic later. I don't have in mind the primary goal of portability between Oracle and SQL Server. But I always keep in mind the performance of SQL code. Always. And I firmly believe that this responsibility should belong to any programmer, whether a database programmer or not. However, for us, database programmers, it is easier to work on this because it is somehow clearer to measure performance than for an application developer, as things are generally measurable.

This earlier rule should raise an error if a specific product specified for deletion from the source system does not exist at the destination, as coming through the data transfer process. It's somehow absurd since this product does not exist in the target. What to signalize to a ghost? Based on the above assumption, only the products already in the destination through *"Speedy"* are eligible for deletion.

What happens if the product is already at its destination but not via the data migration system? Let's say it's a product that Joanna added in the "*Yellow Panther*" and by Angelique in the "*Shoes are everywhere*!" Well, we could imagine many ways to solve this. And this is not an impossible solution, especially if we have existing data when *"Speedy"* starts to work. But this is another story that raises other questions from the beginning. However, if the data transfer process is in place, this should not happen again!

Let's move back to the second consistency rule. This rule checks the portal header, too, as the first one. The goal is to enforce uniqueness by using a SQL rule. Let's look at the second example.

Speedy, a data transfer system. A SQL Exercise

Listing 4-5 Rule 02: The product identifier should be uniquely specified

```
-- SQL Server version
INSERT INTO M_Consistency_Rules (Rule_Id, Rule_Name, Rule_SQL)
VALUES (2,
'The_Product_Identifier_Should_Be_Uniquely_Specified',
 'UPDATE Gate_Header SET Error_Id = 2 FROM Gate_Header dest
 WHERE EXISTS (SELECT 1 FROM Gate_Header sr WHERE
sr.Product_Identifier = dest.Product_Identifier GROUP BY
sr.Product_Identifier HAVING COUNT(*) > 1)') ;
 -- Oracle version. Don't forget to commit!
INSERT INTO M_Consistency_Rules (Rule_Id, Rule_Name, Rule_SQL)
VALUES (2,
'The_Product_Identifier_Should_Be_Uniquely_Specified',
 'UPDATE Gate_Header dest SET Error_Id = 2
 WHERE EXISTS (SELECT 1 FROM Gate_Header sr WHERE
sr.Product_Identifier = dest.Product_Identifier GROUP BY
sr.Product_Identifier HAVING COUNT(*) > 1)') ;
```

This rule is necessary. The gate header cannot contain the same product twice. You mention one product in the gate header once and mention the details after. Logically, the gate header cannot allow product duplicates.

Now it's time for SQL statement number three! Let's see this rule and move the focus to the details table for the primary entity, our magical shoe! Let's check some shoe details as of now. We just wanted to be sure the product shoe is uniquely determined.

Listing 4-6 Rule 03: The attribute name is wrong

```
-- SQL Server version
INSERT INTO M_Consistency_Rules (Rule_Id, Rule_Name, Rule_SQL)
VALUES (3, 'The_Attribute_Name_Is_Wrong',
 'UPDATE Gate_Details  SET Error_Id = 3 FROM Gate_Details  dest
 WHERE NOT EXISTS (SELECT 1 FROM M_Attributes sr WHERE
sr.Attribute_Name = dest.Attribute_Name)') ;
 -- Oracle version. Don't forget to commit!
INSERT INTO M_Consistency_Rules (Rule_Id, Rule_Name, Rule_SQL)
VALUES (3, 'The_Attribute_Name_Is_Wrong',
 'UPDATE Gate_Details  dest SET Error_Id = 3
 WHERE NOT EXISTS (SELECT 1 FROM M_Attributes sr WHERE
sr.Attribute_Name = dest.Attribute_Name)') ;
```

This rule checks the validity of attribute names. These are predefined in the metadata table M_Attributes. In this case, the attribute name should be unique. However, we can better classify attributes, and sometimes the attribute names can be unique in combination with other fields in the metadata table, like some types eventually. For simplicity, in this situation, using a SQL consistency rule is the best solution for forcing the attribute name's uniqueness.

So what's going on here, rule number three? Check the M_Attributes metadata table and examine the values for the Attribute_Name column. These values are representative of the same Attribute_Name column in the Gate_Details table. It's like a foreign key constraint, but between different systems. On the other hand, the metadata objects can be part of the target database or not. It is not a must for sure. Remember that we are talking about two distinct databases and a way to communicate between them. Hence, this rule is better because it allows any of the options, is independent.

Let's look at the next example, rule number four, and imagine all sorts of inconsistencies coming through the gate. The following rule is to check the length of the string attributes. You can see in the table with source details (see Listing 2-5), the value for the product's properties is 4000 characters maximum, typical for a string. However, inside the target, each property has a size, which is variable depending on the attribute. The portal has a generic field for all data elements with a length of 4000. This 4000 field should host them all. We do not consider numeric, date, or lobes data types, for these other columns in the input would be required.

Imagine a string attribute that has a length of 40 in the target. The same data element can come from the source through the gate with a size of 45 characters. If Johnny leaves this passthrough, he'll have a problem. We will undoubtedly receive a known type error during the data migration process that exceeds the maximum length. Angelique will not be happy if, through absurdity, she sees these types of Oracle errors or even lovely messages taken over by Johnny and his team. Realizing and anticipating this possibility, Johnny constructs this rule to check from the beginning the length of any string attribute from the source relative to the value already set in the target property definition (that 40 is well known and stable). This value exists in the M_Attributes metadata table. The target is the reference, and what is coming from the source shall be synchronized with the destination specs.

Thus, this standard error will never occur. The size will be treated accordingly from the beginning before *"Speedy"* starts.

Looking back at the attribute definition metadata table, you can see the string size for each target attribute written in the M_Attributes metadata table (see Listing 2-3) in the Attribute_Length field. Keep in mind that there is maintenance involved. If, for example, the size of the property changes in the target, the attribute metadata table should reflect this change. The consistency rule will automatically consider the new value.

Let's see this one!

Listing 4-7 Rule 04: The length of the string is too large

```
-- SQL Server version
INSERT INTO M_Consistency_Rules (Rule_Id, Rule_Name, Rule_SQL)
VALUES (4, 'The_Length_Of_The_String_Is_Exceeded',
'UPDATE Gate_Details SET Error_Id = 4 FROM Gate_Details dest
INNER JOIN M_Attributes sr ON sr.Attribute_Name =
dest.Attribute_Name
WHERE LEN(dest.Attribute_Value) > sr.Attribute_Length AND
sr.Attribute_Data_Type = ''STRING''') ;
-- Oracle version. Don't forget to commit!
INSERT INTO M_Consistency_Rules (Rule_Id, Rule_Name, Rule_SQL)
VALUES (4, 'The_Length_Of_The_String_Is_Exceeded',
'UPDATE Gate_Details dest SET Error_Id = 4
WHERE EXISTS (SELECT 1 FROM M_Attributes sr WHERE
sr.Attribute_Name = dest.Attribute_Name AND
LENGTH(dest.Attribute_Value) > sr.Attribute_Length AND
sr.Attribute_Data_Type = ''STRING'')') ;
```

Let's add more examples. You can expand this list later. I invite you to do this! Here is another rule, This_Attribute_Should_Be_Numeric. You can see the Attribute_Data_Type field in the attribute metadata table. Most data items are of type string, but there is the numeric attribute called "measure". In a real system, there could be a wide variety of possible data types. We limit the area to the most common, for obvious reasons.

Usually, to cover all types of attributes with better accuracy, we could have added a few additional fields in the gate for other data types, such as date or time, numeric, and possibly lob. For example, we could have added a new attribute_value field, such as numeric_value_attribute, to count the import detail table's numeric attributes. However, in this scenario, there is only Attribute_Value of a string with 4000. The goal is to describe how to build such a system relatively quickly. Of course, sometimes the complexity of any transfer system can go far beyond this simple structure, but sometimes such a design can suffice.

In conclusion, Johnny must verify this rule for numerics: if the attributes are numeric. Take a look below. Don't forget to run in the database:

Listing 4-8 Rule 05: This Attribute Should Be Numeric

```
-- SQL Server version
INSERT INTO M_Consistency_Rules (Rule_Id, Rule_Name, Rule_SQL)
VALUES (5, 'This_Attribute_Should_Be_Numeric',
'UPDATE Gate_Details SET Error_Id = 5 FROM Gate_Details dest
INNER JOIN M_Attributes sr ON sr.Attribute_Name =
dest.Attribute_Name
WHERE ISNUMERIC(dest.Attribute_Value) = 0 AND
sr.Attribute_Data_Type = ''NUMERIC''') ;
-- Oracle version. Don't forget to commit!
INSERT INTO M_Consistency_Rules (Rule_Id, Rule_Name, Rule_SQL)
VALUES (5, 'This_Attribute_Should_Be_Numeric',
'UPDATE Gate_Details dest SET Error_Id = 5
WHERE EXISTS (SELECT 1 FROM M_Attributes sr WHERE
sr.Attribute_Name = dest.Attribute_Name AND
LENGTH(TRIM(TRANSLATE(dest.Attribute_Value, ''.0123456789'', ''
''))) IS NOT NULL AND sr.Attribute_Data_Type = ''NUMERIC'')') ;
```

You can see that there are differences between the syntaxes for some SQL rules due to various reasons, like different functions that can handle multiple situations. For SQL Server, the "isnumeric" function detects if a string's content represents a numeric value. Simultaneously, for Oracle, there is a combination of specific Oracle functions that reach the same result. Checking the string's content to see if it is numeric is not a standard functionality and variable depending on the database system. Anyway, this is not so important, as portability is not necessarily the number one priority. What can ensure more similarity between the various relational database systems than the SQL language itself?

Now, let's finally define the last two SQL consistency rules related to suppliers or manufacturers. Suppose that usually, these providers should already exist on the target. For example, Angelique and her managers ask Johnny not to create new suppliers or manufacturers in the software *"Shoes are everywhere"* through *"Speedy."* The assumption is that they should exist. Business specifications guide the world of programmers, whether we like it or not! The verification process will update the gate with an error if a manufacturer or supplier in the accounting system does not exist in the manufacturing module. However, there is also the possibility to allow the creation of suppliers or producers from the source.

This duality means that we need to specify the behavior in another metadata table, a table that will define the settings, depending on the business (see Listing 4-3).

Let's define these two settings.

Listing 4-9 Settings for accepting new suppliers or manufacturers

```
-- Same script for Oracle and SQL Server.
INSERT INTO M_Settings(Setting_Id, Setting_Name,
Setting_Value, Setting_Description)
VALUES (1, 'ALLOW_NEW_MANUFACTURERS_FROM_SOURCE', 'YES', 'You
can create new manufacturers as part of the data migration
process. Accepted values YES or NO');
INSERT INTO M_Settings(Setting_Id, Setting_Name,
Setting_Value, Setting_Description)
VALUES (2, 'ALLOW_NEW_SUPPLIERS_FROM_SOURCE', 'NO', 'You can
create new suppliers as part of the data migration process.
Accepted values YES or NO');
```

I hope the meaning of the settings is straightforward. Accept the possibility to create new manufacturers or suppliers in the application "*Shoes are everywhere*" if it only exists in the "*Yellow Panther*" system. The settings' names are relevant, allow a new manufacturer from the source, or allow new suppliers. If the value of the parameter is YES, we accept the possibility of new target suppliers. Otherwise, the source system is not reliable enough to add new vendors. Sometimes the target uses source lookup data; otherwise not, it depends on the business context.

Consequently, after adding these two settings and managing two possible scenarios, we can imagine two consistency rules regarding the gateway.

Let's see them:

Listing 4-10 Rule 06: This Supplier Does Not exist

```
-- SQL Server version
INSERT INTO M_Consistency_Rules (Rule_Id, Rule_Name, Rule_SQL)
VALUES (6, 'This_Suplier_Does_Not_Exists_In_The_Target',
'UPDATE Gate_Details SET Error_Id = 6 FROM Gate_Details dest
WHERE dest.Attribute_Name = ''SUPPLIER_CODE'' AND
(SELECT Setting_Value FROM M_Settings WHERE Setting_Name =
''ALLOW_NEW_SUPPLIERS_FROM_SOURCE'') = ''NO''
AND NOT EXISTS (SELECT 1 FROM Suppliers sr WHERE
UPPER(sr.Supplier_Code) = UPPER(dest.Attribute_Value))') ;
-- SQL Server version
INSERT INTO M_Consistency_Rules (Rule_Id, Rule_Name, Rule_SQL)
VALUES (7, 'This_Manufacturer_Does_Not_Exists_In_The_Target',
'UPDATE Gate_Details SET Error_Id = 7 FROM Gate_Details dest
WHERE dest.Attribute_Name = ''MANUFACTURER_CODE'' AND
```

```
(SELECT Setting_Value FROM M_Settings WHERE Setting_Name =
''ALLOW_NEW_MANUFACTURERS_FROM_SOURCE'') = ''NO''
AND NOT EXISTS (SELECT 1 FROM Manufacturers sr WHERE
UPPER(sr.Manufacturer_Code) = UPPER(dest.Attribute_Value))') ;
    -- Oracle version. Don't forget to commit!
    INSERT INTO M_Consistency_Rules (Rule_Id, Rule_Name, Rule_SQL)
    VALUES (6, 'This_Suplier_Does_Not_Exists_In_The_Target',
    'UPDATE Gate_Details dest SET Error_Id = 6
    WHERE dest.Attribute_Name = ''SUPPLIER_CODE'' AND
    (SELECT Setting_Value FROM M_Settings WHERE Setting_Name =
''ALLOW_NEW_SUPPLIERS_FROM_SOURCE'') = ''NO''
AND NOT EXISTS (SELECT 1 FROM Suppliers sr WHERE
UPPER(sr.Supplier_Code) = UPPER(dest.Attribute_Value))') ;
    -- Oracle version. Don't forget to commit!
    INSERT INTO M_Consistency_Rules (Rule_Id, Rule_Name, Rule_SQL)
    VALUES (7, 'This_Manufacturer_Does_Not_Exists_In_The_Target',
    'UPDATE Gate_Details dest SET Error_Id = 7
    WHERE dest.Attribute_Name = ''MANUFACTURER_CODE'' AND
    (SELECT Setting_Value FROM M_Settings WHERE Setting_Name =
''ALLOW_NEW_MANUFACTURERS_FROM_SOURCE'') = ''NO''
AND NOT EXISTS (SELECT 1 FROM Manufacturers sr WHERE
UPPER(sr.Manufacturer_Code) = UPPER(dest.Attribute_Value))') ;
```

These are the seven rules, but the magic number seven doesn't make sense here! It's just a coincidence. We shouldn't stop at seven; despite this number's mythical significance, we should reach a higher value and try to anticipate everything. If we expect all possible errors in ideal product development, the system would be perfect!

Now that we have these seven rules and are part of the M_Consistency_Rules metadata table, we will make a quick selection from this table and see all the nicely aligned SQL rules get the exact meaning of the purpose. See the query that you should execute: "*select Rule_SQL from M_Consistency_Rules;*"

Let's look at the Oracle version first.

Listing 4-11 The set of consistency rules in Oracle

```
-- The set of consistency rules: Oracle version
-- The first rule required access to the staging table and
cannot be checked now but next chapter, after setting the
staging area.
UPDATE Gate_Header dest SET Error_Id = 1
```

```
WHERE dest.To_Delete = 1 AND NOT EXISTS
(
    SELECT 1 FROM Staging_Products sr
    WHERE sr.Product_Identifier = dest.Product_Identifier
) ;
UPDATE Gate_Header dest SET Error_Id = 2
WHERE EXISTS
(
    SELECT 1 FROM Gate_Header sr
    WHERE sr.Product_Identifier = dest.Product_Identifier
    GROUP BY sr.Product_Identifier HAVING COUNT(*) > 1
) ;
UPDATE Gate_Details  dest SET Error_Id = 3
WHERE NOT EXISTS
(
    SELECT 1 FROM M_Attributes sr
    WHERE sr.Attribute_Name = dest.Attribute_Name
) ;
UPDATE Gate_Details dest SET Error_Id = 4
WHERE EXISTS
(
    SELECT 1 FROM M_Attributes sr
    WHERE sr.Attribute_Name = dest.Attribute_Name
    AND LENGTH(dest.Attribute_Value) > sr.Attribute_Length
    AND sr.Attribute_Data_Type = 'STRING'
) ;
UPDATE Gate_Details dest SET Error_Id = 5
WHERE EXISTS
(
    SELECT 1 FROM M_Attributes sr
    WHERE sr.Attribute_Name = dest.Attribute_Name
AND LENGTH(TRIM(TRANSLATE(dest.Attribute_Value,'.0123456789',
' '))) IS NOT NULL
    AND sr.Attribute_Data_Type = 'NUMERIC'
) ;
```

```
UPDATE Gate_Details dest SET Error_Id = 6
WHERE dest.Attribute_Name = 'SUPPLIER_CODE' AND
(SELECT Setting_Value FROM M_Settings WHERE Setting_Name =
'ALLOW_NEW_SUPPLIERS_FROM_SOURCE') = 'NO'
AND NOT EXISTS
(
    SELECT 1 FROM Suppliers sr
    WHERE UPPER(sr.Supplier_Code) =UPPER(dest.Attribute_Value)
) ;
UPDATE Gate_Details dest SET Error_Id = 7
WHERE dest.Attribute_Name = 'MANUFACTURER_CODE' AND
(SELECT Setting_Value FROM M_Settings WHERE Setting_Name =
'ALLOW_NEW_MANUFACTURERS_FROM_SOURCE') = 'NO'
AND NOT EXISTS
(
    SELECT 1 FROM Manufacturers sr
    WHERE UPPER(sr.Manufacturer_Code) =
UPPER(dest.Attribute_Value)
) ;
```

Try and run each consistency rule in Oracle. You won't see row updates, which means the data is clean according to what Johnny had already anticipated. None of the mistakes Johnny assumed are present. Jean-Luc and Johnny are true masters of programming, aren't they! You can take a look at each rule and try to build others. Imagine what other bad things could happen!

Let's not forget the sister SQL Server database system and see the specific Microsoft rules below.

Listing 4-12 The set of consistency rules in SQL Server

```
-- The collection of consistency rules: SQL Server version
-- The first rule required access to the staging table and
cannot be checked now but next chapter, after setting the
staging area.
UPDATE Gate_Header SET Error_Id = 1 FROM Gate_Header dest
WHERE dest.To_Delete = 1 AND NOT EXISTS
(
    SELECT 1 FROM Staging_Products sr
    WHERE sr.Product_Identifier = dest.Product_Identifier
) ;
```

```
UPDATE Gate_Header SET Error_Id = 2 FROM Gate_Header dest
WHERE EXISTS
(
    SELECT 1 FROM Gate_Header sr
    WHERE sr.Product_Identifier = dest.Product_Identifier
    GROUP BY sr.Product_Identifier HAVING COUNT(*) > 1
) ;
UPDATE Gate_Details  SET Error_Id = 3 FROM Gate_Details dest
WHERE NOT EXISTS
(
    SELECT 1 FROM M_Attributes sr
    WHERE sr.Attribute_Name = dest.Attribute_Name
) ;
UPDATE Gate_Details SET Error_Id = 4 FROM Gate_Details dest
INNER JOIN M_Attributes sr
    ON sr.Attribute_Name = dest.Attribute_Name
WHERE LEN(dest.Attribute_Value) > sr.Attribute_Length
AND sr.Attribute_Data_Type = 'STRING' ;
UPDATE Gate_Details SET Error_Id = 5 FROM Gate_Details dest
INNER JOIN M_Attributes sr
    ON sr.Attribute_Name = dest.Attribute_Name
WHERE ISNUMERIC(dest.Attribute_Value) = 0
AND sr.Attribute_Data_Type = 'NUMERIC' ;

UPDATE Gate_Details SET Error_Id = 6 FROM Gate_Details dest
WHERE dest.Attribute_Name = 'SUPPLIER_CODE' AND
(SELECT Setting_Value FROM M_Settings WHERE Setting_Name =
'ALLOW_NEW_SUPPLIERS_FROM_SOURCE') = 'NO'
AND NOT EXISTS
(
    SELECT 1 FROM Suppliers sr
    WHERE UPPER(sr.Supplier_Code) =UPPER(dest.Attribute_Value)
) ;

UPDATE Gate_Details SET Error_Id = 7 FROM Gate_Details dest
WHERE dest.Attribute_Name = 'MANUFACTURER_CODE' AND
```

```
(SELECT Setting_Value FROM M_Settings WHERE Setting_Name =
'ALLOW_NEW_MANUFACTURERS_FROM_SOURCE') = 'NO'
  AND NOT EXISTS
  (
      SELECT 1 FROM Manufacturers sr
      WHERE UPPER(sr.Manufacturer_Code) =
UPPER(dest.Attribute_Value)
  ) ;
```

For people with a partial understanding of the distinction between data and metadata, look at the tables starting with M_, the metadata tables. Look at the table M_Attributes and M_Consistency_Rules. These are metadata tables and store data descriptions, such as M_Attributes, to see the attributes. For example, take a look at the suppliers. There are providers of lookup tables with values such as "Eagle Nice" or "Lala Shoes" (see Listing 2-4). These represent data, various values for some concrete suppliers. In the suppliers' table, you can see multiple characteristics of the suppliers. Subsequently, these suppliers are mentioned and attached to the products by the supplier identifier Supplier_Id that is one characteristic of the product as seen from the table Products. These are all examples of data. The table M_Attributes and all the tables starting with M_ do not store data but data about data. Looking at the values within this table (see Listing 2-3) and check the row SUPPLIER_CODE.

To conclude this elementary revision of a primary concept, very simplistically speaking, a metadata row corresponds, in general, to a data column. We, database guys, are used with metadata because we know to read from the system tables (see SQL Server) or data dictionary (see Oracle). These are system metadata managed by the database management system. In such systems as replication/data migration/ETL data warehouse, we have a custom metadata set of objects. This layer of custom metadata is part of any process as the one above because it describes data and methods between various systems, so such thing as unified metadata does not exist. *"Shoes are everywhere"* possess an internal metadata system. The same considerations apply to *"Yellow Panther." "Speedy"* may technically be part of one of the two, now integrated into the target. However, the data in *"Yellow Panther"* is in another place, and there is no standard metadata layer. So this needs to be developed custom. The metadata structure in any data transfer system is one of the critical components of such a product. I felt the need to review all these distinctions for some people who may not have so much experience.

If the M_Attributes is a classic custom metadata table describing data about data, let's look at the second table, M_Consistency_Rules. This table is even more fascinating! This metadata table is active if we can call it, compared with

M_Attributes, a passive table. In the M_Consistency_Rules table, we have SQL statements that, once executed, act against the data. In this table, you can see the process of check against the gate, not just a data description of the data. In this sense, the two metadata tables are so different. One is passive, describing the data, and the second one is active, defines processes, and is effectively used to act against data.

I just wanted to make this parenthesis here to explain these fundamental differences between various types of information: data, passive metadata, and, even more, active metadata.

How to violate a SQL consistency rule?

Now we are almost there, and the gate is ready and sealed. No one can enter without a visa! Anyway, if you remember, the variety of films and series where entries considered insurmountable are never as such; there is always a way to open any door. Despite all the measures taken, new errors are still possible to show up during the process. That is why you need to be aware that the SQL consistency rules list is dynamic and eligible for continuous expansion.

The next step is to prepare some samplings and try to see these consistency rules in action effectively.

Now that we can agree with the idea that there is no perfect gate, only better gates. In our case, a better entry is a gateway with a set of consistent SQL rules attached to it. As a result, the probability of errors or inconsistencies is lower.

Now, look at the set of SQL consistency rules. Think of database constraints once more! When any student attends one SQL course and is learning about database constraints, after understanding their purpose, after learning how to add database constraints to tables or columns, what is the next step in the learning process? The next step is always the same; try to simulate and create false data to violate these database constraints. In this way, the student will effectively understand what the database constraints are and how they work. Similarly, I will add new products to the gate with the specific purpose of violating these SQL consistency rules.

What will I do now? First, I will remove the gate data to add later at the end of this chapter and add some other data to illustrate these consistency rules' usefulness. We will try to break these constraints! Let's do this!

Listing 4-13 New sampling for the gate

```
-- Same script for Oracle and SQL Server.
DELETE Gate_Details;
DELETE Gate_Header;
-- Remove this rule because it references staging area, not
created yet.
DELETE M_Consistency_Rules WHERE Rule_Id = 1;


INSERT INTO Gate_Header (Product_Identifier, Business_Code)
VALUES ('AT12_TS_098', 'AT12_TS_098');
INSERT INTO Gate_Header (Product_Identifier, Business_Code)
VALUES ('NM94_AX_121', 'NKS_LRM_093');
INSERT INTO Gate_Details (Gate_Detail_Id, Product_Identifier,
Attribute_Name, Attribute_Value)
VALUES (1, 'AT12_TS_098', 'PRODUCTNAME', 'Adidas Samba Rose
Core Black');
INSERT INTO Gate_Details (Gate_Detail_Id, Product_Identifier,
Attribute_Name, Attribute_Value)
VALUES (2, 'AT12_TS_098', 'MEASURE', 'Fourty');
INSERT INTO Gate_Details (Gate_Detail_Id, Product_Identifier,
Attribute_Name, Attribute_Value)
VALUES (3, 'AT12_TS_098', 'TYPE_CODE', 'One nice product type
but a bit long, beyond 20');
INSERT INTO Gate_Details (Gate_Detail_Id, Product_Identifier,
Attribute_Name, Attribute_Value)
VALUES (4, 'AT12_TS_098', 'GENDER', 'Unisex');
INSERT INTO Gate_Details (Gate_Detail_Id, Product_Identifier,
Attribute_Name, Attribute_Value)
VALUES (5, 'NM94_AX_121', 'PRODUCT_NAME', 'Nike Zoom Pegasus
Turbo 2');
INSERT INTO Gate_Details (Gate_Detail_Id, Product_Identifier,
Attribute_Name, Attribute_Value)
VALUES (6, 'NM94_AX_121', 'GENDER', 'Female');
INSERT INTO Gate_Details (Gate_Detail_Id, Product_Identifier,
Attribute_Name, Attribute_Value)
VALUES (7, 'NM94_AX_121', 'COLOR', 'Pink');
```

Now, run this script on the gate, and the result is that the data has some consistency issues. If you see the first material, the attribute name is

PRODUCTNAME, instead of PRODUCT_NAME, the content of the measure attribute is not numeric, and the length of the property PRODUCT_CODE is higher than 20, the value allowed for the product code, as you can see in M_Attributes metadata table. All the others should be okay.

To continue, previous considerations about possible error handling options could become more evident. For example, the second product is clean, and it does not break any consistency rules while the first one does. Should we only consider the second one for the data migration process and somehow take the first one out of the gate and isolate it somewhere and send it back to Jean-Luc for verification? Should we stop everything and fix and try again after Jean-Luc investigates? At least two options are available here.

Now, we need to do one last thing. We do not have the logic to process these rules. I never started any procedure or function. No code yet. What a nightmare! Now is the time for that, and the first part of the process is to build a functionality that should process these consistency rules. Technically, it should execute SQL statements, make updates, and finally do one action or another, depending on which is the best approach, as seen above.

Let's build this logic now!

Checking the first results

Finally, after so many design considerations, it's time for the first part of SQL development. I'm sorry it took so long for passionate programmers. My plan today was to present from scratch a model of a data transfer system based entirely on SQL. Lots of stories here. Should I be sorry about that?

Johnny leads the developers' team working for the software system "*Shoes are everywhere,*" manufacturing IT applications. Jean-Luc leads the IT team for an accountancy system called "*Yellow Panther.*" They worked together to meet the integration between the two systems on a site; the footwear company named "*Yellow Shoe.*" Johnny built a gateway to Panther and created SQL coherence rules based on checking this portal's consistency. Jean-Luc developed a process in the "*Yellow Panther*" to fill the entrance. Now we will see the first part of the process, the logic created by Johnny's team, to check these consistency rules.

Here it is. Let's see the SQL Server version first:

Listing 4-14 Check the gate consistency for SQL Server

```
-- The process of checking the gate, SQL Server version
DECLARE
    @v_Rule_Id              INT,
    @v_Rule_SQL             NVARCHAR(4000),
```

```
        @v_Count                  INT,
        @v_The_Gate_Is_Consistent NVARCHAR(3);
        UPDATE Gate_Details
        SET Error_Id = NULL
        WHERE Error_Id IS NOT NULL;
        UPDATE Gate_Header
        SET Error_Id = NULL
        WHERE Error_Id IS NOT NULL;
        DECLARE C_Consistency_Rules CURSOR FOR
        SELECT Rule_Id, Rule_SQL
        FROM M_Consistency_Rules
        ORDER BY 1;
BEGIN
        OPEN C_Consistency_Rules;
        FETCH NEXT FROM C_Consistency_Rules
        INTO @v_Rule_Id, @v_Rule_SQL;
        WHILE @@FETCH_STATUS = 0
        BEGIN
                EXECUTE sp_executesql @v_Rule_SQL;
                FETCH NEXT FROM C_Consistency_Rules
                INTO @v_Rule_Id, @v_Rule_SQL;
        END;

        CLOSE C_Consistency_Rules;
        DEALLOCATE C_Consistency_Rules;

        SELECT @v_Count = COUNT(*) FROM
        (
                SELECT Error_Id FROM Gate_Header
                WHERE Error_Id IS NOT NULL
                UNION ALL
                SELECT Error_Id FROM Gate_Details
                WHERE Error_Id IS NOT NULL
        ) a;
        IF @v_Count > 0
                SET @v_The_Gate_Is_Consistent = 'NO';
```

```
        ELSE
                SET @v_The_Gate_Is_Consistent = 'YES';
        PRINT @v_The_Gate_Is_Consistent;
    END;
```

The logic is quite simple. Let's analyze the steps in order:

♣ First, Johnny reset the error identifier to NULL for the entire gate. It is a safety measure; the input is volatile and recreated each time. Initially, there should be no errors. This initialization is the starting point for both the header and the details.

♣ After that, it declares and opens the cursor with the SQL statements that define the consistency rules. Then, it retrieves the dedicated variable each time for each SQL statement.

♣ Then Johnny executes each SQL statement described by the consistency rule. The result of each SQL statement will be a gate update, either header or detail. The error takes the value of the rule identifier when the update returns any rows.

♣ Finally, the process calculates a count. If it is greater than zero, this count will imply that there are errors, which means that the gate is not consistent. The NO value of the dedicated variable will explain the mistakes, and further investigations are needed. If YES, this means that the gateway is clean and that the data migration process can begin.

If there are errors, the *"Speedy"* process can hold until all the errors are corrected. Another option is to isolate the lines with consistency errors and start the *"Speedy"* with the correct data. The isolation process is not an easy task, but it is a possibility.

As you can see, there are errors. The data transfer system cannot start. Before continuing to and understand the mistakes, let's describe the Oracle version of the logic. See it below:

Listing 4-15 Check gate consistency Oracle

```
-- The process of checking the gate, Oracle version
SET SERVEROUTPUT ON
DECLARE
    v_Rule_Id                   INT;
    v_Rule_SQL                  VARCHAR2(4000);
    v_Count                     INT;
    v_The_Gate_Is_Consistent    VARCHAR2(3);
    CURSOR C_Consistency_Rules IS
```

```
    SELECT Rule_Id, Rule_SQL
    FROM M_Consistency_Rules
    ORDER BY 1;
BEGIN
    UPDATE Gate_Details
    SET Error_Id = NULL
    WHERE Error_Id IS NOT NULL;
    UPDATE Gate_Header
    SET Error_Id = NULL
    WHERE Error_Id IS NOT NULL;
    COMMIT;
    OPEN C_Consistency_Rules;
    LOOP
    FETCH C_Consistency_Rules INTO v_Rule_Id, v_Rule_SQL;
        EXIT WHEN C_Consistency_Rules%NOTFOUND;
        EXECUTE IMMEDIATE v_Rule_SQL;
        COMMIT;
    END LOOP;

    CLOSE C_Consistency_Rules;
    SELECT COUNT(*) INTO v_Count FROM
    (
        SELECT Error_Id FROM Gate_Header
        WHERE Error_Id IS NOT NULL
        UNION ALL
        SELECT Error_Id FROM Gate_Details
        WHERE Error_Id IS NOT NULL
    ) a;
    IF v_Count > 0 THEN
        v_The_Gate_Is_Consistent  := 'NO';
    ELSE
        v_The_Gate_Is_Consistent  := 'YES';
    END IF;
    DBMS_OUTPUT.PUT_LINE (v_The_Gate_Is_Consistent);
END;
/
```

Executing the above logic, John will see the response NO, meaning the gateway is not consistent. Consequently, he will run a query to check to see what the issues are. Here is his SQL query below:

Listing 4-16 Check the list of errors

```
-- Same script for Oracle and SQL Server.
SELECT h.Product_Identifier, rh.Rule_Name AS Error_Name,
NULL AS Attribute_Name, NULL AS Attribute_Value,
'product' AS error_type
FROM Gate_Header h INNER JOIN M_Consistency_Rules rh
    ON rh.Rule_id = h.Error_Id
WHERE h.Error_Id IS NOT NULL
UNION
SELECT  d.Product_Identifier,  rd.Rule_Name  AS  Error_Name,
d.Attribute_Name, d.Attribute_Value, 'attribute' AS error_type
FROM Gate_Details d INNER JOIN M_Consistency_Rules rd
            ON rd.Rule_id = d.Error_Id
WHERE d.Error_Id IS NOT NULL;
```

The results show the three errors described earlier, all at a detailed level. Let's see them below!

Table 4-1 The list of errors

Product identifier	Error name	Attribute Name	Attribute Value
AT12_TS_098	The Attribute Name Is Wrong	PRODUCTNAME	Adidas Samba Rose Core Black
AT12_TS_098	The Length Of The String Is Exceeded	TYPE_CODE	One nice type code but a bit long, beyond 20
AT12_TS_098	This Attribute Should Be Numeric	MEASURE	Forty

Johnny will see that the gate data has the following inconsistencies:

♣ One attribute name is wrong. The name of the attribute that specifies the product's name is PRODUCT_NAME and not PRODUCTNAME.

♣ The length of a type code is greater than 20, so the string's length is longer than it should be. This finding avoids a well-known error during the data transfer process.

♣ The measure should be numeric and is not.

Johnny will talk to Jean-Luc, eventually, send him an email, and ask him to investigate. Jean-Luc will review his logic accordingly. After a while, Jean-Luc will execute his internal process and fill the gate again. The data transfer system will not start until the input is clean and error-free.

And this is the end of this chapter! I have a request for you. It is quite essential, so I will bold for you not to forget. Before starting the new section, don't forget to **remove the gate's data again (detail and header) and execute Listing 4-17 to fill the gate once more with the original products**. Let's do that, to be sure no one will forget!

Listing 4-17 Rebuild the source area

```
-- Same script for Oracle and SQL Server.
DELETE Gate_Details;
DELETE Gate_Header;


INSERT INTO Gate_Header (Product_Identifier, Business_Code)
VALUES ('AT12_TS_098', 'AT12_TS_098');
INSERT INTO Gate_Header (Product_Identifier, Business_Code)
VALUES ('NM94_AX_121', 'NKS_LRM_093');
INSERT INTO Gate_Header (Product_Identifier, Business_Code)
VALUES ('AT12_RE_106', 'AT12_RE_106');
INSERT INTO Gate_Header (Product_Identifier, Business_Code)
VALUES ('NM92_DD_191', 'NKS_BKM_135');
INSERT INTO Gate_Details (Gate_Detail_Id, Product_Identifier,
Attribute_Name, Attribute_Value)
VALUES (1, 'AT12_TS_098', 'PRODUCT_NAME', 'Black Adidas
Torsion original ZX flux');
INSERT INTO Gate_Details (Gate_Detail_Id, Product_Identifier,
Attribute_Name, Attribute_Value)
VALUES (2, 'AT12_TS_098', 'GENDER', 'Male');
INSERT INTO Gate_Details (Gate_Detail_Id, Product_Identifier,
Attribute_Name, Attribute_Value)
```

```
    VALUES (3, 'AT12_TS_098', 'COLOR', 'Black');
    INSERT INTO Gate_Details (Gate_Detail_Id, Product_Identifier,
Attribute_Name, Attribute_Value)
    VALUES (4, 'AT12_TS_098', 'TYPE_CODE', 'AS');
    INSERT INTO Gate_Details (Gate_Detail_Id, Product_Identifier,
Attribute_Name, Attribute_Value)
    VALUES (5, 'NM94_AX_121', 'PRODUCT_NAME', 'Nike Zoom Pegasus
Turbo 2');
    INSERT INTO Gate_Details (Gate_Detail_Id, Product_Identifier,
Attribute_Name, Attribute_Value)
    VALUES (6, 'NM94_AX_121', 'GENDER', 'Female');
    INSERT INTO Gate_Details (Gate_Detail_Id, Product_Identifier,
Attribute_Name, Attribute_Value)
    VALUES (7, 'NM94_AX_121', 'COLOR', 'Pink');
    INSERT INTO Gate_Details (Gate_Detail_Id, Product_Identifier,
Attribute_Name, Attribute_Value)
    VALUES (8, 'NM94_AX_121', 'TYPE_CODE', 'AS');
    INSERT INTO Gate_Details (Gate_Detail_Id, Product_Identifier,
Attribute_Name, Attribute_Value)
    VALUES (9, 'NM94_AX_121', 'SUPPLIER_CODE', 'LS');
    INSERT INTO Gate_Details (Gate_Detail_Id, Product_Identifier,
Attribute_Name, Attribute_Value)
    VALUES (10, 'AT12_RE_106', 'PRODUCT_NAME', 'Adidas Samba Rose
Core Black');
    INSERT INTO Gate_Details (Gate_Detail_Id, Product_Identifier,
Attribute_Name, Attribute_Value)
    VALUES (11, 'AT12_RE_106', 'GENDER', 'Unisex');
    INSERT INTO Gate_Details (Gate_Detail_Id, Product_Identifier,
Attribute_Name, Attribute_Value)
    VALUES (12, 'AT12_RE_106', 'COLOR', 'Black');
    INSERT INTO Gate_Details (Gate_Detail_Id, Product_Identifier,
Attribute_Name, Attribute_Value)
    VALUES (13, 'AT12_RE_106', 'TYPE_CODE', 'AS');
    INSERT INTO Gate_Details (Gate_Detail_Id, Product_Identifier,
Attribute_Name, Attribute_Value)
    VALUES (14, 'AT12_RE_106', 'SUPPLIER_CODE', 'EN');
    INSERT INTO Gate_Details (Gate_Detail_Id, Product_Identifier,
Attribute_Name, Attribute_Value)
    VALUES (15, 'AT12_RE_106', 'MANUFACTURER_CODE', 'MLS');
```

```
INSERT INTO Gate_Details (Gate_Detail_Id, Product_Identifier,
Attribute_Name, Attribute_Value)
    VALUES (16, 'NM92_DD_191', 'PRODUCT_NAME', 'Nike Lance Cycling
Shoes Men 41');
INSERT INTO Gate_Details (Gate_Detail_Id, Product_Identifier,
Attribute_Name, Attribute_Value)
    VALUES (17, 'NM92_DD_191', 'GENDER', 'Male');
INSERT INTO Gate_Details (Gate_Detail_Id, Product_Identifier,
Attribute_Name, Attribute_Value)
    VALUES (18, 'NM92_DD_191', 'COLOR', 'Silver');
INSERT INTO Gate_Details (Gate_Detail_Id, Product_Identifier,
Attribute_Name, Attribute_Value)
    VALUES (19, 'NM92_DD_191', 'TYPE_CODE', 'CS');
INSERT INTO Gate_Details (Gate_Detail_Id, Product_Identifier,
Attribute_Name, Attribute_Value)
    VALUES (20, 'NM92_DD_191', 'SUPPLIER_CODE', 'EN');
INSERT INTO Gate_Details (Gate_Detail_Id, Product_Identifier,
Attribute_Name, Attribute_Value)
    VALUES (21, 'NM92_DD_191', 'MANUFACTURER_CODE', 'FFM');
INSERT INTO Gate_Details (Gate_Detail_Id, Product_Identifier,
Attribute_Name, Attribute_Value)
    VALUES (22, 'NM92_DD_191', 'MEASURE', '41');
```

In the next chapter, we will begin the process of developing the data transfer system.

5 Speedy, development phase, first-round

Ready for a short review?

I described the gateway to a data transfer/migration module as an exit from the Panther system. There are some assumptions. First, consider a target system and a source at a customer's site. Companies, either medium or large, but sometimes even smaller, can have various software applications that work in parallel. This variety of IT systems on a client site is commonplace, despite most software vendors' efforts to cover everything and integrate most business lines into a single unified software application. In my example, the story is at a shoe factory, the "*Yellow Shoes*" plant. There are two software products on this site, which work separately, but require cooperation: the manufacturing software "*Shoes are everywhere*" and the accounting product "*Yellow Panther.*" This scenario is practical and familiar, if I may say so!

In general, software companies that build applications cover their business segment and have their customers. At client locations, these software applications coexist with others. Sometimes life together can be peaceful and neutral, each line of activity can be distinct, and the software products may not interfere with each other. But quite often, the systems need to communicate. The two software products could share a commonplace. There may be a time priority within the company because, for example, products are created first in accounting and then transferred to manufacturing.

Before *"Speedy"* entered the arena, there was a lot of double work. Users like Joanna created the products in accounting, and, in parallel, users like Angelique added the same products to manufacturing. Double work is never pleasant and efficient without mentioning that it leaves a place for inconsistency. Products are the same, so that, being defined twice, even for different purposes, they can end up in situations to misinterpret one product as two in parallel applications.

I want to mention once again that I am not referring to a data warehouse scenario. Although, most of the concepts here are available there as well. However, a data warehouse is more complicated. Various sources require integration into a new historical database, such as the data warehouse. Here's how it is with the seven rings and the ones that control them all, the data warehouse system! It is not the case in this factory, and things are much simpler at the "*Yellow Shoe.*" This scenario has nothing to do with warehouse and historical databases.

Two information systems coexist at the same site. Joanna creates the products in *"Yellow Panther"* for accountancy purposes; Angelique should receive them later to implement the manufacturing activity. The product gets two meanings, the accountancy meaning first and manufacturing after. However, it's the same old shoe!

To remedy these shortcomings, Johnny and his team began designing *"Speedy,"* a data transfer tool. This utility supposes to link the two software systems.

The first concept is the gateway that solved the problem of independence. We analyzed this entrance in previous chapters, and now we already have this portal full of data, ready to be used as input for *"Speedy."* This gateway is a way of connecting to any source system and should be as simple as possible. In this case, a simple table with a master details structure is enough.

I described a mechanism for verifying the input data so that the process controls its consistency through a set of SQL statements. When the checking process runs against the input, the result can be positive or negative, which means that the gate is clean or not. If there are no errors, the data transfer interface is ready. What's next? The next step is to start the process itself and see how it works.

Again, I feel compelled to warn you not to expect sensational news or technological miracles. I'm sure you are curious about the design and development process, the next step. Well, it won't be anything special, just simple things. Old-fashioned SQL technique in action, you'll see! I am sure you also believe that simplicity, readability, performance are the quality criteria in IT and not anything else!

Look at ABBA! BBC just voted ABBA's Waterloo Eurovision the best song of all time. When you go to karaoke, for example, ABBA is always there; it is still present. Well, at least in Europe, to speak like the Americans or the British! The first time I was in the US, I was surprised to hear their memories of their trip to Europe, as Europe is a country or something. I understood the meaning of the Atlantic ocean, which separates two worlds! Hence, I understood why an American never says phrases like I am going to France or Spain, he is going to Europe. For me, it was a fun lesson to learn! Just as a curiosity, don't ask me why the British say they are going to Europe unless their Channel is like the Atlantic Ocean! I never understood, looking at the map! This mystery is deeply rooted in the souls of the British people.

Returning to ABBA, look at the simplicity of their songs! See the philosophy and how unique the beauty of life is, even after so many years! You can watch the Mamma Mia musical and see how a band's songs make the script of a film that covers all the complexities of life from love, hate, betrayal, jealousy, friendship, etc.! Now, don't shoot me, please! ABBA is ABBA, and SQL is SQL! Music is music, but IT and databases are not the same thing. How boring can SQL be compared to ABBA! But this is the beauty of the analogy, which allows you to build bridges between entirely different worlds. ABBA quality is beyond any suspicion in music. I could say a similar statement about SQL in the software world when it comes to data. Well, the analogy somehow stops in the sense that somewhere in the future, a new model and new languages or other revolutionary developments will make SQL obsolete while ABBA will live forever! Consequently, ABBA wins even here, against SQL!

Let's end this introduction to this chapter and start the work! However, I never forget that my goal is to promote my favorite technology, which is SQL. I want to show that you can still do so many things with the SQL language! If they don't want to spend their money on technology just because they are new or preferred by some architects or managers, people and companies can still remember SQL. When they continue to use massive, local, or cloud relational databases, they are still relational databases. And relational databases mean the use of the SQL language. It doesn't matter if it's with Oracle, SQL Server in PostgreSQL, or anything else.

Moreover, for these systems, such as *"Speedy,"* a data transfer product, many companies choose to use expensive and modern visual tools or inadequate technologies because they feel that SQL is outdated. Sometimes these new technologies may be needed. But I am very confident that the classic SQL language can often solve problems specific to its approach. Well, in the end, it's always a matter of choice. Sometimes, that's why there is marketing! In the decisions taken by the companies' management, often the criteria have little to do with the reality on the ground! It's time to get to work!

Staging area, Product's status

Like *"Speedy,"* a data transfer system aims to fill the target area and move the products into the manufacturing system, products already defined in the accountancy. The gateway is a simple structure of a master-detail model that mirrors a part of the source, containing only what is relevant for the target.

This entry will be periodically supplemented by Jean-Luc's logic at the source site. New shoe items may bring new properties, or maybe certain product features may change. This information must be present in the manufacturing system. For example, perhaps a shoe item has changed its type or has a new trade name, or a commercial shoe name changes its text, or a pair of shows disappear from accounting! The three classic actions of adding, modifying, deleting will apply to the products entirely or some of the attributes. It is necessary to be able to answer some simple questions, such as:

♣ Check the status of the product? By product status, I understand his state related to the target? Is the product **new** in the destination system? The product is not yet part of the target system, which means that it is present at the gate for the first time. In this case, everything is new, the product, as well as all the corresponding attributes. In such cases, in general, there is only one action, add, insert, add!

♣ Is the product already part of the target? The status of the item can be present or **existing**; from the target point of view. The shoe item had been before at the gate and is already in the target. Now there are some changes to the source, and they need to get to the destination. Here is the classic edit, update, etc.

♣ Was the product removed from the accountancy system? If yes, do we need to remove it from the target as well? Or maybe we only need to signalize that the product is part of the destination but does not belong to the source anymore? There are many possible ways to solve this problem.

♣ Let's look at other hypothetical topics for discussion. Are the elements always created in the source system? Or is it possible that some products are exclusively part of the target, which means they are not in the accounting system? If so, there are specific products that are not part of the source. *"Speedy"* may not consider these products or register them as target products, which means products owned by the destination.

I am talking about the status of the product, a new concept. Imagine you go to a health clinic. You arrive at the reception. Almost any receptionist, generally with a big smile on their face, first asks you a question: have you ever been here? It's almost like a stereotype, always the same question first. Why is that? Well, we are all part of the IT crowd; we are aware that maybe the receptionist has a software system in front of the desk and wants to know if you are already in it. One wants to see if you are an existing customer or not, which means you are a new customer. The same goes for the manufacturing application. The product status check is at the top of the list when the transfer process begins.

However, detecting the item's status and other things that will follow, for example, product attributes, is not an easy task. Many solutions are possible. We need to identify the conditions and changes in the product header or details. Where do we do this? Again, the choices are multiple. One of them is related to the (possible) need for a **staging** area. The intermediate zone is a crucial component of the data migration process.

Let's look at a general definition taken from Wikipedia to avoid any misunderstandings.

Speedy, a data transfer system. A SQL Exercise

"A staging area (otherwise staging point, staging base, or staging post) is a location where organisms, people, vehicles, equipment, or material are assembled before use. It may refer to:

Data management

Main article: staging (data)

Intermediate storage area between the sources of information and the data warehouse (DW) or data mart (DM). It is usually temporary, and its contents can be erased after the DW/DM has been loaded successfully.

Software development

Main article: Deployment environment

A stage or staging environment is an environment for testing that exactly resembles a production environment. It seeks to mirror a real production environment as closely as possible and connect to other production services and data, such as databases."

It's a vague definition, and maybe I can extend it somehow. Well, a subjective extension, don't consider me the master of the concept, please! I see the staging area as an atelier, a workshop or laboratory where we prepare the future, as a training camp where we train the champions for their big matches that will follow. In my example, as we will see, it is like the first floor we have to go up to get home to our apartment on the second one.

Do we need a staging area? If I think about it better, I would say this is a necessity. Perhaps a more precise question is this: do we need a physical and nominal staging area? Here the answer may vary; there is no single answer. It depends on the architecture and implementation of systems such as an ETL or a data migration utility. In any case, we certainly need a place to identify these changes. Moving data from one place to another incrementally means, first of all, detecting the status of the change. If that place is memory or a physical space, such as a database or schema, this is an implementation detail. Indeed, there must be a room in which the process takes place. This comparison occurs. This process will happen if entities like shoe items coming from the accountancy are new to the target, or in a change or eventually in a removal process.

I don't propose to answer this question now because many solutions are possible, and they are relative to various projects, implementations, desired architectures, specific businesses, and, why not, subjective preferences! Honest people know how much individual preferences influence their decisions, even in objective worlds like IT. As part of a process of objective reasoning, this personal element is part of the human nature to which we all bow, regardless of whether or not we accept this fatality. I am not an exception, and I propose a staging area driven by the SQL language, a relational database, stand-alone, or I included in the target. I do not claim that this is the universal solution, the best of all possible solutions. But I do think that, quite often, this is a reliable solution that can achieve acceptable results. And this is what I will propose in my example, a SQL-based staging area!

Thus, my recommendation for SQL-based physical storage is understandable. As for what to use, there is all the freedom in the world! It can be anything from Oracle or SQL Server to PostgreSQL or Maria Db etc. In our examples, in the beginning, we will continue until the end with both Oracle and SQL Server.

What is such a data transfer? It is a process where the goal is relatively straight: data movement. There is a source, then a gateway that maps the source system already filled with information, and there is a target. In general, there are no users to manipulate data in such a scenario, not too much interaction, no user interface. It's just a process that should somehow run automatically. It can be driven by specific jobs or run by some responsible users like Angelique. What reason could someone have to use anything other than logic written in a database? Why should one use SQL logic embedded in Java or C#? I know this is a common choice; some people write better SQL using Java! This decision will involve a lot of debate and reasoning. There are also statistics of people who use one technology or another in addition to neutrality and objectivity. In general, this is a crucial factor. Before analyzing the architectures, let's look at the available people!

Let's analyze *"Speedy,"* the proposed solution! The goal is simple: to transfer data from one place to another between two relational databases. Why would anyone use anything other than SQL? I don't see many advantages because even if you use Java or C #, you still use SQL, whether you like it or not! I can't believe that SQL embedded in Java can be better than SQL written by a good SQL programmer, in PL SQL or Transact SQL! Anyway, I admit my degree of subjectivity being a SQL programmer. In conclusion, such systems, in my opinion, should be SQL-based because the goal is simple, data transfer between various points.

Now, when I clarify what the organization area will be, there are several options. The intermediate zone can be either a new Oracle schema, a SQL Server schema or database, or a set of objects from the same target schema or database. Sometimes a memory area can do the job, there are many options on the table. Everything is possible.

Finally, I will go to the first step required by the designer/architect/developer of the data transfer system. Johnny decides it's time to build the staging area. He did this and managed to create one according to our needs!

Let's start with the SQL Server version, not that it matters but we need to have an order so I try to follow the order SQL Server and then Oracle, if you don't mind! You can add yours, whatever will be.

Speedy, a data transfer system. A SQL Exercise

Listing 5-1 The staging area SQL Server

```sql
-- The staging area design: SQL Server version
CREATE TABLE Executions
(
    Execution_Id          INT IDENTITY(1, 1) NOT NULL,
    Start_Date            SMALLDATETIME,
    End_Date              SMALLDATETIME,
    Execution_Status      NVARCHAR(20)
);


ALTER TABLE Executions
ADD CONSTRAINT Pk_Executions PRIMARY KEY (Execution_Id);
CREATE TABLE Staging_Products
(
    Staging_Product_Id    INT IDENTITY(1, 1) NOT NULL,
    Product_Identifier    NVARCHAR(20)  NOT NULL,
    Execution_Id          INT NOT NULL,
    Business_Code         NVARCHAR(20),
    Product_Status        INT,
    To_Delete             INT
);
ALTER TABLE Staging_Products ADD CONSTRAINT
Pk_Staging_Products PRIMARY KEY (Staging_Product_Id);
ALTER TABLE Staging_Products ADD CONSTRAINT
Uq_Staging_Products_Identifier UNIQUE (Product_Identifier);
ALTER TABLE Staging_Products
ADD CONSTRAINT Fk_Staging_Products_Executions
FOREIGN KEY (Execution_Id) REFERENCES Executions
(Execution_Id);
CREATE TABLE Staging_Attributes
(
    Staging_Detail_Id     INT IDENTITY(1, 1) NOT NULL,
    Staging_Product_Id    INT NOT NULL,
    Attribute_Name        NVARCHAR(255) NOT NULL,
    Attribute_Value       NVARCHAR(4000) NOT NULL,
    Attribute_Link        INT NOT NULL,
```

```
    Execution_Id              INT NOT NULL,
    Attribute_Status          INT,
    To_Delete                 INT
);
ALTER TABLE Staging_Attributes
ADD CONSTRAINT Pk_Staging_Attributes
PRIMARY KEY (Staging_Detail_Id);
ALTER TABLE Staging_Attributes
ADD CONSTRAINT Fk_Staging_Attr_Identifiers FOREIGN KEY
(Staging_Product_Id) REFERENCES Staging_Products
(Staging_Product_Id);


ALTER TABLE Staging_Attributes
ADD CONSTRAINT Fk_Staging_Attr_Executions
FOREIGN KEY (Execution_Id) REFERENCES Executions
(Execution_Id);
```

At first sight, the staging area is relatively similar to the gate. Before continuing, please keep in mind that this is a simple example, and the particularities of other data migration systems might be very different, so the complexity much higher. Consequently, this model does not cover everything; it is a basic model. This design is not a universal solution to any data migration process and cannot be.

However, I can say that a simple model like this can cover a moderate and medium system quite well. If anyone understood certain aspects described here and used them in his/her projects, I would be delighted! The goal is purely educational, and the proposed solution is not to change projects but to open horizons or clarify existing ones.

The staging area comprises two similar tables, a header (Staging_Products) and a detail (Staging_Attributes). What do we have here? Let's recap!

♣   The staging header is the product's image, the shoe object, and has an artificial primary key (the surrogate key from the staging is always good to have a distinct one), the Staging_Product_Id column.

♣   The Staging_Products table contains the Product_Identifier field. Please remember the gate and check the data in it. The product identifier received from Jean-Luc is the **business key** that allows the connection between the source area, defined by the entrance and the staging area. Based on this field, Johnny will undoubtedly know that the staging area is consistently connected to the portal. The connection between the two spaces, the source area defined by the gate and the staging zone, is made through the Product_Identifier field. We discussed this a lot when analyzing the need for the source's central entity's uniqueness, perhaps Jean-Luc's most essential task.

♣ The product code contains information that could be important because it would give meaning from a business perspective. I went to a few factories many years ago, and I know that these product codes are sometimes very relevant from a business point of view. This field is occasionally descriptive but can be useful. It provides intelligibility and significance to the footwear. Sometimes this can be the same as the Product_Identifier. Using such business-relevant information for such strong technical reasons is an open topic!

♣ The product status (Product_Status) is an essential, artificial field. I have already discussed this sensitive attribute earlier from the beginning. It shows the state of the shoe item. The product that comes from the gate can be "new," i.e., shoes sent for the first time from accounting. In this case, everything is entirely new for the staging area. It is like a newcomer coming to the door for the first time! Welcome! The status may already be present, which means that the product is "updated," as it came earlier from the source through the portal. This product already exists in the staging area. Now, due to possible changes to the source system, it is transmitted back through the gate. The status could be "*delete*d," the product is no longer present in the source area. Maybe Joanna removed this product, accidentally or not! Depending on this, some actions may occur in the transfer process. Notice the column's status *nullability*. This flag is essential for the understanding of the entire data transfer utility. If the product status is null, the product is not part of the current execution.

♣ There is also a third table, called Executions. This table is a kind of evidence, like a log, and allows identifying an execution. For instance, Angelique regularly performs data transfers and the data streams from the source to the target by staging, as we will see later. Johnny was aware that he had to store these executions for various purposes. That's why he created this table. However, it's not a necessity, but almost! Johnny considered it a kind of timestamp and decided to record every data process runs. A history of executions is beneficial for all sorts of purposes. Thus, identifying these runs is not mandatory, but you can almost consider it as such!

♣ The second table stores the products' attributes. The first two columns are artificial, and there is the key for the detail and the reference to the product, the foreign key (Staging_Product_Id). As mentioned earlier, Johnny preferred to have a separate column key for the staging and not use the unique product identifier that comes from the gate. There are some advantages to this approach.

♣ The pair attribute name and attribute values correspond to the same combination in the gate. The correspondence is evident. The essential information at the detailed level is here. A wide variety of attributes add value to the system.

♣   Finally, let's see the new field status once again, but at the detail level, the attribute's state. The same values apply; a property can be new to the staging area; it can be updated or required for deletion. Similarly, see the status's nullability. If the state is null, this means the attribute is not affected by the current import. You will understand much better a bit later when seeing the related logic.

Now, before we continue, let's mention a similar version of the staging area for Oracle. I prefer to use the traditional ways, so I use sequences for Oracle and identity for SQL Server!

Listing 5-2 The staging area Oracle

```
-- The staging area design: Oracle version
CREATE SEQUENCE Seq_Executions;
CREATE SEQUENCE Seq_Staging_Products;
CREATE SEQUENCE Seq_Staging_Attributes;

CREATE TABLE Executions
(
    Execution_Id          INT NOT NULL,
    Start_Date            DATE,
    End_Date              DATE,
    Execution_Status      VARCHAR2(20)
);
ALTER TABLE Executions
ADD CONSTRAINT Pk_Executions PRIMARY KEY(Execution_Id);
CREATE TABLE Staging_Products
(
    Staging_Product_Id    INT NOT NULL,
    Product_Identifier    VARCHAR2(20)  NOT NULL,
    Execution_Id          INT NOT NULL,
    Business_Code         VARCHAR2(20),
    Product_Status        INT,
    To_Delete             INT
);
ALTER TABLE Staging_Products
ADD CONSTRAINT Pk_Staging_Products PRIMARY KEY
(Staging_Product_Id);
```

```
ALTER TABLE Staging_Products
ADD CONSTRAINT Uq_Staging_Products_Identifier
UNIQUE (Product_Identifier);
ALTER TABLE Staging_Products
ADD CONSTRAINT Fk_Staging_Products_Executions
FOREIGN KEY (Execution_Id) REFERENCES Executions
(Execution_Id);
CREATE TABLE Staging_Attributes
(
    Staging_Detail_Id        INT NOT NULL,
    Staging_Product_Id       INT NOT NULL,
    Attribute_Name           VARCHAR2(255) NOT NULL,
    Attribute_Value          VARCHAR2(4000) NOT NULL,
    Attribute_Link           INT NOT NULL,
    Execution_Id             INT NOT NULL,
    Attribute_Status         INT,
    To_Delete                INT
);


ALTER TABLE Staging_Attributes
ADD CONSTRAINT Pk_Staging_Attributes PRIMARY KEY
(Staging_Detail_Id);
ALTER TABLE Staging_Attributes
ADD CONSTRAINT Fk_Staging_Attr_Identifiers
FOREIGN KEY (Staging_Product_Id) REFERENCES Staging_Products
(Staging_Product_Id);
ALTER TABLE Staging_Attributes
ADD CONSTRAINT Fk_Staging_Attr_Executions
FOREIGN KEY (Execution_Id) REFERENCES Executions
(Execution_Id);
```

Solid earth versus passing wind

The staging area is minimalist. Johnny added the fundamentals and essentials needed for his purpose. Of course, it could add many additional features for a complete system. And it will certainly take this as a starting point later. In general, an IT system is like a living beam. First, he is a child, then he grows up and becomes an adult, and eventually, he will retire! Nevertheless, what Johnny has done now is enough to get a reasonable idea of managing such a system.

From a structural point of view, the staging area is similar to the gateway, somehow reflecting the source space. What is the difference between the two if you compare quickly? Well, there are some significant differences. The structure is similar, but that is pretty much. Let's see what these differences are!

First, the source area or gate is **volatile**. Johnny's team fills the entrance each time and, before that, cleans (truncates) the source area. This action makes his life much more comfortable because he does not care about what was before (at the entrance). The source area's gateway is like an empty box for the accounting team and is always open, waiting for a new beginning. Therefore, every time Jean-Luc takes out a new set of shoe items and is ready to deliver them to the portal, he replaces what existed before and refills it.

Of course, a consistent implementation will archive the gateway before starting any logic. Moreover, the archiving step will take place just before the verification process. There are so many other things needed for a complete mechanism. But this is just another example, as part of the basics.

The staging area, on the contrary, is a **permanent** location. You can understand the reason for this difference by looking at the significance of the status fields. The status of the product or the attribute can be either new, updated, or deleted. In essence, this state makes a big difference between source and staging. The whole set of shoes with their details from Jean-Luc's system exists in the staging area for detection.

For a better understanding, let's imagine that now, at this moment, *"Speedy"* begins. Jean-Luc already filled the gate with four products, if you remember! These items are ready for delivery to the data manufacturing database through the transfer process. These four pairs of shoes with their details are present at the gate and prepared for the transfer in the first instance. After a while, maybe five more items will fill the accounting database portal, and two of them are among the first four. How many products will exist in the staging area? If we count, we will get four-plus three pairs of shoes, so a total of seven products. Four materials were already present, two of them will be in an update, and three new products will be on the way, so seven in total! Three shoe items are new to the staging area in the second data transfer, two are in an update, and two are unaffected! You will understand this simple algorithm much better when you will execute the set of SQL statements later in the process.

Now, let's look at the differences between the staging area and the gate:

♣ The staging area is permanent compared to the gate. The source area (mirror) is volatile. This distinction makes a big difference.

♣ The entrance partially reflects the source area and stores the latest products requested by Angelique. Staging is a complete set of products that go through the transfer process from the beginning till now, the entire history of shoe items. For example, maybe 10,000 products were moved through the data transfer process for a year and were part of the Panther. Now, the last cycle will deliver four pairs of shoes. Perhaps you can see the difference between the 10,000 items processed during *"Speedy's"* lifetime and the last four ones just received from the *"Yellow Panther."*

♣ The two zones are similar, but the staging area has an additional field called *status* for both the product and the attribute. Based on the comparisons, this field will detect the quality of the product or property. This one will show if the product is new, updated, or no longer part of the source. The intermediate zone's primary purpose is to detect the product's state or attributes and apply the required changes based on this status.

♣ The staging area is a buffer between the source and the target, and the staging area itself will become a source for the target space later.

♣ The purpose of the execution table is to identify an execution context. The advantage is obvious; in this way, every action, every data movement, every error is identifiable. An import code, start and end date, or an import phase represents minimum requirements. Of course, the table may contain more useful information, but these are the essential elements. Some kind of denormalization is not harmful because the execution identifier is like a timestamp. Therefore, I add this key in both the header and the detail table.

♣ This staging area model can be extended with, for example, an error and a log table. Both must refer to the execution identifier. In this way, we can locate each process or log error and attach them to execution. You can do this with a sophisticated tool, or you can do this with simple SQL, do as you wish!

Finally, the gate represents the source area; the staging space is present, and we have seen the target area. At this moment, Johnny finishes the design and is ready for development. Now it's time for real action, the development process, the second part of this project!

The classic approach in two steps

This simple model of the data transfer/migration system is, after all, a classic approach. Things happen at a shoe factory. We visit the *"Yellow Shoe"* plant; life is like in Star Trek or maybe a little like in Star Wars. Well, by the way, by no means can you associate Star Trek with Star Wars! I'm a Star Trek fan, and I love

Picard. My brother-in-law is a Star Wars fan. He once told me you couldn't be a Star Trek and Star Wars fan at the same time. You are either one or the other.

Consequently, it would be best to choose between the two. I like Star Trek, but I also like Star Wars. I remembered when I was a kid and saw the first episodes of Star Wars. At one point, Han Solo met Luke in search of a ship. They met in a bar full of all sorts of creatures of all kinds, a fantastic world. The same image is available in many Star Trek episodes, like the Promenade! Well, you can imagine a site using a variety of IT systems, each with its users, surviving in a space that is similar to the world of Star Wars or Star Trek. At "*Yellow Shoe,*" at least two systems try hard to work together in harmony, even if there may be different species!

We have completed the design, and now we are in the development stage. From this point of view, in most cases, there are two significant steps involved in such a data migration process:

♣   The first step is the data transfer from the entrance, the source's volatile image at a given time, to the permanent staging area. The logic involved is relatively simple, and the purpose is quite well defined. Johnny needs to detect the entities' status and attributes to know what to transfer to the next stage. To conclude here, the first step is to transfer data from the source area (the gate) to the staging area.

♣   The second and last step is to process the entities, in our case, the products or shoes, from the staging area, take only the objects with a modified status and process them further until the target. The second step is usually much more complicated due to the destination, challenging to reach. Thus, the second step is transferring data from the intermediate area to the target location.

In conclusion, this is the development of a data transfer system, like *"Speedy!"* The scenario is precise, with a source and a target at a client site. In general, we assume a staging area, which acts as an intermediate space between the source area and the destination. The first step of development involves the data transfer from the source zone to the intermediate one. The process is incremental, in the sense that only changing entities affect the staging area. These products acquire a valid status in this zone, mainly with three possible values. Products with a not-null state are ready to participate in the second step, transferring data from stage to target.

Now, let's finish talking. It's time to see some action, right? Let's go to the code! The words are boring; writing code is fascinating! I love them both! I know I'm not a typical programmer, but I can live with that inconvenience! Or maybe I'm old-fashioned! So, it's time for the first step. Johnny is ready for his transfer from the source area through the gate to the staging.

Ready, we're moving! I was almost stuck here!

The way we write logic is, to some extent, irrelevant. Whether it's in a Java or C # system or a database like Oracle or SQL Server, any option is acceptable. It can be anywhere. In this particular context, when everything is in the backend, there are not too many interactions with the user, and when everything is SQL, I see no reason not to use the database itself.

The place of action is part of the equation, but the way we write the code is essential. Programming style matters; this is not something to be ignored. I looked at how this type of logic should be written in my previous book, described the two programming styles in detail in a relational database, and promoted the set-based approach specific to programmers who understand the SQL paradigm. I firmly believe that such a data transfer system should be primarily SQL in a set-based manner. The only necessary thing in such scenarios is the data movement from one place to another, meaning data manipulation, etc.

Before you can start transferring data, you must define the process by specifying an execution identifier. Looking at the staging area design (see Listing 5-1), you can take a look at the Executions table. The first step is the generation of an execution identifier.

You must remember that this step takes place after checking the gate and only if the entrance is clean. If the door has errors of any kind, the process will not start. Joanna, eventually Jean-Luc, will try to fix all the consistency errors. Johnny can review the consistency rules; maybe something is wrong. He can also try to isolate the inconsistencies and remove them from the gate, eventually adding them to another place and delivering them to Jean-Luc for examination. When Johnny starts *"Speedy"* and generates the first execution, the entry is clean according to the set of consistency rules built by the data transfer team. Keep in mind that the SQL consistency rules list is dynamic and can grow continuously because you never know what might happen! The list of check rules can expand with additional SQL statements that may appear from time to time. This extension with new verification rules is an ongoing process, an endless story. As in PL SQL, we prefer not to use OTHERS but to identify the precise reason for an error. A sense of anticipation is so essential for us programmers!

Generate the execution identifier

The first thing Johnny will do is generate the execution identifier. Everything that happens from now on will have a reference in this qualifier.

Listing 5-3 Generate an execution identifier

```
-- SQL Server
INSERT INTO Executions (Start_Date, End_Date,
Execution_Status)
   VALUES (GETDATE(), NULL, 'STARTED');
   -- Oracle
INSERT INTO Executions (Execution_Id, Start_Date, End_Date,
Execution_Status)
   VALUES (Seq_Executions.NEXTVAL, SYSDATE, NULL, 'STARTED');
```

I don't think I need to remind you to commit if you choose the Oracle version! Given this step's simplicity, we've added both versions, Oracle and SQL Server, to a single list, as you can see above. Pick up the one that you consider, of course. Alternatively, you can create one for PostgreSQL or another database system that you can use because things are quite similar. Oracle and SQL Server are just examples.

Now we have begun the process. Let's see what we have. A single id and several time references, as well as a status. Another one? Yes, because the execution itself has its state, and now the process has begun!

Table 5-1 The first data transfer execution

Execution Id	Start Date	End Date	Execution Status
1	11/17/2020	NULL	STARTED

I want to mention a few primary considerations for this table:

♣   This execution_id identifies an execution. If something happens and we need some checks, we have a way of knowing how to say: here it is! That's what happened at that exact moment!

♣   The statement records the start date of the execution.

♣   Initially, the import completion date is null. When the process is complete, this field will receive an update at the current time. Johnny can also determine the length of the process. He can measure the performance, "that import was too long," or "how fast it works," users will appreciate in a way or another. Johnny can validate compliments at work or criticism, depending on the situation.

♣   There is also a status here; these flags surround us! Initially, when the process starts, the state is set to start (STARTED). When the cycle ends, the state will turn into success. If some errors occur during the process, the condition will become, for example, a failure.

The first wave, transfer product data

Now that Johnny is ready to start and has the first execution, it is time to activate the gate. The data from the entrance is available for the journey to the staging. As already mentioned, the process needs to meet some objectives at this stage.

The access gate, as well as the source area, were divided into two segments. The first segment is the header and contains the essential components that define the primary entity, such as the product. This segment includes both business and artificial elements. When we talk about an object's definition, I refer to all sorts of fields or columns, such as surrogate identifiers without commercial significance, but simple identification, generally unique or reference, such as foreign keys, etc.

The second part of the gate is composed of attributes. A wider variety of product features implies a better description of it. Please don't take the example here as one of its kind, because it's simple and try to give yourself an idea to not become a solution on its own. However, starting from a similar model and improving according to the business's needs, it can become a reasonable model to use.

Now, the migration step from gate to staging consists of two sub-steps. The first sub-step is to transfer the product's header definition to the staging area, and the second to move the product's details, the layer of attributes.

Before explaining how to do this, I think it's time for the first photo, data transfer for products. Let's start, as usual, with the SQL Server version.

Listing 5-4 Generate products in staging, SQL Server

```
-- SQL Server version
DECLARE @v_Current_Execution_Id     INT,
    @v_New                          INT,
    @v_Existing                     INT;
SET @v_New      = 1;
SET @v_Existing = 0;


-- 01 Get the current process identifier.
```

```
SELECT @v_Current_Execution_Id = Execution_Id
FROM Executions WHERE Execution_Status = 'STARTED';
-- 02 Reset the status to null for the products.
UPDATE Staging_Products
SET Product_Status = NULL
WHERE Product_Status IS NOT NULL;
-- 03 Add new products from the source. These are new.
INSERT INTO Staging_Products (Product_Identifier,
Business_Code, Execution_Id, Product_Status)
SELECT sr.Product_Identifier, sr.Business_Code,
@v_Current_Execution_Id AS Execution_Id,
@v_New AS Product_Status
FROM Gate_Header sr
WHERE NOT EXISTS
(
    SELECT 1 FROM Staging_Products dest
WHERE sr.Product_Identifier = dest.Product_Identifier
);
-- 04 Set the status to zero for products in an update
process.
UPDATE Staging_Products
SET Product_Status = @v_Existing,
Execution_Id = @v_Current_Execution_Id,
Business_Code = sr.Business_Code, To_Delete = sr.To_Delete
FROM Staging_Products dest INNER JOIN Gate_Header sr
    ON sr.Product_Identifier = dest.Product_Identifier
WHERE Product_Status IS NULL;
```

Here begins the *development* process, for real! Let's look at the above logic, but first of all, run it in your SQL Server schema and see the results by running a simple query against the Staging_Products. What are the components of the above coding? Let's take a closer look and summarize:

♣   First, Johnny captures the current execution based on *status*. As you have noticed, this flag plays a crucial role. Imagine that you have previously performed the process a thousand times. Usually, of these one thousand previous executions, only one should have active status. All others should be over, either successfully or with some errors, but finished. Thus, if the logic is well written, a single process should have active status at some point. So master Babanus will capture the value of this current execution. Alternatively, he can obtain this value as a parameter if this logic is written somewhere in a function or procedure, as is likely to be the case. In a more complex scenario, parallelism can allow many simultaneous executions. My example involves sequencing, which is sufficient to illustrate an incremental and straightforward system of this kind.

♣ The second point is to reset the status. If a data element in the intermediate zone has a null state, it means that the particular product is not affected by the current process. This status quo update has the meaning of the following statement: hey, I want to start a new race. All previous products in the potential list of participants have null status! Those who wish to join now must prepare to line up! In an imaginary universe of a thousand athletes who have entered the race so far, only twenty are lined up and start the new competition. But potentially, any of the one thousand could join the current race. Second, take a look at the null update only for products that have value. This update is good for performance, don't update the whole table. Imagine that in this time, you have over a million products over data migration in the last three years. Updating one million rows to zero instead of five, the one affected in the previous process, makes a massive difference in performance!

♣ Add new products through the data transfer system. These are the pairs of shoes that are new to staging. The target does not know them at all, as well as the stage. When I was a kid, I was a big fan of Steffi Graf. I remembered that she had a famous TV commercial with an Adidas model, Torsion. Even now, this model is popular in the "*Yellow Panther.*" Joanna knows it very well. However, Angelique is not aware of this model in her manufacturing system! All the new product identifiers from the "*Yellow Panther*" are not part of the staging area. Moreover, the product status for these will become one, which means the products are entirely new. Of course, because this is the first execution, all four items will have the status one (new) regarding the staging area.

♣ The last sequence of the code refers to existing products, products already processed in a previous execution and are now part of an update. Based on the Jean-Luc team's unique identifier in the accounting system, either natural or artificial, I mean the Product_Identifier field. Johnny can compare the products in the gate and the staging area. These are the items that will be part of an update process. The business code might change, for example. Consequently, the zero status signalizes that these products are in an update process.

After performing this step, let's classify the products in the intermediate zone. I need to better explain the transfer process from source to staging and the state field's role. Products with null status are those that do not participate in the current execution. The products with the state one (1) are the ones that are new for the "*Shoes are everywhere*" application. They were created in the Panther but are not yet part of the manufacturing module. They will become part of it after this execution. Finally, zero-state products are those that have already been processed some time ago in any previous implementation. Some changes take place in the *"Yellow Panther"* and transfer to the manufacturing system.

Johnny is breathing hard, but he's happy! It completes this first sub-step of the first step, transfers data from the gate to the staging area, respectively transfers the product header definition. There is another part, the last sub-step. Mister Babanus will soon start moving product attributes.

However, before that, let's look at the Oracle version.

Listing 5-5 Generate products in staging, Oracle

```
-- Oracle version
DECLARE
    v_Current_Execution_Id     INT;
    v_New                      INT;
    v_Existing                 INT;
BEGIN
v_New           := 1;
v_Existing      := 0;


-- 01 Get the current process identifier.
SELECT Execution_Id INTO v_Current_Execution_Id
FROM Executions WHERE Execution_Status = 'STARTED';
-- 02 Reset the status to null for the products.
UPDATE Staging_Products
SET Product_Status = NULL
WHERE Product_Status IS NOT NULL;


-- 03 Add new products from the source.
INSERT INTO Staging_Products (Staging_Product_Id,
Product_Identifier, Business_Code, Execution_Id, Product_Status)
SELECT Seq_Staging_Products.NEXTVAL AS Staging_Product_Id,
sr.Product_Identifier, sr.Business_Code, sr.Execution_Id,
sr.Product_Status
FROM
(
    SELECT sr.Product_Identifier, v_Current_Execution_Id AS
    Execution_Id, v_New AS Product_Status, sr.Business_Code
    FROM Gate_Header sr
    WHERE NOT EXISTS
```

```
        (
              SELECT 1 FROM Staging_Products dest
          WHERE sr.Product_Identifier = dest.Product_Identifier
          )
  ) sr;
  -- 04 Set the status to zero for the products in an update
  UPDATE Staging_Products dest
  SET Product_Status = v_Existing,
  Execution_Id = v_Current_Execution_Id,
  Business_Code = (
      SELECT sr.Business_Code FROM Gate_Header sr
      WHERE sr.Product_Identifier = dest.Product_Identifier),
  To_Delete = (
      SELECT sr.To_Delete FROM Gate_Header sr
      WHERE sr.Product_Identifier = dest.Product_Identifier)
  WHERE Product_Status IS NULL
  AND EXISTS
  (
      SELECT 1 FROM Gate_Header sr
      WHERE sr.Product_Identifier = dest.Product_Identifier
  );
      COMMIT;
  END;
  /
```

With a little effort, the logic is similar. We all know that this is not a mystery, but the advantage of a standard, namely SQL. For software companies with the same system but using many databases, such as Oracle and SQL Server, a good compromise between performance and portability is always the right choice. The best way to do this is to think of set-based SQL and to adapt the mindset accordingly. I will no longer support this requirement until SQL disappears from the market or I withdraw! I think the style of set-based programming in a relational database is the foundation of database development. And this style mainly applies to data-intensive applications, such as data migration systems or ETL systems, where the purpose is primarily data transfer. Unfortunately, the data transfer style is often inadequate, with abuse of cursors and structures, using the procedural technique, or, even worse, trying to simulate object-oriented programming style in a relational database!

Before continuing, Johnny quickly makes a selection in the staging area to see the pairs of shoes. He does this for the first time, as he will do quite often from now on. He prepares the result in tabular format, ready for Angelique. She, like almost any business user, loves Microsoft Excel! Johnny executed this query to populate the excel below: *"SELECT Staging_Product_Id AS Id, Product_Identifier AS Product_Id, Execution_Id AS Exec_Id, Business_Code, Product_Status AS Status FROM Staging_Products;"*

Table 5-2 The set of data at the product level in the staging area

Id	Product Id	Exec Id	Business Code	Status
1	AT12_TS_098	1	AT12_TS_098	1
2	AT12_RE_106	1	AT12_RE_106	1
3	NM92_DD_191	1	NKS_BKM_135	1
4	NM94_AX_121	1	NKS_LRM_093	1

See how, in this first run, the staging area is a kind of mirror of the gate and that the status is 1 for all the products, which is obvious because these are new products, arriving for the first time in the staging area via the gate through the data migration system.

Now, the next step is to transfer the attributes for the products. Let's go forward.

The second wave, transfer attributes

Before proceeding, check the list of details for the four products. See Listing 3-3. Each product has some properties, and the verification process validates these attributes at the beginning. The gateway checking mechanism eliminates a lot of possible reasons for inconsistency before the data migration process begins. This check does not mean that *"unexpected things could happen."* Remember Bilbo and his experiences, and he can testify to this statement. And every programmer with some experience is aware that errors can be waiting for you in the corner and can hit you when you don't expect them! But the frequency is reduced by this verification process. The gate should be approximately accurate, at least theoretically. However, like any human work, the IT system itself is imperfect, and there is always room for improvement.

Consequently, Johnny should look for more and more consistent SQL check statements to cover more situations. For this, he may need an ongoing discussion with Angelique and sometimes with Jean-Luc and Joanna. We programmers should learn from users whenever we have the opportunity. For them, it is a luxury because users are generally not interested in seeing the technical side. However, for us, it is crucial to have at least a better understanding of the business. Talking to users is the best thing, but given the modern approach and so many intermediate layers involved, this is becoming a rarity. Developers no longer have access to business users, and this is a loss for them! Johnny is happy; he can talk to Angelique and Joanna, and he has direct access to business knowledge! Not to mention the immediate access to Angelique, which is a bonus for which Johnny is exceptionally grateful!

After examining Listing 3-3, to know what is needed to transfer, and after inspecting the staging area's design in detail, Johnny will continue with the next step.

Let's change the order a bit and first reveal the logic and then analyze what's there. Let's see the transfer of data attributes from the gateway to the intermediate zone using the SQL Server version.

Listing 5-6 Generate product details in staging, SQL Server

```
--Process the product details to staging, SQL Server.
DECLARE
      @v_Current_Execution_Id    INT,
      @v_New                     INT,
      @v_Existing                INT;
SET @v_New            = 1;
SET @v_Existing       = 0;


-- 01 Get the current process identifier.
SELECT @v_Current_Execution_Id = Execution_Id
FROM Executions WHERE Execution_Status = 'STARTED';
-- 02 Reset the status to null for the attributes.
UPDATE Staging_Attributes
SET Attribute_Status = NULL
WHERE Attribute_Status IS NOT NULL;
-- 03 New attributes for new products
```

```
INSERT INTO Staging_Attributes (Staging_Product_Id,
Attribute_Name, Attribute_Value, Attribute_Status,
Attribute_Link, Execution_Id)
SELECT sp.Staging_Product_Id, sr.Attribute_Name,
sr.Attribute_Value, @v_New AS Attribute_Status,
sr.Attribute_Link, @v_Current_Execution_Id AS Execution_Id
FROM Gate_Details sr INNER JOIN Staging_Products sp
    ON sr.Product_Identifier = sp.Product_Identifier
WHERE sp.Product_Status = @v_New
AND NOT EXISTS
(
    SELECT 1 FROM Staging_Attributes atr
    WHERE sp.Staging_Product_Id = atr.Staging_Product_Id
);
-- 04 New attributes for existing products (in an update)
INSERT INTO Staging_Attributes (Staging_Product_Id,
Attribute_Name, Attribute_Value, Attribute_Status,
Attribute_Link, Execution_Id)
SELECT na.Staging_Product_Id, na.Attribute_Name,
sr.Attribute_Value, @v_New AS Attribute_Status,
sr.Attribute_Link, @v_Current_Execution_Id AS Execution_Id
FROM Gate_Details sr INNER JOIN Staging_Products sp
    ON sr.Product_Identifier = sp.Product_Identifier
INNER JOIN
(
    SELECT sp.Staging_Product_Id, sr.Attribute_Name
    FROM Gate_Details sr INNER JOIN Staging_Products sp
        ON sr.Product_Identifier = sp.Product_Identifier
    INNER JOIN Staging_Attributes atr
        ON atr.Staging_Product_Id = sp.Staging_Product_Id
    WHERE atr.Attribute_Status IS NULL
    AND sp.Product_Status = @v_Existing
    EXCEPT
    SELECT Staging_Product_Id, Attribute_Name
    FROM Staging_Attributes
) na
ON na.Staging_Product_Id = sp.Staging_Product_Id
    AND sr.Attribute_Name = na.Attribute_Name;
```

```
-- 05 Existing attributes in an update for products in an
update
    UPDATE Staging_Attributes
    SET Attribute_Status = @v_Existing,
    Execution_Id = @v_Current_Execution_Id,
    Attribute_Value = sr.Attribute_Value, To_Delete = sr.To_Delete
    FROM Staging_Attributes dest INNER JOIN Staging_Products sp
        ON dest.Staging_Product_Id = sp.Staging_Product_Id
    INNER JOIN Gate_Details sr
        ON sr.Product_Identifier = sp.Product_Identifier
    WHERE sp.Product_Status = @v_Existing
    AND dest.Attribute_Name = sr.Attribute_Name
    AND dest.Attribute_Status IS NULL;
```

Wow! It looks like there's more work here! In conclusion, the transfer from the source to the intermediate zone is limited to identifying status and differences. What is the quality of an entity? But the attribute's status of an entity? Is it new, is it in an update, is it to be removed? What are the changes in the staging area from the perspective of the data coming from the gateway? These are just some of the few questions that the developer of a data transfer system should ask! The surveys are about the same. Technologies differ, as well as complexities, from one project to another, etc.

We hope you can take a look at the logic above or, even better, run it on your system and allow yourself to describe the numbered side steps above.

♣ The first sub-step is similar to the previous logic. The meaning of the status is the same: first, the attribute turns into a null value. When we talk about null, we better say, a lack of value, right? In this way, all the lines in the staging area are virgins; they are like newborns. The assumption is: what has been there so far awaits feedback from the gate. After running this logic, all the null-stage area lines are considered *unaffected* by the current execution.

♣ The second sub-step generates new attributes for the latest products. Coincidentally, all articles will fit here in this first round, as all products are new to the staging area, entering the staging for the first time. You can see how the staging header table storing entities are joined by entity identifier, like product in our case, with the gate's details component. See the condition for the product status to be one, which means the logic refers to new products. Furthermore, although this condition may be missing, check the syntax that specifies that it does not exist. Usually, this condition should not occur because, once the product status is one, the Staging_Attributes table should not contain any attributes associated with these products. This second query will add all the 34 properties related to the four products as part of the first data migration import execution.

♣ The next statement looks for new attributes. However, the products already exist in the target from previous executions. In other words, the property status can be new, but for an item in an update. There are not such attributes yet, as this is the first execution in *"Speedy's"* history! I want to explain by example. Suppose the "*Shoes are everywhere*" module already contains one Adidas Torsion shoe generated from "*Yellow Panther*" through *"Speedy."* For any reason, at the time of transmission, there is no color. Thus, in the staging area, for this Adidas Torsion shoe, there was no color specified. Later, the gate will add the black color for the Adidas Torsion shoe in a future execution. Well, this is the type of scenario sought by statement three. The product status will become zero because the product is in an update, and the attribute state is set to one because the attribute is new to the target. Finally, the condition that does not exist will detect any potential properties that have not yet pass through the data transfer system in the intermediate area, such as the missing black color for the Adidas Torsion shoe.

♣ Detecting the last change refers to an actual update, a change in the value of an attribute. You can imagine that the specific Adidas Torsion shoe, which was defined in the target by the gate and staging area as black, is changed from the source system to white. Consequently, there is a product, Adidas Torsion, which is already part of the staging and target, with the color black recorded in both staging and target zones. After a while, the source applies a change and sends white for this product. This change should first be part of the staging area, which is what sub-step four is doing. You can check the update between the detail staging table (Staging_Attributes) and source detail table (Gate_Details), provided the product status is zero, which means the product present in the current import, the equality between the name of the attribute from the gate detail and staging detail (Attribute_Name). This attribute's value becomes the new one, white, and the property's status is zero because it is updated.

These are the facts, friends! The intermediate area is complete, and we are ready with the first step of a simple data transfer interface. I have tried to explain, perhaps often, with too many details, and I think that many systems can improve their capabilities with a simple design like this. Let's see the Oracle version before moving on to the conclusions!

Listing 5-7 Generate product details in staging, Oracle

```
-- Oracle version. Process the product details to staging
DECLARE
        v_Current_Execution_Id          INT;
        v_New                           INT;
```

Speedy, a data transfer system. A SQL Exercise

```
    v_Existing                          INT;
BEGIN
    v_New           := 1;
    v_Existing      := 0;


    -- 01 Get the current process identifier.
    SELECT Execution_Id INTO v_Current_Execution_Id
    FROM Executions WHERE Execution_Status = 'STARTED';
    -- 02 Reset the status to null for the attributes.
    UPDATE Staging_Attributes
    SET Attribute_Status = NULL
    WHERE Attribute_Status IS NOT NULL;
    -- 03 New attributes for new products
INSERT INTO Staging_Attributes (Staging_Detail_Id,
Staging_Product_Id, Attribute_Name, Attribute_Value,
Attribute_Status, Attribute_Link, Execution_Id)
    SELECT Seq_Staging_Attributes.NEXTVAL AS Staging_Detail_Id,
sr.Staging_Product_Id, sr.Attribute_Name, sr.Attribute_Value,
sr.Attribute_Status, sr.Attribute_Link, sr.Execution_Id
    FROM
    (
        SELECT sp.Staging_Product_Id, sr.Attribute_Name,
        sr.Attribute_Value, v_New AS Attribute_Status,
        sr.Attribute_Link, v_Current_Execution_Id AS Execution_Id
        FROM Gate_Details sr INNER JOIN Staging_Products sp
                ON sr.Product_Identifier = sp.Product_Identifier
        WHERE sp.Product_Status = v_New
        AND NOT EXISTS
        (
                SELECT 1 FROM Staging_Attributes atr
        WHERE sp.Staging_Product_Id = atr.Staging_Product_Id
        )
    ) sr;
        -- 04 New attributes for existing products (in an update)
    INSERT INTO Staging_Attributes (Staging_Detail_Id,
Staging_Product_Id, Attribute_Name, Attribute_Value,
Attribute_Status, Attribute_Link, Execution_Id)
```

```
SELECT Seq_Staging_Attributes.NEXTVAL AS Staging_Detail_Id,
sr.Staging_Product_Id, sr.Attribute_Name, sr.Attribute_Value,
sr.Attribute_Status, sr.Attribute_Link, sr.Execution_Id
FROM
(
SELECT sp.Staging_Product_Id, sr.Attribute_Name,
sr.Attribute_Value, v_New AS Attribute_Status,
sr.Attribute_Link, v_Current_Execution_Id AS Execution_Id
FROM Gate_Details sr INNER JOIN Staging_Products sp
    ON sr.Product_Identifier = sp.Product_Identifier
INNER JOIN
(
    SELECT sp.Staging_Product_Id, sr.Attribute_Name
    FROM Gate_Details sr INNER JOIN Staging_Products sp
        ON sr.Product_Identifier = sp.Product_Identifier
    INNER JOIN Staging_Attributes atr
        ON atr.Staging_Product_Id = sp.Staging_Product_Id
    WHERE atr.Attribute_Status IS NULL
    AND sp.Product_Status = v_Existing
    MINUS
    SELECT Staging_Product_Id, Attribute_Name
    FROM Staging_Attributes
) na
        ON na.Staging_Product_Id = sp.Staging_Product_Id
        AND sr.Attribute_Name = na.Attribute_Name
) sr   ;


-- 05 Existing attributes in an update for products in an
update
UPDATE Staging_Attributes dest
SET Attribute_Status = v_Existing,
Execution_Id = v_Current_Execution_Id,
Attribute_Value = (
SELECT sr.Attribute_Value
FROM Gate_Details sr, Staging_Products sp
WHERE sr.Product_Identifier = sp.Product_Identifier
AND sr.Attribute_Name = dest.Attribute_Name
```

```
AND sp.Staging_Product_Id = dest.Staging_Product_Id
AND sp.Product_Status = v_Existing
            )
WHERE dest.Attribute_Status IS NULL
AND EXISTS
(
    SELECT 1 FROM Gate_Details sr, Staging_Products sp
    WHERE sr.Product_Identifier = sp.Product_Identifier
    AND sr.Attribute_Name = dest.Attribute_Name
    AND sp.Staging_Product_Id = dest.Staging_Product_Id
    AND sp.Product_Status = v_Existing
);
COMMIT;
END;
/
```

Johnny will execute the logic and quickly run a query to see the data in the staging area. The data is very similar to the gateway now because it's the first time the system is running, so there is no history. An early guest in a hotel will enter an empty hotel, right?

Well, so many identifiers! This interrogation was John's reflection on the data in the staging area. If I want to talk to Angelique and analyze her from time to time, she will be in complete shadow! I have to do something; otherwise, my secret plan will fail! Master Babanus decided to create a kind of business-friendly view of the stage area to understand Angelique.

Let's see the query.

Listing 5-8 The list of products and attributes in staging

-- The list of products and their details, Oracle and SQL Server
SELECT   h.Product_Identifier   **AS**   Product_Id,   h.Business_Code, d.Attribute_Name, d.Attribute_Value
FROM Staging_Products h **INNER JOIN** Staging_Attributes d
    ON h.Staging_Product_Id = d.Staging_Product_Id
WHERE h.Product_Status **IS NOT NULL**
AND d.Attribute_Status **IS NOT NULL**
ORDER BY h.Product_Identifier, d.Attribute_Name ;

Now the staging area is ready. Angelique is a little confused because she didn't understand the meaning of the staging area. She is eager to see the data in her manufacturing application! And the data isn't there yet, just in an excel presented by Johnny.

Let's see the excel list, and we have finished it with the staging area for now!

Table 5-3 The list of products and attributes in staging

Product Id	Business Code	Attribute Name	Attribute Value
AT12_RE_106	AT12_RE_106	COLOR	Black
AT12_RE_106	AT12_RE_106	GENDER	Unisex
AT12_RE_106	AT12_RE_106	MANUFACTURER_ CODE	MLS
AT12_RE_106	AT12_RE_106	PRODUCT_NAME	Adidas Samba Rose Core Black
AT12_RE_106	AT12_RE_106	SUPPLIER_CODE	EN
AT12_RE_106	AT12_RE_106	TYPE_CODE	AS
AT12_TS_098	AT12_TS_098	COLOR	Black
AT12_TS_098	AT12_TS_098	GENDER	Male
AT12_TS_098	AT12_TS_098s	PRODUCT_NAME	Black Adidas Torsion original ZX flux
AT12_TS_098	AT12_TS_098	TYPE_CODE	AS
NM92_DD_191	NKS_BKM_135	COLOR	Silver
NM92_DD_191	NKS_BKM_135	GENDER	Male
NM92_DD_191	NKS_BKM_135	MANUFACTURER_ CODE	FFM
NM92_DD_191	NKS_BKM_135	MEASURE	41
NM92_DD_191	NKS_BKM_135	PRODUCT_NAME	Nike Lance Cycling Shoes Men 41

NM92_DD_191	NKS_BKM_135	SUPPLIER_CODE	EN
NM92_DD_191	NKS_BKM_135	TYPE_CODE	CS
NM94_AX_121	NKS_LRM_093	COLOR	Pink
NM94_AX_121	NKS_LRM_093	GENDER	Female
NM94_AX_121	NKS_LRM_093	PRODUCT_NAME	Nike Zoom Pegasus Turbo 2
NM94_AX_121	NKS_LRM_093	SUPPLIER_CODE	LS
NM94_AX_121	NKS_LRM_093	TYPE_CODE	AS

Well, just a little patience, my dear! John answered when asked the same question for the tenth time in the last month! Look, you have to catch your breath and be patient once again, my dear! Soon, "*Shoes are everywhere*" will come out of the hunger process!

6 Happy ending for John and Angelique?

There is a lot of agitation at home

At "*Yellow Shoe*," until now, users performed some operations twice, and this unnecessary duplication of work caused a lot of problems for the enterprise. For example, they have managed the same tasks in different places. Joanna added the products to the "*Yellow Panther*" system and worked with the other accountants to control various parameters. On the other hand, in another corner of the company, Angelique was doing about the same operation, at least part of it, adding more or less the same products and covering other segments of the shoe factory, analyzing and determining the manufacturing process!

It's like those national software systems without integration or less integration when the citizen has to define and redefine himself in various software products each time he/she starts a new "career" in a new IT application! I remember the despair on everyone's face when they have to fill in, again and again, personal details such as name, surname, address, etc., with each new beginning!

Joanna and Angelique have to define the same products in the two systems, and the same work has always been so unpleasant and inefficient! But, after all, this is not the greatest tragedy. We can choose to see the water-filled side of the glass! From these shortcomings, more jobs are born. Therefore, there is a specific human component, even if it lacks IT elegance. To remind me of my childhood, I grew up in a communist society led by the famous Ceausescu. I know how many people did so much useless work! I know what it's like to have a community where a lot of people pretend to work. Even today, many jobs around the world involve transmitting different papers from one place to another! Maybe transferring documents from one place to another is not a bad thing, by definition.

There are other more critical issues besides the ones mentioned above. One of them is the risk of low data quality. Joanna will add the product Adidas Torsion Meow with product code 123. For various reasons, Angelique wants to add Adidas Torsion Meow on the other side of the company and add it with another product code, 1233. However, it should be the same Adidas Twist Meow! A report appeared with two pairs of Adidas Torsion Meow shoes on the manager's desk, one with product code 123 and the second with another product code 1233. The manager is confused and does not know what to believe because he trusted both Joanna and Angelique. He called them both and has a long discussion! Finally, this is how the manager decides it is time for a change; after such meetings, the manager finally called Johnny and see what solutions are available! Here's how the idea of *"Speedy"* came about!

Johnny promised Angelique that the days of chaos and anarchy would be over. When Joanna defines a new pair of shoes in the *"Yellow Panther,"* Angelique will see it quite quickly in *"Shoes are everywhere!"* How? Well, that is pretty simple! For example, Angelique will press a button called sync, and all the recently designated products defined in *"Yellow Panther"* will automatically transfer to the other side of the enterprise! The part that belongs to Angelique is to take care of the manufacturing process, the place where she is the best! Eventually, a job running in the background will periodically push the designated products from the accountancy to the manufacturing system! Johnny is not yet sure how to deal with the end of the process, but he will see. Sometimes software application grows almost organically. Ideas come with time, slowly, slowly with the development of the system.

Moreover, as a reward, Angelica is ready to honor John's promise to go to dinner once she gets rid of the annoying task. There is a lot of agitation and excitement at her office. The management could not afford to buy a completely new system that would do accounting and production for various reasons. Johnny Babanus's courage and wisdom managed to find a way to help management get an affordable solution that could do most of the work, keeping what they have. The two systems will work almost like one now, well, at least partially!

After this reminder of the human spirit and the *"Yellow Shoes"* factory's charm, it is time to return to the technical side, return to SQL, and process the database's development. The staging area is ready for the new adventure. It was a target before and will become a source after!

The chameleon or when the source becomes a target

One of the most spectacular sequences in a sport, be it football, tennis, or anything else, is when the defense turns into an attack, in other words, triggering a counterattack. This transformation of a phase into the opposite is part of the beauty of any sport! And this is not a specific feature of the game: we are all a mixture of defense, attack, and counterattack in our daily lives, including private or business.

I remember a great motto when I was on a trip to Cleveland, Ohio. All the buses in Cleveland had the following slogan painted on them: *change is healthy*. I saw this motto in Europe, too, after a while. I love this motto, even if it is quite normal advice for everyone. As individuals, we combine conservatism and liberalism, if you allow me to borrow this terminology, with a purely sociological and psychological meaning, not political. An effort to change seems trivial, but we all know how great our inertia is and how hard we sometimes manage to make specific changes that would make our lives better.

Now, after this parenthesis, combining attack and counterattack in sports with promoting change as a way of life, we can return to *"Speedy,"* phase two. The idea is that the staging area will transform itself into something else, like a chameleon.

In the previous chapter, we populate a destination called the staging area from a gate that simulates the Panther (source area). I presented a logic that does this; I already executed the first part and filled the staging zone. And now, what's next? Some teams defend themselves for a long time in football, trying to deceive the opponents' vigilance and suddenly launch devastating counterattacks! From the prey, they become predators! Surprisingly, in this data transfer system, the reason for filling the staging area is that this intermediate area, which was a target in the first step, will change direction and become a source for a new destination. Prey becomes predator, and the source becomes the target! You can forget about the gate. From now on, it's history until the next execution!

Any such process involves sources and targets, and they are interchangeable! There is always a source and a destination. Moreover, there is a staging area, in general. This one can be physical or pure memory; there are many possible implementations, but the staging area is already part of the game, and this is where the transfer occurs. Therefore, in almost any similar system, there are these two steps. During the first step, the data is prepared and transferred from the source to the staging area. If you remember, the arrow from A to B, where A is the source system and B is the rest area. There is a change of direction in the second step, and remember, we already agree: *change is healthy*! Subsequently, point B, staging, becomes a starting point, and point C, the target, is the final destination. And this is the second step! To paraphrase the title of the subchapter, this is what happens when the source becomes a target! Thus, the staging area has a dual nature in itself. It is a source and a destination as part of the same system, but not simultaneously, but in different project phases.

Angelique's ultimate goal: come home

Angelique's ultimate goal is quite simple: she wants her shoes to come home immediately, without stress! For this, she put some pressure on poor Johnny, not knowing that the pressure is not a burden but a reward! Without realizing it, Johnny's most burning goal was to make Angelique happy at this point in his life. Of course, the reasons are multiple, starting with customer satisfaction, as well as that of professional achievement. However, I feel that you realize that to these neutral reasons is added a sentimental one! It's not hard to guess what's going on in Johnny's soul!

Now is the time to start developing the last step. Before that, I would like to ask readers to review the target system's design, checking all the Listings in Chapter 2. Johnny, *"Speedy's"* designer, needs to be aware of all this before starting his logic. At the same time, he needs to know what is coming from the staging area, his new source in this second phase of work.

The complexity of the two steps is different. The second step is more complicated than the first, in most cases. The explanation is simple. The gate and the staging area have similar structures. Looking at the target, you cannot say the same about the staging and the target, the manufacturing system. The design of the target area is not standard and uniform. It has the typical structure of any conventional relational database. This design is not a normalized structure like the staging (and the gate).

Accordingly, there should be a way to map the staging area's standardized structures to the target area's systems. Trying to copy from a normalized form into a regular one is not necessarily a piece of cake. Sometimes it's quite hard, and Johnny searches for a way to make them look more alike.

Again, there are several ways. One of the most common is to use a layer of **intermediate views**. Master Babanus was quite happy when he realized this and had a beer that night with the boys, his teammates! They got an IPA at their favorite pub, an Irish pub, of course!

The layer of staging views, a shadow of the target

Johnny is aware that he has to rewrite the SQL code, so it will not look like he is writing directly from the normalized staging zone to the destination. Thus, he considers an intermediate layer of views. This new level will map the normalized staging area's design to the target area format. It will simplify the development in the second step and make it easier to read.

If you start with this simple model and grow, which means that you add two or three more tables and finally add another entity of your choice, you will understand and achieve better. When someone tries to explain a complex problem using a simple example, there are some natural limitations. I'm sure your projects' complexity is more significant because real life is more complicated than books! But I hope this example could be useful to some of you!

Johnny introduces this intermediate layer of view before continuing the development process and implementing the transfer from staging to target. These database views will read from the staging area, the standardized model, and map the target zone, a classic data model that is not normalized as the staging. At first glance, the two design structures are so different that data transfer might seem quite challenging. Transforming the staging area so that it is similar to the destination will hide the difficulty and add much better readability to the development process.

How can Johnny implement this layer of database views to reveal the different images of the target area? The staging space has such a normalized design! How can he transfer data from this strict design into a model as free as the target?

Johnny was watching Angelique while she was doing her management reports! He is a database guy and naturally hates Excel. On the other hand, Johnny couldn't stop admiring her for the impressive Excel skills! During his career, visiting various clients, he saw experienced Excel users doing wonders with Microsoft Excel. Suddenly, like a flame, an idea came to his mind! He remembered the (new) features present in almost any database system that implements a pivot and unpivots syntax! This syntax is similar to the one Excel has been using for many years. He thanks Angelique in his mind and hopes to thank her personally later. Johnny starts testing to see if this syntax can help him build the middle ground, the intermediate layer of database staging views. And the answer was yes! The pivot syntax allows the transition from such a standardized structure, such as its staging area, to a free design. This design can exist in any system, whether manufacturing or not.

A reminder! *"Speedy"* is in progress, and Johnny seems in the zone now, like Nadal or Federer in their big matches! He reviews in his mind quickly! There are four products. All are new as this is the first execution.

Consequently, this visualization object will only cover new products, i.e., new ones at the destination, at least for now. Look at the names of the views, which refers to new products. Johnny will start with these for now. Later on, he'll see what happens if some products are updated. For the moment, he took time to cover only the new products, and by recent, he means new to the target system.

After checking all the Lists in Chapter 2, let's remember the target's design and the definition of the attributes. Let's see the miracle that Johnny gets while looking at Angelique! See SQL Server version; first, the intermediate view shows the products' image in the new products' staging area.

Listing 6-1 The staging view maps product target table SQL Server

```
-- New Products Staging views SQL Server version
IF OBJECT_ID('Stg_V_New_Products') IS NOT NULL
    DROP VIEW Stg_V_New_Products
GO
CREATE VIEW Stg_V_New_Products
AS
SELECT Product_Code, Type_Code, Product_Name, Supplier_Code,
Manufacturer_Code, Color, Gender, Measure, Source_Product_Code
FROM
(
SELECT COALESCE(pr.Business_Code, pr.Product_Identifier) AS
Product_Code, attr.Attribute_Name, attr.Attribute_Value,
pr.Product_Identifier AS Source_Product_Code
FROM Staging_Products pr INNER JOIN Staging_Attributes attr
    ON pr.Staging_Product_Id = attr.Staging_Product_Id
INNER JOIN M_Attributes ma
    ON ma.Attribute_Name = attr.Attribute_Name
WHERE pr.Product_Status = 1 AND ma.Target_Object = 'PRODUCTS'

) stg
PIVOT
(
    MAX(Attribute_Value)
FOR Attribute_Name IN (TYPE_CODE, PRODUCT_NAME, SUPPLIER_CODE,
MANUFACTURER_CODE, COLOR, GENDER, MEASURE)
) AS p;
```

Johnny was very proud of his start, the beginning of step 2. Now he checked in the staging area through the intermediate views and noticed that it contained all the relevant data that will allow a subsequent process to fill the target table with product information. Looking at the image above, you can see how the pivot function does the wonders it sees while looking at Angelique working with her excel. This feature allows Johnny to transform the highly normalized segment of the intermediate area that contains all the attributes of the product into an almost exact image of the target table. The games between the staging space and the target area will be much easier to develop later.

Let's analyze a bit of the syntax of the database view! You can see the body of the database view with a join between the two staging tables. The header data is constant and is propagated directly to the outer query. The pivoting operations transform the attributes from the detail table. In this way, this view will return the requested information from the staging area associated with the current execution. The format will be precisely the one in the target zone.

Johnny quickly interrogates the visualization object and sees what he has got! He selected only a few of the fields in the database view and not all of them. Feel free to deeply analyze the entire content of the database view, including artificial data elements. Johnny executed the following query: "*SELECT Product_Code, Product_Name AS Name, Type_Code AS Type, Supplier_Code AS Supplier, Color, Manufacturer_Code AS Man, Gender FROM Stg_V_New_Products;*"

Table 6-1 staging area disguised as a target area!

Product Code	Name	Type	Suppl ier	Color	Man	Gender
AT12_RE_106	Adidas Samba Rose Core Black	AS	EN	Black	MLS	Unisex
AT12_TS_098	Black Adidas Torsion original ZX flux	AS	NULL	Black	NULL	Male
NKS_BKM_135	Nike Lance Cycling Shoes Men 41	CS	EN	Silve r	FFM	Male
NKS_LRM_093	Nike Zoom Pegasus Turbo 2	AS	LN	Pink	NULL	Female

Take a look at the four materials in the most appropriate configuration, ready to update the target table. Check the status column for both products and attributes and note that these are essential artificial fields. See the conditions inside! Both the shoe item's status and the property must have a valid value, which means that they should not be null. In our first case, everything is new so that both flags will be equal to 1. However, you can see how the view processes only the affected products. This view ignores products that do not enter the current execution through the gate.

This intermediate view level that maps staging to the target is not always present; it depends on the design. However, for this type of scenario, this layer is excellent. It allows almost a perfect map between staging and target. This is a classic approach! Let's look at the Oracle version before we continue.

Listing 6-2 The staging view mapping the product target table Oracle

```
-- New Products Staging view Oracle version
CREATE OR REPLACE VIEW Stg_V_New_Products
AS
SELECT Product_Code, Type_Code, Product_Name, Supplier_Code,
Manufacturer_Code, Color, Gender, Measure, Source_Product_Code
FROM
(
SELECT attr.Attribute_Name, attr.Attribute_Value,
COALESCE(pr.Business_Code, pr.Product_Identifier) AS
Product_Code, pr.Product_Identifier AS Source_Product_Code
FROM Staging_Products pr
INNER JOIN Staging_Attributes attr
    ON pr.Staging_Product_Id = attr.Staging_Product_Id
INNER JOIN M_Attributes ma
    ON ma.Attribute_Name = attr.Attribute_Name
WHERE pr.Product_Status = 1 AND ma.Target_Object = 'PRODUCTS'
)
PIVOT
(
    MAX(Attribute_Value)
 FOR Attribute_Name IN ('TYPE_CODE' AS Type_Code,
'PRODUCT_NAME' AS Product_Name, 'SUPPLIER_CODE' AS
Supplier_Code, 'MANUFACTURER_CODE' AS Manufacturer_Code,
    'COLOR' AS Color, 'GENDER' AS Gender, 'MEASURE' AS Measure)
);
```

The mystery of identifiers!

From ancient times, perhaps in the history of humankind, one of the most discussed topics has been the mystery of the concept of identity. For example, in logic, the "*law of identity*," one of the three laws of logic, states that everything is identical with itself. From ancient times, famous Greek philosophers such as Socrates and Aristotle, identity has always been discussed by philosophers.

I'm not a philosopher, although I would like to be one. I'm just a database programmer. However, I love philosophy and have spent several years hoping to understand some of the great thinkers' concepts. I think I understood a drop from an ocean! For instance, when I realized that a simple statement like the one according to any two objects in space, even if it has the same characteristics by absurdity, they still differ in position! Thus, even for this reason, they cannot be identical! However, spending several years trying to understand some of the secrets of philosophy helped me much later in my practical activities. Because IT in general and programming, in particular, are a pragmatic activity. Programmers are not logicians, philosophers, scientists, doctors, or mathematicians. It deals with and solves practical and real problems. Do you think that a pure mathematician would bother his/her mind with Angelique's worries that she has to put her shoes back in the application and that she can introduce them differently than Joanna? Of course not. Mathematicians live in another world, the world of perfect numbers and shapes! Here is a big difference between the pure object of the mind, the mythical number one, compared to a pair of shoes, the thing! A shoe plus a shoe are never two shoes!

However, going back to database identifiers and setting aside philosophy, everyone knows that the world of databases was not indifferent to Socrates' past troubles. The world of databases has widely adopted some of the terminologies of logic, mathematics, and philosophy, and not just the vocabulary!. Each type of database talks about identifiers and uses this phraseology very often. The word id is one of the most common terms for us, children of the database! The product_id column is a good example. Whether we like it or not, we see identifiers everywhere and love this word, even if we don't analyze it philosophically as seriously as a logician!

In general, the identifier has some attributes derived from logic and philosophy, and one of them is one of uniqueness. As in philosophy, mathematics, and the science of reasoning, unique identification allows for distinct and secure contact. Otherwise, we can live in a world full of illusions!

Let's look at the set of systems in discussion and see how many identifiers there are so far. Let's count them and review their significance.

♣ Country_Id. This number refers to a country. It is a numeric value and an artificial identifier for a particular country. Like most synthetic fields, its meaning comes from a natural column(s), the country's name. The name of the country can usually replace the identifier itself, as it should be unique. However, if the country's name accepts duplicates and there could be two countries with the same name India, for example, with identifiers 45 and 91, we would have a rather severe consistency problem. An artificial identifier's meaning makes sense through other information, namely, meaningful information for the business. The identifier is a replacement for some business information, and a number 45 without an associated country name, such as India, is worthless. If the identifier is not necessarily unique, which is sometimes possible, this is another story. And here, sometimes, tragedies can appear in our databases!

♣ Then there is Language_Code in the Languages table, an identifier with the data type string with more meaning than the previous one. This meaning exists now because, traditionally, languages have some shortcuts in the world of geography, and these are generally the same. When specifying a name as FR, it is unusual to think of anything other than the French language.

♣ Type_id, Manufacturer_Code, and Supplier_Id are the remaining identifiers for the lookup tables, some completely artificial, others with some commercial significance.

♣ Then follows the columns Product_Id and Commercial_Code, product identifiers, and commercial codes for products. It is a tradition in relational databases not to use natural fields as identifiers. In general, identifiers are used as primary keys and used in relationships between tables. For example, the most critical column in the "Yellow Shoe" system is not Product_Id, but Code. You can see the unique business constraints attached to the Code, and this Code has some meaning. The uniqueness of the Code is essential in the "Yellow Shoe" application.

♣ On the other hand, if you interrogate the gate, you will notice other identifiers. The Product_Identifier is essential because it uniquely identifies a product in the "Yellow Panther" system. For Johnny, this product identifier can be artificial or natural, and he doesn't know. The only thing that matters to him is that this is an identifier in the strong sense of the word; that is, it possesses the attribute of uniqueness. The Gate_Detail_Id is the artificial identifier of the gate's detail, not a critical one, more for safety purposes. It is good to be sure you can uniquely identify a line in the gate.

♣ In the staging area, other identifiers line up and wait their turn!! There is the Execution_Id, the id of the execution. Furthermore, there is the Staging_Product_Id, the id of the product in the staging area. You can then see the Staging_Detail_Id, the attribute for a product in the staging area. All are artificial, and Staging_Product_Id gets meaningful by associating with Jean-Luc's id, Product_Identifier.

These things are well known to every programmer with some SQL experience, not to mention database developers. Why all this review here in this context? First, a data transfer like *"Speedy"* is not a system in itself but a road. Imagine you want to go somewhere, for example, I would like to travel by car from Luxembourg to Romania. I open Google Maps and add the original location, Luxembourg. Luxembourg is the source of travel, the starting point. Then I add the final destination, Romania, and this is the target. Since I am not a professional driver and cannot drive 2000 km in one fell swoop, I have to add an intermediate point and choose Vienna to spend a night and rest. This trip is a data transfer or migration system; it is a road from one place to another with a few intermediate stops called staging. And imagine that I have to transport items from Luxembourg to Romania, and I have to find a way to identify these items, so I label them. These are the identifiers.

Leaving aside this analogy, what is interesting about these identifiers described above? The fact that they do not recognize each other between the two ends. For example, the Product_Identifier that comes from the accounting system is unknown to the manufacturing system. Johnny or even Angelique have no idea about it; users take them for granted, and Johnny prays to be unique in the source system! Similarly, the Product_id column in the destination is entirely unknown to Jean-Luc, although it is a critical identifier in the manufacturing system. The identifiers in the staging are generally artificial, meaningless. However, Johnny should be familiar with them if *"Speedy"* is part of the manufacturing system to simplify the communication with the *"Yellow Panther."* If not, and the data migration transfer system is separate, these staging identifiers are not familiar with either Johnny and Jean-Luc. There could be a third person, such as Luke Skywalker, my favorite cousin's hero, who runs a third-party application, a data migration system that works separately.

And now, back to where I was, a question arises. The organization area is full of some products, and there is a Stg_V_New_Products view that simulates the central target table with new shoe items. This view contains all business fields in the source system based on identifiers generated by Jean-Luc. But there are three questions, quite critical, that need an additional answer:

♣ The product identifier generated by Jean-Luc, the column Product_Identifier, is the key to the entire source system. This key is easily propagated to the staging, connecting the source system through the staging area's gate. But this identifier is unknown to the manufacturing system, the target area. Johnny realizes that he needs to do something to make it known. The target system must be able to recognize this identifier. There should be a way to find a place in the target database. This field's relevance for the destination will be exactly that: as an indicator for the source system, that's it! The target system must adapt this product source identifier to link the two systems.

♣ In this scenario, the Product_Id in the target is the key to the *"Shoes are everywhere."* We can say that both Product_Id and Code are keys in this case. The first is artificial, but its meaning is given by the second, assuming that the Code has robust business relevance. This identifier is part of the target, which means that it only exists in the manufacturing system. On the other hand, not all products necessarily come from the Panther. Some may be footwear-specific items created by Angelique directly in the "*Shoes are everywhere*"! There must be a way to distinguish between the two products: those generated by Angelique versus Joanna's.

♣   How is Product_Id created? Maybe Johnny thought of a sequence? Or he used the identity property or some other internal method? Or perhaps Johnny thought of the old approach of creating new values using a custom logic? How does Product_id generate if a new product comes from the accounting system?

Somehow these three questions are related. For the source system's entities to become known in the target, for example, the product id, Johnny decides to modify the product's central table and add a new column dedicated to this purpose. The reason is simply the data transfer system: it must become visible inside the destination. Let's update the structure:

Listing 6-3 Add the external product identifier to the target

```
-- Add external (Source) identifier to the target
ALTER TABLE Products
ADD Source_Product_Code VARCHAR(20);
```

After this change, the central target table is linked to the source because it stores the "*Yellow Panther*" identifier. This field has no business significance from a manufacturing perspective and is only a reference to the accounting module. In this central table, from now on, there will be two types of footwear. First, there will be items defined by Angelique, which exist only in the manufacturing system. Somehow the owner is the target if you consider the creator as being the owner. These will have a null value specified for Product_Identifier. Second, there will be products that come from the accounting module, and in a way, Panther owns them. These products will have a value for the Product_Identifier field.

The easiest solution would have been a sequence or column with identity properties to generate new products. However, I did not consider this option because I wanted to have a single script for Oracle and SQL Server. Consequently, I will imagine the classic method for manually generating values.

But an extra layer of materialized views?

Using these staging views can cause performance issues. If the data managed by the database views is medium or large, it's best to stabilize those views somehow. If you have a script or a particular logic like a function and reference the database view multiple times, you might have performance issues. The caching helps but still if there is enough data inside, it takes a while and causes problems. The repeated call of views in an exercise is not the perfect solution. Hence, Johnny considers he can use simple tables or even specific database materialized views.

The performance of such a data transfer system is essential. Johnny doesn't want to let Angelique wait too long until she receives new information from Joanna. The performance of any system is generally the most challenging and difficult part of the process. Whether they are architects, designers, or developers in any technology, the best specialists think about performance from the beginning and not when the system suffers severely due to poor performance. Even in this unfortunate situation, you should rarely accept the unpleasant condition and hope to find room for improvement. Hence, my vision is that performance is a continuous process that goes hand in hand with development. For instance, a good data programmer will continuously fight for better execution times when doing his job. One should think about the system's performance simultaneously as the development and come back regularly to improve things, periodically rewrite the development code if necessary, frequently change, etc.

It is true that we, the programmers, are under the pressure of our managers and the business's pressure. We have to make things work first. However, I believe that we should continuously try to change for better performance whenever we have the opportunity to do so, even if it is not a direct request of a manager. I can say one thing: change is healthy in programming as well. Now, what can healthy mean in this context? We're not talking about human beings now, so it's something else. I would say that healthy means better and better performance. And that means a continuous effort to improve things, to find better ways, and so on. A good programmer will not be satisfied with the mentality: it works. He will try to make things work better!

Database performance is analyzed based on several factors, such as the amount of data or the process's difficulty. One is to work in a complex data migration system with multiple entities and hundreds of attributes, and complicated logic. Another thing is to have a completely smooth and straightforward process, with not too many complex processing operations. One is to process two or three pairs of shoes, and one is to transfer hundreds of such products periodically. An application developer can process data procedurally and atomically. He/she can use cursors, scalar functions, or triggers for each step. On the other hand, a database developer can manage everything holistically and based on sets. The performance will differ substantially.

In our example, if there are large executions with many products, repeated use of logical views could cause serious performance issues and increase execution time. A great way to improve performance and reduce runtime is to use tables or materialized views instead of database views. For example, suppose this view is called three or more times in logic. Often is better to copy the database view to a table and use the table instead. It makes a huge difference!

Johnny wants to avoid the call to view the Stg_V_New_Products database in this process. Thus, he decides to create a table. Subsequently, Master Babanus will copy the contents of the database view into the table. He could use a temporary or permanent table or a materialized view. This feature could seriously improve the performance. Everything to get the promised dinner with Angelique, some people might say when they see Johnny dreaming! He could dream of his database table or dream of Angelique. No one can tell us except him!

Let's see the table created for this purpose:

Listing 6-4 The table used as a materialized view

```
-- Products Staging database table (mv) for new products
CREATE TABLE Stg_Mv_New_Products
(
        Product_Code              VARCHAR(20) NOT NULL,
        Type_Code                 VARCHAR(20),
        Product_Name              VARCHAR(255),
        Supplier_Code             VARCHAR(20),
        Manufacturer_Code         VARCHAR(20),
        Color                     VARCHAR(100),
        Gender                    VARCHAR(10),
        Measure                   INT,
        Type_Id                   INT,
        Supplier_Id               INT,
        Product_Id                INT,
        Source_Product_Code       VARCHAR(20)
);
```

What do you notice in this table? First, the columns are almost identical to those of the Stg_V_New_Products database view. Nevertheless, if you review the target system's design, see Listing 2-1; you can see a few additional columns like Type_Id and Supplier_Id and the mysterious Product_Id column.

This table will be more than a copy of the intermediate database view contents, but Johnny will try to add even more information. How will this information be obtained? If materialized views are an option, we may need a new secondary step in logic, either themselves or simple tables. You will be amazed to see the effectiveness of this extra step!

So right now, the Stg_V_ New_Products view mirrors the staging area for actual execution. Second, the Stg_Mv_ New_Products table is a kind of database materialized view. Ultimately, there are some new columns Type_Id and Supplier_Id, and these are related to the lookup target tables called Types and Suppliers.

You can also check the target identifier specified here. It doesn't come from the source. When filling this intermediate table with data from the staging area, Johnny will also handle the target product identifier. Let's see how this works!

Listing 6-5 Generate one last intermediate layer

```
-- Using a table (materialized view) for performance reasons
DELETE Stg_Mv_New_Products;


INSERT INTO Stg_Mv_New_Products (Product_Code, Type_Code,
Product_Name, Supplier_Code, Manufacturer_Code, Color, Gender,
Measure, Type_Id, Supplier_Id, Source_Product_Code)
SELECT p.Product_Code, p.Type_Code, p.Product_Name,
p.Supplier_Code, p.Manufacturer_Code, p.Color, p.Gender,
p.Measure, t.Type_Id, s.Supplier_Id, p.Source_Product_Code
FROM Stg_V_New_Products p LEFT OUTER JOIN Suppliers s
    ON s.Supplier_Code = p.Supplier_Code
LEFT OUTER JOIN Product_Types t
    ON p.Type_Code = t.Type_Code;
```

This second step is not mandatory, as mentioned earlier. However, I noticed that it dramatically improves performance, and I highly recommend it. Using the table instead of the database view everywhere during logic is a great benefit. On the other hand, there is the cost of the population in the table. As always, the developer will measure the cost against benefits and make the right decision. I can advise as such: if you reference the view multiple times, you better create the table and use it instead. If you reference the database view, let's say one-two times, then you can skip the table. I do not think it's worth it.

In addition to performance, this additional step provides the chance to gather all potential information for this table, including target identifiers that can correlate the source with the target. The external join syntax on the left will allow the product type, supplier, and even the target product identifier to update the table.

This additional step will simplify the last step, that of the target population. Now is finally the time for Angelique to see some real stuff in the manufacturing application. Because shoes are everywhere, right? What a profound reality!

Angelique's surprise: sometimes she is on her own

Finally, we reach the first end. The supreme goal is to populate the Products table based on data from the Stg_Mv_New_Products table. Let's look at the SQL Server version first.

Listing 6-6 Generate the products in the target, SQL Server version

```
-- Generate the new items in the target, SQL Server version
DECLARE @v_Max_Product_Id    INT;
-- 01 Store the last product identifier in the target
SELECT @v_Max_Product_Id = MAX(Product_Id) FROM Products;
-- 02 Add new products from the staging to the target
INSERT INTO Products (Product_Id, Code, Name, Type_Id,
Supplier_Id, Manufacturer_Code, Color, Gender, Measure,
Source_Product_Code)
SELECT COALESCE(@v_Max_Product_Id, 0) + ROW_NUMBER() OVER
(ORDER BY p.Code) AS Product_Id, p.Code, p.Name, p.Type_Id,
p.Supplier_Id, p.Manufacturer_Code, p.Color, p.Gender,
p.Measure, Source_Product_Code
    FROM
    (
        SELECT Product_Code AS Code, Product_Name AS Name,
        Type_Id, Supplier_Id, Manufacturer_Code, Color, Gender,
        Measure, Source_Product_Code
        FROM Stg_Mv_New_Products
    ) p;
-- 03 Update product identifier in the mv (Stg_Mv_New_Products)
UPDATE Stg_Mv_New_Products
SET Product_Id = sr.Product_Id
FROM Stg_Mv_New_Products dest INNER JOIN Products sr
    ON sr.Code = dest.Product_Code ;
```

Here is the situation: it is a new beginning! After such a long journey and a long wait, Angelique and her manufacturing colleagues will see the first results. The products created by Joana and her team as part of the "*Yellow Panther*" software system are now in Manufacturing. The transfer took place last night. Angelique woke up this morning, went to the gym, drank her coffee, and went to the office. She turned on her computer and connected to "*Shoes are everywhere.*" She looked at the list of products, organized by default after the creation date, and suddenly saw some new pairs of shoes. Johnny wanted to surprise her and did not tell her the day before that he would run the data migration system for the first time in the evening. And that's what he did! Angelique was amazed. These new products from "*Yellow Panther*" are now available in "*Shoes are everywhere.*"

Looking at the logic above, we can quickly describe it:

♣ We store the latest product identifier in a variable (see the variable @ v_Max_Product_Id).

♣ The SQL procedure's source object is the materialized view Stg_Mv_New_Products, which stores the staging area's current details. We are familiar with this table; it contains information in the database view with a similar name. The target table is the Products table, the central table of the manufacturing system.

♣ We insert the new footwear, if any. The product status is the field Product_Status in table Stg_Mv_New_Products. If it has the value one, the product is a new one. The logic will insert the product into the target table. In this first execution, all products are unknown to the target. Consequently, this insert statement applies to all four products.

♣ The third statement will update the mv table with the new target product identifier (Product_Id column). This way, we synchronize the mv table accordingly. Use of Product_Id later may or may not be required. As a result, even this update may or may not be necessary.

♣ There might be a new set of update instructions to update the target table's attributes for existing products. An existing product is a product in an update. The meaning of the value zero in the field Product_Status is that of a shoe item in an update. The attributes in the table Products might change if the status for the property is one. However, for now, we do not have such products because this is the first execution. This scenario will be for later.

It's time to see the Oracle version; take a look below. Again, you can see how similar the logic in Oracle and SQL Server is. This similarity stems from the strength of the SQL standard and the set-based approach. I know both database systems relatively well and can say a few words about them. In general, we choose a kind of first basic database system. After completing the SQL logic and performing the appropriate testing, the translation process begins. Once the SQL logic is ready, the translation process is relatively accessible. If the programming code is mostly procedural and not set-based, because some programmers cannot eliminate this bad habit, the translation process can become quite complicated and risky. Portability is useful when developing multiple systems and writing SQL programming codes in numerous models for different clients. However, performance is ahead of portability if you have to choose. At least that's my opinion. So, I don't necessarily recommend thinking about portability as the primary goal. We recommend that you first analyze performance, which is essential. However, the first way to perform well in a relational database is to write set-based. Set-based coding ensures good performance. However, the set-based approach will have other consequences. One is that the process of translating from one database system to another will be much easier.

Here is the mighty Oracle!

Listing 6-7 Generate the products in the target, Oracle

```
-- Generate the products in the target, Oracle version
DECLARE
    v_Max_Product_Id          INT;
    v_Count                   INT;
BEGIN
    -- 01 Store the last product identifier in the target
    SELECT COUNT(*) INTO v_Count FROM Products;
    IF v_Count > 0 THEN
            SELECT MAX(Product_Id) INTO v_Max_Product_Id
            FROM Products;
    ELSE
            v_Max_Product_Id    := 0;
    END IF;
    -- 02 Add new products from the staging to the target
    INSERT INTO Products (Product_Id, Code, Name, Type_Id,
Supplier_Id, Manufacturer_Code, Color, Gender, Measure,
Source_Product_Code)
    SELECT v_Max_Product_Id + ROW_NUMBER() OVER (ORDER BY p.Code)
AS Product_Id, p.Code, p.Name, p.Type_Id, p.Supplier_Id,
p.Manufacturer_Code, p.Color, p.Gender, p.Measure,
Source_Product_Code
    FROM
    (
        SELECT Product_Code AS Code, Product_Name AS Name,
        Type_Id, Supplier_Id, Manufacturer_Code, Color, Gender,
        Measure, Source_Product_Code
        FROM Stg_Mv_New_Products
    ) p;
```

```
-- 03 Update product identifier in Stg_Mv_New_Products
UPDATE Stg_Mv_New_Products dest
SET Product_Id = (SELECT sr.Product_Id
FROM Products sr WHERE sr.Code = dest.Product_Code)
WHERE EXISTS
(
    SELECT 1 FROM Products sr
    WHERE sr.Code = dest.Product_Code
);
COMMIT;
END;
/
```

Angelique looks into her system and can now see two types of products:

♣   The target products. These are the products created by Angelique or any of her teammates. You can tell that the target owns these products. Commercially, some of these products may not be relevant from an accounting point of view.

♣   The migrated products. These are the products from the *"Yellow Panther."* These have already been processed in the accounting system and migrated to the new system. In addition to the accounting perspective, the products will gain relevance for manufacturing. After migration, these products acquire new meanings, and information about them becomes much more diverse. Finally, Angelique will update the products and add manufacturing meanings. The cycle is complete.

Periodically, once new products become available in Joanna's accounting, and Angelique needs them in manufacturing, they will migrate through the simple system described above. Moreover, once there are some changes in *"Yellow Panther,"* some products already present in *"Shoes are everywhere"* need an update. Any change to any shoe (product) that exists in the target system is a product update. This update could mean adding a new attribute, updating an existing property (already added before), or even removing a detail, if acceptable.

You can see four products if you want to query table products (select * from Products). By checking the staging area, you can see that these four products' status is 1, which means new. Consequently, all four products are new to the destination.

To better understand the difference, suppose Angelique adds a new product directly into *"Shoes are everywhere."* Before explaining this, let's simulate Angelique's work using an insert statement. See below:

Speedy, a data transfer system. A SQL Exercise

Listing 6-8 Add a target shoe item SQL Server

```
-- Add a target shoe product, SQL Server version
DECLARE @v_Max_Product_Id    INT;
-- 01 Store the last product identifier in the target
SELECT @v_Max_Product_Id = MAX(Product_Id) FROM Products;
-- 02 Add new products from the staging to the target
INSERT INTO Products (Product_Id, Code, Name, Type_Id,
Supplier_Id, Manufacturer_Code, Color, Gender, Measure,
Source_Product_Code)
SELECT COALESCE(@v_Max_Product_Id, 0) + 1 AS Product_Id, 'ABC'
AS Code, 'Angelique shoe item Adidas' AS Name, 2 AS Type_Id, 2
AS Supplier_Id, NULL AS Manufacturer_Code, 'Silver' AS Color,
'Female' AS Gender, 42 AS Measure, NULL AS Source_Product_Code ;
```

I think it's time to launch a query against the product table. This table is the most important in the manufacturing system, and most of our efforts are to complete this accounting table. Consequently, it deserves a little respect. So, let's query it ("*SELECT Code, Name, Source_Product_Code FROM Products*") and move the results in excel. See the data below:

Table 6-2 staging area disguised as a target area!

Code	Name	Source Product Code
AT12_RE_106	Adidas Samba Rose Core Black	AT12_RE_106
AT12_TS_098	Black Adidas Torsion original ZX flux	AT12_TS_098
NKS_BKM_135	Nike Lance Cycling Shoes Men 41	NM92_DD_191
NKS_LRM_093	Nike Zoom Pegasus Turbo 2	NM94_AX_121
ABC	Angelique shoe item Adidas	NULL

Can you see the big difference between the four new accounting products and the fifth one created by Angelique? The source_Product_Code is null for the ABC item. Consequently, ABC is a product developed within the target that owns it. ABS is a target material and exists only in "*Shoes are everywhere*"; it has nothing to do with Joanna and accountancy.

146

For consistency, let's generate one target material for the Oracle version too.

Listing 6-9 Add a target shoe item Oracle version

```
-- Add a target shoe product, Oracle version
DECLARE
    v_Max_Product_Id            INT;
BEGIN
-- 01 Store the last product identifier in the target
SELECT MAX(Product_Id) INTO v_Max_Product_Id FROM Products;


-- 02 Add new products from the staging to the target
INSERT INTO Products (Product_Id, Code, Name, Type_Id,
Supplier_Id, Manufacturer_Code, Color, Gender, Measure,
Source_Product_Code)
SELECT COALESCE(v_Max_Product_Id, 0) + 1 AS Product_Id, 'ABC'
AS Code, 'Angelique shoe item Adidas' AS Name, 2 AS Type_Id, 2
AS Supplier_Id, NULL AS Manufacturer_Code, 'Silver' AS Color,
'Female' AS Gender, 42 AS Measure,
    NULL AS Source_Product_Code FROM dual;
        COMMIT;
    END;
/
```

Complete an execution

The target area is updated, and this was the ultimate goal of our data transfer system. There is one more thing to do before you have a final trial. I call this process the completion. The last step of the data migration is a final update to the Executions table.

Two things are still needed before the process is complete, first execution.

♣ If the import succeeds, the flag must change its value to signal success. If you remember, the Execution_Status column was initially active. That is, the execution is in progress. The column's value will remain unchanged as long as the data migration continues to be as such. Two things could happen during the process. The import could fail due to an unexpected error. In such a case, the flag should transform into failure, for example. The second situation is when the execution is a success. In such a case, the column will receive a similar value, such as "success."

♣ The date that means the end of the process will be the current date. This way, we will know when the process begins and when it ends. This information defines a log of events. On the other hand, this information is needed for long-term imports when measuring execution times. Large data transfers can cause performance issues, and we always need to have the possibility to measure and compare after trying different things to improve.

Here is the last part of the process, the so-called completion.

Listing 6-10 Complete the import

```
-- Complete the execution, SQL Server version
UPDATE Executions
SET End_Date = GETDATE(), Execution_Status = 'SUCCESS'
WHERE Execution_Status = 'STARTED' ;


-- Complete the import, Oracle version
UPDATE Executions
SET End_Date = SYSDATE, Execution_Status = 'SUCCESS'
WHERE Execution_Status = 'STARTED' ;
```

Let's make a selection from the Executions table. See what the table looked like at the beginning.

Table 6-3 Executions table! First time

Execution Id	Start Date	End Date	Execution Status
1	27-FEB-21	NULL	STARTED

Now let's see what the data looks like after the completion process:

Table 6-4 Executions table! End

Execution Id	Start Date	End Date	Execution Status
1	27-FEB-21	27-FEB-21	SUCCESS

You can see the difference and better understand the meaning of this table. The finalization logic creates the record representing an execution in the first instance, with a value for the start date and the flag value "started." This registration was

148

the first step of the process, after the gate check process. Then *"Speedy"* does its job, and, finally, the last stage of the process is an update of the same record in which the end date becomes the current date at that time, and the state becomes "success." Of course, the date information should display the time as well, not just the date.

Angelique is happy now that she received the first products from Joanna. She can see everything! The next question is: what happens when Joanna changes some of these products already in manufacturing? Any attribute of any kind? This attribute could be accounting specific, so no transfer to manufacturing is required. But if the property has an ordinary meaning, it may be necessary to propagate the change. Or if Joanna eliminates a shoe item from accounting? Does Angelique need to follow her and delete the product from manufacturing? Or maybe she needs to signal the change somehow? Many options are on the table. We cannot cover all of them. But later on, we need to analyze this topic a bit, of updates from one system to another, and the various options a data transfer can offer in implementing these updates.

7 The joy comes from the code, not the word

By the time we get to El Dorado

The IT world in our shoe factory is improving with the new system. However, before deciding on this solution, which is a compromise, the leadership has long reflected alternative options. The decision was not an easy one. The footwear company originally intended to buy a completely new software system to replace the previous two. Remember that they still need a data migration process, but a different application type, even in such a scenario. Let's call this a one-time data migration process.

There is a big difference between a migration process that runs once and initializes a new system, on the one hand, and a data transfer system like *"Speedy"* that runs continuously and incrementally. For example, let's assume that a company changes the manufacturing system to a better one. In most cases, the new ones are better; we can give them credit for that, even if it doesn't always happen! Replacing a software product A with a new product B requires a lot of effort and data within the organization. Among other tasks, one of the most important is the use of existing data.

What does this thing mean? As mentioned in the previous paragraph, another scenario for our site would have been to dismiss both *"Yellow Panther"* and the *"Shoes are everywhere"* and replaced them with a new ERP system that covers both lines of activity. In this situation, Joanna and Angelique will work together on a new software product. Let's call it *"El Dorado."* As we know, almost all major software enterprises promise these types of *"El Dorado."* systems that will cover every aspect of the customer.

A new system that will replace the two existing ones is an option that requires a one-time data migration process. This data migration process aims to initialize the new *"El Dorado"* system with data from existing applications. If this were possible, retaining data from old structures such as *"Yellow Panther"* and *"Shoes Are Everywhere"* requires a one-time data migration system that will transfer data from the two old systems to the new *"El Dorado"* product. This process involves all sorts of transformations and techniques and could be a severe challenge. After implementing the new system, including this one-time data migration, the new *"El Dorado"* will control everything. Theoretically, life will be more comfortable and better for the customer. There will be a completely new system that will do everything, accounting, manufacturing, and the future will be brighter for the shoe factory. Unfortunately, even if the management would consider this option, they realized that this alternative solution is not so accessible from various points of view.

Hence, management chooses not to buy "*El Dorado*." As a result, they will continue to use the two existing applications. Joanna and Angelique will continue to be in the same position as before. However, they will have increased responsibilities, as you already know, and will find out later.

The two systems will remain as they are and work together. The integration will not be perfect, i.e., it will not replace a new system, but it will somewhat simulate a partial "*El Dorado*." The two software applications will be sisters, and the manufacturing process will be like an accounting extension. There is no "*El Dorado*," so there is no new system with a one-time data migration process. Instead, the two existing systems will continue to survive in their natural habitat, the shoe factory. The difference is that they will be linked and integrated through a transfer process that will ensure continuous collaboration between the two software products. And this link is *"Speedy!"*

The two types of systems are different. We can't compare them. *"Speedy"* requires a continuous transfer between "*Yellow Panther*" and "*Shoes are Everywhere*." Conclusion: this constant data transfer will ensure a good connection between the two systems until close to reaching an adequate integration level. The integration will not be not complete but sufficient to achieve the customer's goal. "*Yellow Panther*" will handle the accounting, "*Shoes are everywhere*" will be responsible for the manufacturing, and *"Speedy"* will periodically transfer information from accounting to manufacturing. The process is continuous and incremental. These are the main features of the process. The advantage is that the customer's site changes are minimal, and the cost is quite reasonable.

Joanna: some red shoes turn green

Returning to the first execution in the last chapter, we can mention the four products already existing in the destination system propagated by *"Speedy's"* process. You witnessed the first execution earlier.

These data imports can take place in several ways. For example, Angelique can call the data transfer system at the touch of a button. Alternatively, the process can run in the background through a job, with the desired frequency, such as daily or hourly. These are irrelevant and quite common details. What is essential is to see the incrementality at work!

Now is the time for the second execution. Joanna made some changes to a shoe item. Besides, she is ready to send a new product to the target. In conclusion, two products are part of the second execution. One shoe is entirely new to the target, while the second pair of shoes is already at the destination, as it was part of the first execution. As a result, the second product will be in an update.

The Adidas Torsion shoe type, with the code AT12_TS_098, will undergo some changes. Joanna will change the supplier, the manufacturer and update the color to white instead of black. She will send this information through the gate. Besides, a new pair of shoes is ready for the source area, with a (new) code NKS_BBB_138. It's another type of Nike, as you can see, looking at the product code.

After Joanna has made her changes, she pressed her famous button during the day, and, very quickly, her changes were visible on Angelique's computer. Some users might say, like in the old times, that is a miracle! Of course, there is no miracle involved, although some people might say that programming itself is a wonder, and this simple data transfer system is a good example. Anyway, for this miracle to happen, SQL code is written by people like Jean-Luc and Johnny!

The first part of the process is the completion of the entrance. Jean-Luc will run his process inside the Panther, and it will generate the gate. This one will contain two header entries, the new and updated product, and the associated details. Conclusion: completing a structure as simple as the set of gate tables was relatively easy for an experienced specialist like Jean-Luc. Let's see the results:

Table 7-1 Gate header (second execution, incremental)

Product Identifier	Business Code
AT12_TS_098	AT12_TS_098
NKS_BBB_138	NKS_BBB_138

Above, you can see the gate header. Comparing with the staging area and checking the list of product codes already in the target, you can easily see that a product is new in staging and target (NKS code). On the contrary, the other product code is already present in the destination, and the product code starts with AT12. If you remember the product's status, either 1 (new) or 0 (an update), you can already draw some conclusions.

Let's see the details of these products.

Table 7-2 Gate details (second execution, incremental)

Product Identifier	Attribute Name	Link	Attribute Value
AT12_TS_098	PRODUCT_NAME	1	White Adidas Torsion ZX
AT12_TS_098	SUPPLIER_CODE	1	LS
AT12_TS_098	MANUFACTURER_CODE	1	MLS
AT12_TS_098	COLOR	1	White
AT12_TS_098	COMMERCIAL_CODE	1	Miau11
AT12_TS_098	COMMERCIAL_NAME	1	Miau Steffi
AT12_TS_098	COMMERCIAL_MANUFACTURER	1	FFM
AT12_TS_098	LANGUAGE_CODE	1	EN
AT12_TS_098	COMMERCIAL_CODE	2	BlueWz1
AT12_TS_098	COMMERCIAL_NAME	2	The first blue Wizzard
AT12_TS_098	COMMERCIAL_MANUFACTURER	2	MLS
AT12_TS_098	LANGUAGE_CODE	2	EN
NKS_BBB_138	PRODUCT_NAME	1	Nike Zoom Vaillant Boom
NKS_BBB_138	GENDER	1	Female
NKS_BBB_138	COLOR	1	Green
NKS_BBB_138	TYPE_CODE	1	AS
NKS_BBB_138	SUPPLIER_CODE	1	EN
NKS_BBB_138	COMMERCIAL_CODE	1	NIK_TAURIEL
NKS_BBB_138	COMMERCIAL_NAME	1	Nike golden elves

NKS_BBB_138	COMMERCIAL_MANUFA CTURER	1	MLS
NKS_BBB_138	LANGUAGE_CODE	1	EN

Here is the list of attributes extracted from the "*Yellow Panther*" according to the logic written by Jean-Luc. The existing pair of Adidas shoes in the transfer system has eight characteristics in the gate. Some of these attributes may be new, while others may be in an update. Their status will vary between one (new) and zero (existing, in an update). The Nike pair of shoes is brand-new to the destination. Consequently, all attributes are unknown to the target, with the value for status equal to one.

Before I continue, I will add the scripts here so that readers can quickly reproduce this in their environments. The SQL files are identical regardless of the database system you use. In the absence of Jean-Luc's logic, a set of SQL insert statements will be a suitable replacement. Let's see below:

Listing 7-1 The Gate, the source area (second execution, incremental)

```
-- Same script for Oracle and SQL Server. Don't forget to
commit if running on Oracle.
DELETE Gate_Details;
DELETE Gate_Header;


-- Product in update
INSERT INTO Gate_Header (Product_Identifier, Business_Code)
VALUES ('AT12_TS_098', 'AT12_TS_098');
-- New product
INSERT INTO Gate_Header (Product_Identifier, Business_Code)
VALUES ('NKS_BBB_138', 'NKS_BBB_138');
-- Changed attribute
INSERT INTO Gate_Details (Gate_Detail_Id, Product_Identifier,
Attribute_Name, Attribute_Value)
VALUES (1, 'AT12_TS_098', 'PRODUCT_NAME', 'White Adidas
Torsion ZX');
-- New attribute
INSERT INTO Gate_Details (Gate_Detail_Id, Product_Identifier,
Attribute_Name, Attribute_Value)
VALUES (2, 'AT12_TS_098', 'SUPPLIER_CODE', 'LS');
```

```
-- New attribute
INSERT INTO Gate_Details (Gate_Detail_Id, Product_Identifier,
Attribute_Name, Attribute_Value)
  VALUES (3, 'AT12_TS_098', 'MANUFACTURER_CODE', 'MLS');
-- Changed attribute
INSERT INTO Gate_Details (Gate_Detail_Id, Product_Identifier,
Attribute_Name, Attribute_Value)
  VALUES (4, 'AT12_TS_098', 'COLOR', 'White');

-- New attribute
INSERT INTO Gate_Details (Gate_Detail_Id, Product_Identifier,
Attribute_Name, Attribute_Value, Attribute_Link)
  VALUES (5, 'AT12_TS_098', 'COMMERCIAL_CODE', 'Miau11', 1);
-- New attribute
INSERT INTO Gate_Details (Gate_Detail_Id, Product_Identifier,
Attribute_Name, Attribute_Value, Attribute_Link)
  VALUES (6, 'AT12_TS_098', 'COMMERCIAL_NAME', 'Miau Steffi',
1);
-- New attribute
INSERT INTO Gate_Details (Gate_Detail_Id, Product_Identifier,
Attribute_Name, Attribute_Value, Attribute_Link)
  VALUES (7, 'AT12_TS_098', 'COMMERCIAL_MANUFACTURER', 'FFM',
1);
-- New attribute
INSERT INTO Gate_Details (Gate_Detail_Id, Product_Identifier,
Attribute_Name, Attribute_Value, Attribute_Link)
  VALUES (8, 'AT12_TS_098', 'LANGUAGE_CODE', 'EN', 1);
-- New attribute
INSERT INTO Gate_Details (Gate_Detail_Id, Product_Identifier,
Attribute_Name, Attribute_Value, Attribute_Link)
  VALUES (9, 'AT12_TS_098', 'COMMERCIAL_CODE', 'BlueWz1', 2);
-- New attribute
INSERT INTO Gate_Details (Gate_Detail_Id, Product_Identifier,
Attribute_Name, Attribute_Value, Attribute_Link)
  VALUES (10, 'AT12_TS_098', 'COMMERCIAL_NAME', 'The first blue
wizzard', 2);
-- New attribute
```

```
INSERT INTO Gate_Details (Gate_Detail_Id, Product_Identifier,
Attribute_Name, Attribute_Value, Attribute_Link)
    VALUES (11, 'AT12_TS_098', 'COMMERCIAL_MANUFACTURER', 'MLS',
2);
    -- New attribute
INSERT INTO Gate_Details (Gate_Detail_Id, Product_Identifier,
Attribute_Name, Attribute_Value, Attribute_Link)
    VALUES (12, 'AT12_TS_098', 'LANGUAGE_CODE', 'EN', 2);
    -- New attribute
INSERT INTO Gate_Details (Gate_Detail_Id, Product_Identifier,
Attribute_Name, Attribute_Value)
    VALUES (13, 'NKS_BBB_138', 'PRODUCT_NAME', 'Nike Zoom Vaillant
Boom');
    -- New attribute
INSERT INTO Gate_Details (Gate_Detail_Id, Product_Identifier,
Attribute_Name, Attribute_Value)
    VALUES (14, 'NKS_BBB_138', 'GENDER', 'Female');
    -- New attribute
INSERT INTO Gate_Details (Gate_Detail_Id, Product_Identifier,
Attribute_Name, Attribute_Value)
    VALUES (15, 'NKS_BBB_138', 'COLOR', 'Green');
    -- New attribute
INSERT INTO Gate_Details (Gate_Detail_Id, Product_Identifier,
Attribute_Name, Attribute_Value)
    VALUES (16, 'NKS_BBB_138', 'TYPE_CODE', 'AS');
    -- New product
INSERT INTO Gate_Details (Gate_Detail_Id, Product_Identifier,
Attribute_Name, Attribute_Value)
    VALUES (17, 'NKS_BBB_138', 'SUPPLIER_CODE', 'EN');
    -- New attribute
INSERT INTO Gate_Details (Gate_Detail_Id, Product_Identifier,
Attribute_Name, Attribute_Value)
    VALUES (18, 'NKS_BBB_138', 'COMMERCIAL_CODE', 'NIK_TAURIEL');
    -- New attribute
INSERT INTO Gate_Details (Gate_Detail_Id, Product_Identifier,
Attribute_Name, Attribute_Value)
    VALUES (19, 'NKS_BBB_138', 'COMMERCIAL_NAME', 'Nike golden
elves');
    -- New attribute
```

```
INSERT INTO Gate_Details (Gate_Detail_Id, Product_Identifier,
Attribute_Name, Attribute_Value)
VALUES (20, 'NKS_BBB_138', 'COMMERCIAL_MANUFACTURER', 'MLS');
-- New attribute
INSERT INTO Gate_Details (Gate_Detail_Id, Product_Identifier,
Attribute_Name, Attribute_Value)
VALUES (21, 'NKS_BBB_138', 'LANGUAGE_CODE', 'EN');
```

The entry is full. What's next?

Please note the comment above each insert statement. These comments show the status of each attribute. Of course, this logic will automatically detect the item's state by comparing the staging area with the gateway. I checked the staging area before and mentioned the condition for each property. In doing so, I wanted to make the reader aware of this flag's importance that signals the data's status from the gate to the staging area.

Looking at the above situation, you can also review the volatility of the gate. See how the SQL script deletes the source area before refilling it with the new information. The source area is volatile, and Jean Luc's logic always fills it from scratch. Volatility is the gate's primary nature; this is the mirror of the current set of products and attributes at a given time.

After filling the source's entrance, what is the next step? Do you remember the first execution? Before starting the transfer process, there is an additional step to check the gate's consistency. Alternatively, and even better, we can consider this verification process as the first step in the data transfer process. And all is done with pure SQL, nothing else!

Let's review the flow; there are three steps:

♣   Check the gateway's consistency. If there are errors, the system may shut down. A review verification process will analyze the entrance. Usually, Joanna and Jean-Luc are responsible for this task. Alternatively, the wrong lines could be isolated and checked separately, while the rest of the good lines will continue. However, this could be risky, as it is not always so easy to isolate everything. Due to the gate's simple structure, a specific correlation between some lines could be a challenge to separate them correctly.

♣   If the gateway is clean, the staging area will become a destination for the gate. The process will detect changes that are new for staging, which is in an update. The staging zone and the gate structures are similar, except that the source area is volatile, while the staging area is permanent. Thus, based on a similar design, the complexity of logic is moderate.

♣ Finally, the target itself is updated based on the changes in the staging. Here is the most challenging part of the logic.

Check the gateway consistency, a necessary prerequisite

Starting with the first step, checking the gate, I will change the method. Instead of using the error_id column as part of the entry, as I did in chapter four, I will use the separate set of tables that store errors: Gate_Header_Errors and Gate_Details_Errors. In Chapter Four, we updated the entrance. Alternatively, we could insert SQL errors into the specific error tables. This new approach allows us to track error records over time. This history does not give us a significant advantage, given that these are all anticipated errors. However, another advantage of this approach is that we can isolate the errors and manage the flow separately. In this case, the data transfer process can continue, while the logic sends the errors to the "*Yellow Panther*" team for further investigation.

After this short review, let's look at SQL Server's logic and check the data's consistency.

Listing 7-2 Check gate consistency SQL server (second execution, incremental)

```
-- The process of checking the gate, SQL Server version
DECLARE
        @v_Rule_Id              INT,
        @v_Rule_SQL             NVARCHAR(4000),
        @v_Count                INT,
        @v_The_Gate_Is_Consistent NVARCHAR(3);


        UPDATE Gate_Details
        SET Error_Id = NULL
        WHERE Error_Id IS NOT NULL;
        UPDATE Gate_Header
        SET Error_Id = NULL
        WHERE Error_Id IS NOT NULL;


        DECLARE C_Consistency_Rules CURSOR FOR
        SELECT Rule_Id, Rule_SQL
```

```
    FROM M_Consistency_Rules
    ORDER BY 1;
BEGIN
    OPEN C_Consistency_Rules;
    FETCH NEXT FROM C_Consistency_Rules
INTO @v_Rule_Id, @v_Rule_SQL;

    WHILE @@FETCH_STATUS = 0
    BEGIN
        EXECUTE sp_executesql @v_Rule_SQL;
        FETCH NEXT FROM C_Consistency_Rules
        INTO @v_Rule_Id, @v_Rule_SQL;
    END;

    CLOSE C_Consistency_Rules;
    DEALLOCATE C_Consistency_Rules;
    SELECT @v_Count = COUNT(*) FROM
    (
        SELECT Error_Id FROM Gate_Header
        WHERE Error_Id IS NOT NULL
        UNION ALL
        SELECT Error_Id FROM Gate_Details
        WHERE Error_Id IS NOT NULL
        ) a;
    IF @v_Count > 0
    BEGIN
        SET @v_The_Gate_Is_Consistent = 'NO';
        INSERT INTO Gate_Header_Errors
        (Product_Identifier, Error_Id)
        SELECT Product_Identifier, Error_Id
        FROM Gate_Header WHERE Error_Id IS NOT NULL
        UNION
        SELECT Product_Identifier, Error_Id
        FROM Gate_Details WHERE Error_Id IS NOT NULL;
```

```
INSERT INTO Gate_Details_Errors (Gate_Detail_Id,
Product_Identifier, Attribute_Name, Attribute_Value, To_Delete,
Error_Id)
SELECT Gate_Detail_Id, Product_Identifier, Attribute_Name,
Attribute_Value, To_Delete, Error_Id
    FROM Gate_Details WHERE Error_Id IS NOT NULL
    UNION
    SELECT d.Gate_Detail_Id, d.Product_Identifier,
d.Attribute_Name, d.Attribute_Value, d.To_Delete, h.Error_Id
    FROM Gate_Details d INNER JOIN Gate_Header_Errors h
        ON h.Product_Identifier = d.Product_Identifier
    WHERE h.Error_Id IS NOT NULL ;
END
ELSE
        SET @v_The_Gate_Is_Consistent = 'YES';
    PRINT @v_The_Gate_Is_Consistent;
END;
GO
```

After running this SQL script, you can see the message; YES, confirming that there are no errors, so the gate is clean. We recommend that you try to simulate some consistency errors to see how it works. I also advise you to create some new SQL consistency rules that will allow you to increase the complexity. All these are part of your homework, if you decide to be, let's say, an active reader! I am sure that a student or a junior developer might expand this system and add their contribution.

Let's not forget Johnny because he did all these things! This new logic left the error column in the source tables and added the new error tables. This solution is somehow mixed. First, Johnny updated the error in the source area, and then he copied the errors from the error tables. Another possible way would have been to rewrite the consistency rules to update the error column in the source area, inserting the error tables directly. You can consider another test to rewrite the existing consistency rules and add the errors straight into the set of dedicated tables. In this case, you can remove the error column from the source area.

The set of error tables is now historical, so the anticipated errors are tracked. If this is not necessary, you can delete the table first.

See the Oracle version of the gateway verification logic:

Listing 7-3 Check gate consistency Oracle (second execution, incremental)

```
-- The process of checking the gate, Oracle
SET SERVEROUTPUT ON
DECLARE
    v_Rule_Id                   INT;
    v_Rule_SQL                  VARCHAR2(4000);
    v_Count                     INT;
    v_The_Gate_Is_Consistent    VARCHAR2(3);

    CURSOR C_Consistency_Rules IS
    SELECT Rule_Id, Rule_SQL
    FROM M_Consistency_Rules
    ORDER BY 1;
BEGIN
    UPDATE Gate_Details
    SET Error_Id = NULL
    WHERE Error_Id IS NOT NULL;
    UPDATE Gate_Header
    SET Error_Id = NULL
    WHERE Error_Id IS NOT NULL;
    COMMIT;

    OPEN C_Consistency_Rules;
    LOOP
    FETCH C_Consistency_Rules INTO v_Rule_Id, v_Rule_SQL;
        EXIT WHEN C_Consistency_Rules%NOTFOUND;
        EXECUTE IMMEDIATE v_Rule_SQL;
        COMMIT;
    END LOOP;
    CLOSE C_Consistency_Rules;

    SELECT COUNT(*) INTO v_Count FROM
    (
        SELECT Error_Id FROM Gate_Header
        WHERE Error_Id IS NOT NULL
```

```
            UNION ALL
            SELECT Error_Id FROM Gate_Details
            WHERE Error_Id IS NOT NULL
    ) a;
    IF v_Count > 0 THEN
            INSERT INTO Gate_Header_Errors
            (Product_Identifier, Error_Id)
            SELECT Product_Identifier, Error_Id
            FROM Gate_Header WHERE Error_Id IS NOT NULL
            UNION
            SELECT Product_Identifier, Error_Id
            FROM Gate_Details WHERE Error_Id IS NOT NULL;
  INSERT INTO Gate_Details_Errors (Gate_Detail_Id,
Product_Identifier, Attribute_Name, Attribute_Value, To_Delete,
Error_Id)
  SELECT Gate_Detail_Id, Product_Identifier, Attribute_Name,
Attribute_Value, To_Delete, Error_Id
  FROM Gate_Details WHERE Error_Id IS NOT NULL
  UNION
      SELECT d.Gate_Detail_Id, d.Product_Identifier,
      d.Attribute_Name, d.Attribute_Value, d.To_Delete,
      h.Error_Id
      FROM Gate_Details d INNER JOIN Gate_Header_Errors h
            ON h.Product_Identifier = d.Product_Identifier
      WHERE h.Error_Id IS NOT NULL ;
      UPDATE Gate_Details
      SET Error_Id = NULL
      WHERE Error_Id IS NOT NULL;
      UPDATE Gate_Header
      SET Error_Id = NULL
      WHERE Error_Id IS NOT NULL;
      COMMIT;

      v_The_Gate_Is_Consistent  := 'NO';
  ELSE
      v_The_Gate_Is_Consistent  := 'YES';
  END IF;
```

```
    DBMS_OUTPUT.PUT_LINE (v_The_Gate_Is_Consistent);
END;
/
```

Similarly, if you use Oracle, try the same exercises, increase the target area's complexity, finally add more SQL consistency rules, change the SQL rules to insert them in the error tables, and don't choose to update the source table instead.

We have covered a specific chapter, (four), which analyzes the error checking mechanism. This time, we did not add any inconsistencies to test the verification mechanism again. You can do this independently on your own. At the end of the book, I will add some recommendations to help readers simulate more situations to understand better how to build similar cases. At this point, our gateway is clean, and the *"Speedy's"* process can begin.

The first stop: staging, the life that comes from the entrance!

Now is the time to understand how this data transfer utility is a **continuous** and **incremental** process. Because the gate is clean, the process's two steps can begin, always in the same order. In the first execution, everything was new, by definition. Subsequent runs could always bring new elements but could also update existing ones. And this is the case in the second import if you remember the example above, where one pair of shoes is (new) for the target, and the other is not.

First of all, we must not neglect the administrative aspects of the system. It's always good to identify our executions, so let's generate a new execution identifier.

Listing 7-4 Generate a new import identifier (second execution, incremental)

```
-- SQL Server
INSERT INTO Executions (Start_Date, End_Date,
Execution_Status)
VALUES (GETDATE(), NULL, 'STARTED');
-- Oracle
INSERT INTO Executions (Execution_Id, Start_Date, End_Date,
Execution_Status)
VALUES (Seq_Executions.NEXTVAL, SYSDATE, NULL, 'STARTED');
```

Speedy, a data transfer system. A SQL Exercise

The execution identifier is like a timestamp used in many places in the process. For a better understanding, let's query the Executions table, see the data below:

Table 7-3 Executions list

Execution Id	Start Date	End Date	Execution Status
1	27-FEB-21	27-FEB-21	SUCCESS
2	28-FEB-21	NULL	STARTED

See the difference between the two runs. The first one ended successfully, as you can see if you look at the column status. The second is ongoing, as seen in the same column. The second import is the current one, and the end date is null, which means that the process is in progress. Usually, there should be a single execution in progress if we consider that *"Speedy"* is sequential. Of course, parallelism is an excellent facility, and we can imagine a more complex and advanced system of this type, using parallelism and allowing many simultaneous executions. However, my example is much simpler, and I assure you that it can cover many situations. It is often enough for these systems to run sequentially, and the implementation is much simpler.

To conclude the topic, this example assumes that there is only one active import at a time. If an error occurs, the status column must be set immediately to failure.

What about the great link?

I think you should now notice the presence of an additional field in the source area. The source detail table, Gate_Details, contains an Attribute_Link field with a default value of 1. Jean-Luc did not even complete this field during the first run, which means that he used the default value. Indeed, this was not necessary. If you check the gateway data in the second round, you will see that this field is only present in an individual situation. What is the meaning of this column in the source area? Why do we need this extra field?

If you check the M_Attributes metadata table, where Johnny defined the attributes, you might see Attribute_Type, single or multiple. We have already explained this property's meaning in the first chapters, saying that a metadata attribute is *simple* if it is one per entity, such as the color that can be one per product. Alternatively, the type is *multiple* if there can be numerous properties per entity. If you look, this is precisely the case with commercial names. A product can have many such alternate names. A commercial name has many fields, such as a code, a name, a manufacturer, and so on.

Thus, a shoe item may have a list of commercial names. The commercial code is unique; indeed, remember there is a primary key on it. But, if there are two or many commercial names attached to a product, how can we know which of them belong to which commercial code? If you check a commercial code, you can see that it has three additional fields. There are commercial names, commercial manufacturers, and language codes. All these fields are related. For one commercial code, there are associated fields like name, manufacturer, and language.

In our example, there is the product AT12_TS_098, which has two commercial codes Miau Steffi and BlueWz1. These are the keys. However, apart from these, each of these codes contains the rest of the properties. There must be a way to specify for each of these additional fields whose keys belong. And now we reach the purpose of the Attribute_Link. This column represents a link, and the intention is to attach the secondary properties to the attribute key, the commercial code. The commercial code is the key, and the rest of the three properties are secondary to this code. The association is through the link.

See for yourself. Look at the commercial code Miau Steffi with the value for Attribute_Link equal to one (1). Check for the rest of the fields with the Attribute_Link equal to 1. The commercial name is Miau Steffi, the manufacturer code is FFM, and the language code is EN. For the second commercial code, BlueWz1, you can see the value two (2) for the link. Checking the rest of the information by looking at the link, you can see the code's name is "The first blue wizard," the commercial manufacturer is MLS, and the language code is EN.

The link's role is crucial, almost like the great link in Deep Space 9! Only that we are not discussing changelings here, but simple fields and attributes in a design. When he builds his logic and fills the gate, Jean-Luc checks the commercial codes and, if he detects that there are many such commercial names for the product, he uses the link, otherwise not. You can see that the second product, with the code NKS_BBB_138, has no link attached even if there are commercial codes. There is only one commercial code, so there is no need for the link delimiter. The logic will see that the rest of the additional fields are attached to this one.

Of course, maybe it was better to fill the link, not rely on the default value. Try this yourself and modify the scripts to use the link and complete with the value one if there are no more sets.

The wind that disappears against the earth that remains

Looking at the sub-title above, we can recognize the difference between the staging area and the source's gateway. The staging area is like the terrain; it stays there forever. It is constantly changing, of course, but it is permanent. The source area is like the wind. It comes, shakes everything around, and move on to the next phase.

Now, enough with the metaphors. I know I am not a typical programmer, as I talk too much. Many people tell me this, and now many readers! I remembered that I had a very quiet colleague, like many programmers, by the way. He sat for hours without saying a word! However, when he was fit, he talked and was funny and friendly! Sometimes, after quiet hours, to get him out of the way, I would approach his office and ask him philosophical questions, such as "David, do you believe in love at first sight?" I can assure you that the effect was quite funny for everyone!

Well, let's get to work. Maybe I shouldn't push my luck so hard, should I? The source gate is ready for processing. Let's see the next step.

First, let's generate the product identifiers in staging. Let's examine the code again. Start as usual with the SQL Server version.

Listing 7-5 Generate the Product to Staging (second execution, incremental)

```
-- SQL Server version
DECLARE
    @v_Current_Execution_Id    INT,
    @v_Count                   INT,
    @v_New                     INT,
    @v_Existing                INT;
SET @v_New      = 1;
SET @v_Existing = 0;
SELECT @v_Count = COUNT(*) FROM Executions
WHERE Execution_Status = 'STARTED';
-- 01 Get the current process identifier.
IF @v_Count = 1
BEGIN
    SELECT @v_Current_Execution_Id = Execution_Id
```

```
FROM Executions WHERE Execution_Status = 'STARTED';
-- 02 Reset the status to null for the products.
UPDATE Staging_Products
SET Product_Status = NULL
WHERE Product_Status IS NOT NULL;


-- 03 Add new products from the source.
INSERT INTO Staging_Products (Product_Identifier,
Business_Code, Execution_Id, Product_Status)
SELECT sr.Product_Identifier, sr.Business_Code,
@v_Current_Execution_Id AS Execution_Id,
@v_New AS Product_Status
FROM Gate_Header sr
WHERE NOT EXISTS
(
        SELECT 1 FROM Staging_Products dest
WHERE sr.Product_Identifier = dest.Product_Identifier
);
-- 04 Set the status to zero for the updated products
UPDATE Staging_Products
SET Product_Status = @v_Existing,
Execution_Id = @v_Current_Execution_Id,
Business_Code = sr.Business_Code, To_Delete = sr.To_Delete
FROM Staging_Products dest INNER JOIN Gate_Header sr
        ON sr.Product_Identifier = dest.Product_Identifier
WHERE Product_Status IS NULL;
END ;
ELSE
-- There should not be two simultaneous executions.
SELECT 1;
GO
```

First, you can see that the script is similar to the one in Listing 5-4. However, the consequences of its execution are different. Now is the time to look at this logic step by step. See how the instructions are labeled. We have four instructions. I will analyze them all again.

♣   Instruction 01. Get the current import identifier in a variable. In this example, we assume that data migration is sequential. I'm sure we all know the famous Oracle errors when we enter a value from a table or a query into a variable, and there are many rows! To avoid this, it is always good to calculate a count. At least that's what I do. However, there should be a single import with the "STARTED" flag. Separately, there should be a way to change this status. If the execution is a failure, then the flag should change to "FAILURE" instead of "STARTED."

♣ Instruction 02. Reset the product status in staging. Initially, all existing products are eligible for an update. This step is one of the keys to the process. All products with the status flag set to null are not players of the current game!

♣ Add new shoe items. If a specific product identifier coming from the "*Yellow Panther*" through the gate does not exist in the Staging area, it is new to staging. These pairs of shoes will be inserted and will have status 1 (one). Product status 1 means a new product. At the first execution, all four items were new because this was the first import. In this second version, the NKS_BBB_138 pair of shoes is an example of a new product.

♣ Finally, you can see the last part of this step that explains the process incrementality. If there are Product identifier-based matches in the Staging area versus the gateway, these are the products in an update. The status of these products will become 0 (zero). The footwear product using the identifier AT12_TS_098 is one such item.

After executing this logic, you will understand the staging area's role and the data migration process's incrementality feature. Let's see the data, in the Staging_Products table, after executing the step. Please run a select statement against the table Staging_Products ("*select Product_Identifier AS Product_Id, Business_Code AS Code, Product_Status, Execution_Id AS Exec_Id, Staging_Product_Id AS Id from Staging_Products*").

Table 7-4 Staging products

Product Id	Code	Product Status	Exec Id	Id
AT12_RE_106	AT12_RE_106	NULL	1	1
AT12_TS_098	AT12_TS_098	0	2	2
NM92_DD_191	NKS_BKM_135	NULL	1	3
NM94_AX_121	NKS_LRM_093	NULL	1	4
NKS_BBB_138	NKS_BBB_138	1	2	5

Now, as in the Sherlock Holmes novels, I will unravel a lot of mysteries. Dear Watson, I will clarify some of your questions, and I will dispel many misunderstandings. Therefore, pay special attention to the analysis that will follow:

♣ First, one statistic: there are five products in the Staging area now. Easy to follow, no headaches.

♣ Check passive products. Three of them have been part of the Staging area since the first execution. They are not part of the second execution. I call them passive! You can quickly check the status of the Product that remains NULL. Products AT12_RE_106, NM92_DD_191, and NM94_AX_121 are three of the four products in the first import which do not participate in the second execution. Look at the null state and see the execution identifiers with the no value. The query that identifies passive products is here ("select * from Staging_Products where Product_Status is null").

♣ Verify new products. The product NKS_BBB_138 is one such item. How can you check this in the staging table? Well, "Cherchez la femme," as in the famous French proverb. If this is one, the shoe item is new to my eyes. Thus, there is only one product in the current import that is new for staging. The query that identifies the new products is here (select * from Staging_Products where Product_Status = 1).

♣ Take a look at the products in an update. AT12_TS_098 is an updated product. You can quickly check if the interface created this Product in the first import and updates the same products in the second import. See the zero flag and verify the execution identifier that becomes two of one, which means that the last product update occurs in the second run. The query that identifies the updated products is here (select * from Staging_Products where Product_Status = 0).

Now you can better understand the importance of such a flag. It is the cornerstone of the system. This indicator is reset each time at the beginning of each step. Potentially, all elements that already exist in the Staging area potentially incomplete! Subsequently, there are two phases of this first step. Firstly, we detect new products in the staging area. The second phase consists of identifying the pairs of shoes that already exist in the staging. Something has changed in the Panther, and this change applies to the target soon. As a result, the logic changes the status to either one or zero. The others are passive, have zero flags, and practically do not participate in the current process.

All these manipulations of the flags are done based on the product identifier, the key to the whole system. That is why I insisted on the previous chapters on the importance of a business key in the source system. By being sure of the source entity's uniqueness of entities, we can be sure about the product's consistency.

Speedy, a data transfer system. A SQL Exercise

Before we continue, let's once again describe the Oracle version of the same logic.

Listing 7-6 Generate Product in Staging (second execution, incremental) Oracle

```
-- Oracle version
DECLARE
        v_Current_Execution_Id          INT;
        v_Count                         INT;
        v_New                           INT;
        v_Existing                      INT;
BEGIN
        v_New       := 1;
        v_Existing  := 0;

        SELECT COUNT(*) INTO v_Count FROM Executions
        WHERE Execution_Status = 'STARTED';
        IF v_Count = 1 THEN
                -- 01 Get the current process identifier.
                SELECT Execution_Id INTO v_Current_Execution_Id
                FROM Executions WHERE Execution_Status = 'STARTED';
                -- 02 Reset the status to null for the products.
                UPDATE Staging_Products
                SET Product_Status = NULL
                WHERE Product_Status IS NOT NULL;
            -- 03 Add new products from the source.
        INSERT INTO Staging_Products (Staging_Product_Id,
Product_Identifier, Business_Code, Execution_Id, Product_Status)
SELECT Seq_Staging_Products.NEXTVAL AS  Staging_Product_Id,
sr.Product_Identifier, sr.Business_Code, sr.Execution_Id,
sr.Product_Status
        FROM
        (
        SELECT sr.Product_Identifier, v_Current_Execution_Id AS
Execution_Id, v_New AS Product_Status, sr.Business_Code
        FROM Gate_Header sr
        WHERE NOT EXISTS
            (
```

```
    SELECT 1 FROM Staging_Products dest
      WHERE sr.Product_Identifier = dest.Product_Identifier
      )
) sr;
-- 04 Set the status to zero for the products in an update
UPDATE Staging_Products dest
SET Product_Status = v_Existing,
Execution_Id = v_Current_Execution_Id,
Business_Code = (SELECT sr.Business_Code FROM Gate_Header sr
WHERE sr.Product_Identifier = dest.Product_Identifier),
To_Delete = (SELECT sr.To_Delete FROM Gate_Header sr
WHERE sr.Product_Identifier = dest.Product_Identifier)
WHERE Product_Status IS NULL
AND EXISTS
(
    SELECT 1 FROM Gate_Header sr
    WHERE sr.Product_Identifier = dest.Product_Identifier
);
    COMMIT;
    ELSE
    -- There should not be two simultaneous executions.
        NULL;
    END IF;
END;
/
```

Before continuing, let's run a query against the Staging_Products table. You'll see the five products, and by checking the Product_status flag, you'll quickly identify that three of them are passive products and two are active. By active, I mean that they participate in the current process. One is new for the target of these two, the one with the value of the one flag, and one is in an update, having the value of the flag equal to zero.

We always get lost in the details

Now that we clarified the staging area's product status, let's continue investigating the second flag. The first flag is the product one and specifies the product status in the staging area. The second flag is the attribute flag. The footwear product has a set of properties, and the next question is referring to these in the same context. What is the visibility of the product attributes? In other words, a product can be either new or in an update or not participating in the current execution. The same question applies to any product detail. Let's explain the problem.

If the footwear product is entirely new for staging and target, then things are clear. Everything is new. Consequently, the status of all attributes will always be one (1). Once a product is 1 for the first time in staging, all the properties that belong to that item will be entirely brand-new for the staging area.

The question arises when we discuss the properties of footwear products that are in an update. The attributes may possess all the possible values for these products: new, in an update, or delete. A first-time detail can mean an insert statement if it involves inserting it into an attribute table. On the other hand, a new attribute can mean an update if the table already contains a record.

Now, let's run the second sub-step of the first part of the data transfer system. I'm sure you remember that we have two parts, in general. The first part is the data transfer from the source area (via the gate) to the staging zone. The second part is the process that moves the data from the staging area to the target.

There are two products affected in this current run: one is new to staging, and the second is in an update. The first sub-step was handling the product. Now the manipulation of the attribute will follow. Let's see the logic again.

Listing 7-7 Generate Attributes to Staging (second execution) SQL Server

```sql
-- SQL Server version.
DECLARE
        @v_Count                INT,
        @v_Current_Execution_Id INT,
        @v_New                  INT,
        @v_Existing             INT;


SET @v_New      = 1;
SET @v_Existing = 0;
SELECT @v_Count = COUNT(*) FROM Executions
WHERE Execution_Status = 'STARTED';
IF @v_Count = 1
BEGIN
    -- 01 Get the current process identifier.
    SELECT @v_Current_Execution_Id = Execution_Id
```

```sql
FROM Executions WHERE Execution_Status = 'STARTED';
-- 02 Reset the status in staging area
UPDATE Staging_Attributes
SET Attribute_Status = NULL
WHERE Attribute_Status IS NOT NULL;
-- 03 Add new attributes for the latest products
INSERT INTO Staging_Attributes (Staging_Product_Id,
Attribute_Name, Attribute_Value, Attribute_Status,
Attribute_Link, Execution_Id)
SELECT sp.Staging_Product_Id, sr.Attribute_Name,
sr.Attribute_Value, @v_New AS Attribute_Status,
sr.Attribute_Link, @v_Current_Execution_Id AS Execution_Id
FROM Gate_Details sr INNER JOIN Staging_Products sp
    ON sr.Product_Identifier = sp.Product_Identifier
WHERE sp.Product_Status = @v_New
AND NOT EXISTS
(
    SELECT 1 FROM Staging_Attributes atr
    WHERE sp.Staging_Product_Id = atr.Staging_Product_Id
);
-- 04 Add new attributes for products in an update
WITH new_attributes (Staging_Product_Id, Attribute_Name)
AS
(
    SELECT sp.Staging_Product_Id, sr.Attribute_Name
    FROM Gate_Details sr INNER JOIN Staging_Products sp
        ON sr.Product_Identifier = sp.Product_Identifier
    INNER JOIN Staging_Attributes atr
        ON atr.Staging_Product_Id = sp.Staging_Product_Id
    WHERE atr.Attribute_Status IS NULL
    AND sp.Product_Status = @v_Existing
    EXCEPT
    SELECT Staging_Product_Id, Attribute_Name
    FROM Staging_Attributes
)
```

```
INSERT INTO Staging_Attributes (Staging_Product_Id,
Attribute_Name, Attribute_Value, Attribute_Status,
Attribute_Link, Execution_Id)
SELECT na.Staging_Product_Id, na.Attribute_Name,
sr.Attribute_Value, 1 AS Attribute_Status, sr.Attribute_Link,
@v_Current_Execution_Id AS Execution_Id
FROM Gate_Details sr INNER JOIN Staging_Products sp
        ON sr.Product_Identifier = sp.Product_Identifier
    INNER JOIN new_attributes na
        ON na.Staging_Product_Id = sp.Staging_Product_Id
        AND sr.Attribute_Name = na.Attribute_Name;


    -- 05 Attributes in an update for products in an update
    UPDATE Staging_Attributes

    SET Attribute_Status = @v_Existing, Execution_Id =
@v_Current_Execution_Id, Attribute_Value = sr.Attribute_Value
        FROM Staging_Attributes dest INNER JOIN Staging_Products
sp
            ON dest.Staging_Product_Id = sp.Staging_Product_Id
        INNER JOIN Gate_Details sr
            ON sr.Product_Identifier = sp.Product_Identifier
    WHERE sp.Product_Status = @v_Existing
    AND dest.Attribute_Name = sr.Attribute_Name
    AND dest.Attribute_Status IS NULL;
END
ELSE
    -- There should not be two simultaneous executions.
    SELECT 1;
GO
```

I will continue to describe the flow. This time, we are in the second phase of the first step, updating the staging area. Nevertheless, unlike the first round, there are modified products. Initially, everything was new for both staging and target, but now there are new products and updated products. This second execution shows the main feature of the process, which is continuous and incremental:

♣   This second sub-step will affect the detail table, where the attributes are normalized. The Staging_Attributes table is the one in question. The first thing we need to reset the attributes' status. See the condition where this is not null. The clause is useful for performance. Imagine you have ten million rows here. And only ten of them are affected by the current execution, so only ten are not null. If you update to null without the where clause, you will update ten million lines. If you update with the where clause, you update ten lines. Keep that in mind! These little things make the difference in a good quality SQL code!

♣   Add the new attributes in the Staging area for the latest products. This scenario applies to the footwear product NKS_BBB_138. Because NKS_BBB_138 is brand new, all its characteristics are unknown to staging. You can see the two conditions, a bit redundant, I admit. Once the footwear product's status is one (1), all attributes' states are one. However, in addition to this condition, which should be sufficient, another is based on the identifier Staging_Product_Id. Of course, the two conditions are more or less equivalent. The statement labeled 02 was the SQL statement that generates all the Staging area attributes during the first run.

♣   Now check the SQL statements numbered 03 and 04. The SQL statement 03 is an inner join between the staging table with products (Staging_Products) and the source area (Gate_Details). Furthermore, check another inner join with the staging table with the attributes (Staging_Attributes). The joins are for the products in an update (see the condition Product_Status equal to zero). The data that does not have a particular property in the staging area was not propagated yet from the "Yellow Panther," even if the shoe item already exists in target. You can see the condition that does not exist based on the Attribute_Name column. The purpose of this third statement is to check for new attributes of already migrated products.

♣   The last sub-step, numbered 04, investigates the existing properties for existing products. See the current import identifier value, look at the status value becoming zero, and see how the new value replaces the old one.

♣   I repeat, considering the linearity, assume there is one execution in progress. A cleansing process should clean the imports in progress and reset the flag to failure. The assumption of linearity is present in my example for simplicity.

♣   Refer to the attribute link field in the staging zone. This field inherits the gateway link identifier. The purpose of this link now becomes clear: to allow the correct correlation of several attributes that use many additional characteristics. See the commercial code as an attribute with a key, the code, and a few secondary fields. These secondary fields are attached to the code, and the attribute link is what makes this connection.

In this way, this simplified logic covers as many scenarios as possible from one source to one target. It first resets the status, checks for new data items, and then verify existing products with new features or properties in an update. The only missing scenario is when a deletion could take place at the source, which should somehow affect the destination.

What is interesting is for you to take a look at the attributes in progress during this execution. To have meaning, Johnny needs to add an inner join between the product header table and details table to show the product identifier. The attributes are irrelevant without the products, right?

The query is simple, and Johnny said "Eureka" when finished, like his famous Greek ancestors:

Listing 7-8 The list of active attributes

```
-- List of active attributes
SELECT h.Product_Identifier, d.Attribute_Name,
d.Attribute_Status AS Status, d.Attribute_Value
FROM Staging_Attributes d INNER JOIN Staging_Products h
    ON h.Staging_Product_Id = d.Staging_Product_Id
WHERE d.Attribute_status IS NOT NULL
ORDER BY h.Staging_Product_Id, d.Staging_Detail_Id
```

Here are the results, as anticipated in Listing 7-1. See below:

Table 7-5 List of active attributes in Staging

Product Identifier	Attribute Name	Status	Attribute Value
AT12_TS_098	PRODUCT_NAME	0	White Adidas Torsion ZX
AT12_TS_098	COLOR	0	White
AT12_TS_098	SUPPLIER_CODE	1	LS
AT12_TS_098	MANUFACTURER_CODE	1	MLS
AT12_TS_098	COMMERCIAL_CODE	1	Miau11
AT12_TS_098	COMMERCIAL_NAME	1	Miau Steffi
AT12_TS_098	COMMERCIAL_MANUFACTURER	1	FFM
AT12_TS_098	LANGUAGE_CODE	1	EN
AT12_TS_098	COMMERCIAL_CODE	1	BlueWz1

AT12_TS_098	COMMERCIAL_NAME	1	The first blue Wizzard
AT12_TS_098	COMMERCIAL_MANUFA CTURER	1	MLS
AT12_TS_098	LANGUAGE_CODE	1	EN
NKS_BBB_138	PRODUCT_NAME	1	Nike Zoom Vaillant Boom
NKS_BBB_138	GENDER	1	Female
NKS_BBB_138	COLOR	1	Green
NKS_BBB_138	TYPE_CODE	1	AS
NKS_BBB_138	SUPPLIER_CODE	1	EN
NKS_BBB_138	COMMERCIAL_CODE	1	NIK_TAURIEL
NKS_BBB_138	COMMERCIAL_NAME	1	Nike golden elves
NKS_BBB_138	COMMERCIAL_MANUFA CTURER	1	MLS
NKS_BBB_138	LANGUAGE_CODE	1	EN

See the attributes' status. Most of them have the status one (1), which means they are new attributes. Some of them have the status zero (0), which indicates the entity is in an update. Now let's look at a similar version of Oracle.

Listing 7-9 Generate the Attributes in Staging (second execution) Oracle

```
-- Oracle version.
DECLARE
    v_Count                   INT;
    v_Current_Execution_Id    INT;
    v_New                     INT;
    v_Existing                INT;
BEGIN
```

Speedy, a data transfer system. A SQL Exercise

```
v_New  := 1;
v_Existing   := 0;

SELECT COUNT(*) INTO v_Count FROM Executions
WHERE Execution_Status = 'STARTED';
IF v_Count = 1 THEN
-- 01 Get the current process identifier.
        SELECT Execution_Id INTO v_Current_Execution_Id
        FROM Executions WHERE Execution_Status = 'STARTED';
        -- 02 Reset the status in staging area
        UPDATE Staging_Attributes
        SET Attribute_Status = NULL
        WHERE Attribute_Status IS NOT NULL;
-- 03 Add new attributes for the latest products
    INSERT INTO Staging_Attributes (Staging_Detail_Id,
Staging_Product_Id, Attribute_Name, Attribute_Value,
Attribute_Status, Attribute_Link, Execution_Id)
    WITH sr (Staging_Product_Id, Attribute_Name, Attribute_Value,
Attribute_Status, Attribute_Link, Execution_Id)
        AS
        (
    SELECT sp.Staging_Product_Id,sr.Attribute_Name,
sr.Attribute_Value, v_New AS Attribute_Status,
sr.Attribute_Link, v_Current_Execution_Id AS Execution_Id
        FROM Gate_Details sr INNER JOIN Staging_Products sp
                ON sr.Product_Identifier = sp.Product_Identifier
        WHERE sp.Product_Status = v_New
        AND NOT EXISTS
        (
                SELECT 1 FROM Staging_Attributes atr
        WHERE sp.Staging_Product_Id = atr.Staging_Product_Id
        )
        )
    SELECT Seq_Staging_Attributes.NEXTVAL AS Staging_Detail_Id,
sr.Staging_Product_Id, sr.Attribute_Name, sr.Attribute_Value,
    sr.Attribute_Status, sr.Attribute_Link, sr.Execution_Id
        FROM sr;
```

```
-- 04 Add new attributes for products in an update
INSERT INTO Staging_Attributes (Staging_Detail_Id,
Staging_Product_Id, Attribute_Name, Attribute_Value,
Attribute_Status, Attribute_Link, Execution_Id)
      WITH new_attributes (Staging_Product_Id, Attribute_Name)
      AS
      (
      SELECT sp.Staging_Product_Id, sr.Attribute_Name
      FROM Gate_Details sr INNER JOIN Staging_Products sp
            ON sr.Product_Identifier = sp.Product_Identifier
      INNER JOIN Staging_Attributes attr
            ON attr.Staging_Product_Id = sp.Staging_Product_Id
      WHERE attr.Attribute_Status IS NULL
      AND sp.Product_Status = v_Existing
      MINUS
      SELECT Staging_Product_Id, Attribute_Name
            FROM Staging_Attributes
      )
      SELECT Seq_Staging_Attributes.NEXTVAL AS
Staging_Detail_Id, na.Staging_Product_Id, na.Attribute_Name,
sr.Attribute_Value,
      v_New AS Attribute_Status, sr.Attribute_Link,
      v_Current_Execution_Id AS Execution_Id
      FROM Gate_Details sr INNER JOIN Staging_Products sp
            ON sr.Product_Identifier = sp.Product_Identifier
      INNER JOIN new_attributes na
            ON na.Staging_Product_Id = sp.Staging_Product_Id
      AND sr.Attribute_Name = na.Attribute_Name;

            -- 05 Attributes in an update
      UPDATE Staging_Attributes dest
      SET Attribute_Status = v_Existing,
      Execution_Id = v_Current_Execution_Id,
      Attribute_Value = (
            SELECT sr.Attribute_Value
      FROM Gate_Details sr, Staging_Products sp
      WHERE sr.Product_Identifier = sp.Product_Identifier
```

```
AND sr.Attribute_Name = dest.Attribute_Name
AND sp.Staging_Product_Id = dest.Staging_Product_Id
AND sp.Product_Status = v_Existing
           )
WHERE dest.Attribute_Status IS NULL
AND EXISTS
(
       SELECT 1 FROM Gate_Details sr, Staging_Products sp
       WHERE sr.Product_Identifier = sp.Product_Identifier
       AND sr.Attribute_Name = dest.Attribute_Name
       AND sp.Staging_Product_Id = dest.Staging_Product_Id
       AND sp.Product_Status = v_Existing
);
COMMIT;
END IF;
END;
/
```

This SQL block above ends the first part, and now comes the second. We finally reached the last piece of the puzzle, transferring data from the staging area to the target zone.

8 Speedy: an incremental process

Home sweet home!

As we have already seen, the second phase of the process is to update the target area. We start this second and last phase by checking the staging zone. Two tables define this area: the table with products (main entities) and the table with attributes (details). Even if the staging table could be quite large, maybe thousands of products, after all, it is not so relevant. Of this variety of thousands of products, only a few of them could be part of the current execution. We used the active-passive terminology to distinguish between them. Active products are footwear items that participate in the current process, and passive products do not participate. For example, there may be four products in the recent run out of several thousand products, and only these four are relevant.

The status field is the key to the process. Products with a valid status, zero or one, are those affected by current imports. On the other hand, null (status) products are passive and not part of the recent execution. I repeated this to emphasize the importance of the status field in the process.

Before we start updating the target tables, we need to update the middle zone; the materialized view layer. As mentioned earlier, this is not mandatory but useful. If you have some data, it will minimize the amount of information to be processed. The Stg_Mv_Products table is much more powerful, if I may say so, than the Stg_V_Products view. You can ask the optimizer!

If you go back to Chapter 6, we had a single view and the associated table. Now is the time for more. First, take a look at the attribute metadata table and check the field Target_Object ("*select Attribute_Name, Target_Object from M_Attributes*"). Let's see them again:

Table 8-1 List of extensive attributes

Attribute_Name	Target_Object
TYPE_CODE	PRODUCTS
SUPPLIER_CODE	PRODUCTS
MANUFACTURER_CODE	PRODUCTS

PRODUCT_NAME	PRODUCTS
COLOR	PRODUCTS
GENDER	PRODUCTS
MEASURE	PRODUCTS
COMMERCIAL_CODE	COMMERCIAL_NAMES
COMMERCIAL_NAME	COMMERCIAL_NAMES
COMMERCIAL_MANUFACTURER	COMMERCIAL_NAMES
LANGUAGE_CODE	COMMERCIAL_NAMES

There are two target tables: Products and Commercial_Names. The first four shoe items contained only information from the Product table (see first round). Alternatively, if you examine the second type of attribute, you will see some new properties that reference the second table. See the metadata table above and how the target object can be either the Products table or Commercial_Names.

Build the database views layer

Consequently, the second execution brought several commercial names. They must be transferred from accountancy to manufacturing. Thus, there is an additional part of the logic now, the SQL code that will handle commercial names. Moreover, one material in an update process means we need to review the SQL logic accordingly. If in Chapter 6, we had a single view and the associated table, now we will have four of them. As described in chapter 6, the first execution illustrates the database view Stg_V_New_Products and the related table Stg_Mv_New_Products. These objects' purpose is to switch from the staging area's normalized view to the target's free design (a usual, typical design). However, the four products were new in the first part, and the data was from one target table, Products. The database view and table cover these. Now, Johnny will create separate database views for products in an update and an additional target table (the table Commercial_Names). Thus, four database views are required. Let's see this set of database views first and start with the SQL Server version.

Listing 8-1 The list of database views, SQL Server

```
-- New Products Staging views SQL Server version
IF OBJECT_ID('Stg_V_New_Products') IS NOT NULL
    DROP VIEW Stg_V_New_Products
GO
CREATE VIEW Stg_V_New_Products
AS
SELECT Product_Code, Type_Code, Product_Name, Supplier_Code,
Manufacturer_Code, Color, Gender, Measure, Source_Product_Code
FROM
(
SELECT COALESCE(pr.Business_Code, pr.Product_Identifier) AS
Product_Code, attr.Attribute_Name, attr.Attribute_Value,
pr.Product_Identifier AS Source_Product_Code
FROM Staging_Products pr INNER JOIN Staging_Attributes attr
    ON pr.Staging_Product_Id = attr.Staging_Product_Id
INNER JOIN M_Attributes ma
    ON ma.Attribute_Name = attr.Attribute_Name
WHERE pr.Product_Status = 1
AND ma.Target_Object = 'PRODUCTS'
) stg
PIVOT
(
    MAX(Attribute_Value)
    FOR Attribute_Name IN (TYPE_CODE, PRODUCT_NAME,
SUPPLIER_CODE, MANUFACTURER_CODE, COLOR, GENDER, MEASURE)
) AS p
GO
-- Products in an update Staging views SQL Server version
IF OBJECT_ID('Stg_V_Upd_Products') IS NOT NULL
    DROP VIEW Stg_V_Upd_Products
GO
CREATE VIEW Stg_V_Upd_Products
AS
SELECT Product_Code, Type_Code, Product_Name, Supplier_Code,
Attribute_Status, Manufacturer_Code, Color, Gender, Measure,
Source_Product_Code
```

```
FROM
(
    SELECT COALESCE(pr.Business_Code, pr.Product_Identifier)
AS Product_Code, attr.Attribute_Status,attr.Attribute_Name,
attr.Attribute_Value,
pr.Product_Identifier AS Source_Product_Code
FROM Staging_Products pr INNER JOIN Staging_Attributes attr
    ON pr.Staging_Product_Id = attr.Staging_Product_Id
INNER JOIN M_Attributes ma
    ON ma.Attribute_Name = attr.Attribute_Name
WHERE pr.Product_Status = 0
AND ma.Target_Object = 'PRODUCTS'
AND attr.Attribute_Status IS NOT NULL
) stg
PIVOT
(
    MAX(Attribute_Value)
    FOR Attribute_Name IN (TYPE_CODE, PRODUCT_NAME,
SUPPLIER_CODE, MANUFACTURER_CODE, COLOR, GENDER, MEASURE)
) AS p
GO
-- New Commercial Codes for products Staging view Oracle
version
IF OBJECT_ID('Stg_V_New_Commercial_Names') IS NOT NULL
    DROP VIEW Stg_V_New_Commercial_Names
GO
CREATE VIEW Stg_V_New_Commercial_Names
AS
SELECT Source_Product_Code, Commercial_Code, Commercial_Name,
Commercial_Manufacturer, Language_Code, Attribute_Link
FROM
(
    SELECT attr.Attribute_Name, attr.Attribute_Link,
    attr.Attribute_Value, pr.Product_Identifier AS
    Source_Product_Code
    FROM Staging_Products pr INNER JOIN Staging_Attributes
attr
            ON pr.Staging_Product_Id = attr.Staging_Product_Id
```

```
    INNER JOIN M_Attributes ma
            ON ma.Attribute_Name = attr.Attribute_Name
        WHERE pr.Product_Status = 1
AND ma.Target_Object = 'COMMERCIAL_NAMES'
) stg
PIVOT
(
    MAX(Attribute_Value)
    FOR Attribute_Name IN (COMMERCIAL_CODE, COMMERCIAL_NAME,
    COMMERCIAL_MANUFACTURER, LANGUAGE_CODE)
) AS p
GO
-- New Commercial Codes for products Staging view Oracle
version
IF OBJECT_ID('Stg_V_Upd_Commercial_Names') IS NOT NULL
    DROP VIEW Stg_V_Upd_Commercial_Names
GO
CREATE VIEW Stg_V_Upd_Commercial_Names
AS
SELECT Source_Product_Code, Commercial_Code, Commercial_Name,
Commercial_Manufacturer, Language_Code, Attribute_Status,
Attribute_Link
FROM
(
SELECT attr.Attribute_Status, attr.Attribute_Link,
attr.Attribute_Name, attr.Attribute_Value,
pr.Product_Identifier AS Source_Product_Code
    FROM Staging_Products pr INNER JOIN Staging_Attributes
attr
            ON pr.Staging_Product_Id = attr.Staging_Product_Id
        INNER JOIN M_Attributes ma
            ON ma.Attribute_Name = attr.Attribute_Name
        WHERE pr.Product_Status = 0
AND ma.Target_Object = 'COMMERCIAL_NAMES'
AND attr.Attribute_Status IS NOT NULL
) stg
PIVOT
```

```
(
    MAX(Attribute_Value)
FOR Attribute_Name IN (COMMERCIAL_CODE, COMMERCIAL_NAME,
COMMERCIAL_MANUFACTURER, LANGUAGE_CODE)
) AS p
GO
```

I will explain these four database views shortly. You can easily see the similarities between them. Everyone uses the pivot function to switch from the staging area's standardized design to any target's free structure. Again, the status is what makes the distinction and drives this layer of views.

♣ The Stg_V_New_Products database view manages the attributes for new products that are part of the Products table. You can see the join with the M_Attributes metadata table and the condition that the target object is the products table. Furthermore, please see the query condition Product_Status = 1, which means the products are new.

♣ Stg_V_Upd_Products database view records product attributes in an update. The property itself can be a new one or in an update. That is why this database view contains an additional field, attribute status. In the first database view, since the products are new, all attributes are also brand-new.

♣ The Stg_V_New_Commercial_Names database view contains additional information about new products. By additional information, I understand commercial names. See the condition Target_Object = COMMERCIAL_NAMES and Product_Status = 1.

♣ The last database view is Stg_V_Upd_Commercial_Names. The scope is quite clear. This database view takes care of additional information (commercial names) for products in an update. You can see the attribute status field again, which means the attribute can be new or updated.

This layer is optional and may be completely missing. However, the advantage of this switch from one design to another is readability. The complexity of the second phase logic is significantly lower by using this switch using these database views. Otherwise, direct writing in the target tables from the intermediate area's highly standardized design would have been challenging. The pivot syntax allows us to simulate the target area as it is, another chameleon! Life is full of surprises, and I can hear Angelique saying, "You see, the pivot is Excel, and your SQL code uses it too. Although you criticize Excel, you still use it whether you recognize it or not!"

As an exercise, try to insert directly from the normalized design into the target objects' set and see the difference. Without using the pivot functionality, you will see that the logic is not straightforward, and the performance will not be the best. This step and this technique are beneficial here.

Before we continue, let's look at the Oracle version. There is not much difference, but consistency is consistency. All exercises will come from both systems, and there are no exceptions unless the syntax is identical. Unfortunately, this is not always possible!

Listing 8-2 The list of database views, Oracle

```sql
-- New Products Staging view Oracle version
CREATE OR REPLACE VIEW Stg_V_New_Products
AS
SELECT Product_Code, Type_Code, Product_Name, Supplier_Code,
Manufacturer_Code, Color, Gender, Measure, Source_Product_Code
FROM
(
SELECT COALESCE(pr.Business_Code, pr.Product_Identifier) AS
Product_Code, attr.Attribute_Name, attr.Attribute_Value,
pr.Product_Identifier AS Source_Product_Code
    FROM Staging_Products pr INNER JOIN Staging_Attributes
attr
        ON pr.Staging_Product_Id = attr.Staging_Product_Id
    INNER JOIN M_Attributes ma
        ON ma.Attribute_Name = attr.Attribute_Name
    WHERE pr.Product_Status = 1
AND ma.Target_Object = 'PRODUCTS'
)
PIVOT
(
    MAX(Attribute_Value)
    FOR Attribute_Name IN ('TYPE_CODE' AS Type_Code,
'PRODUCT_NAME' AS Product_Name, 'SUPPLIER_CODE' AS
Supplier_Code, 'MANUFACTURER_CODE' AS Manufacturer_Code,
'COLOR' AS Color, 'GENDER' AS Gender, 'MEASURE' AS Measure)
);
-- Products in an update Staging views Oracle version
CREATE OR REPLACE VIEW Stg_V_Upd_Products
AS
```

Speedy, a data transfer system. A SQL Exercise

```sql
SELECT Product_Code, Type_Code, Product_Name, Supplier_Code,
Attribute_Status, Manufacturer_Code, Color, Gender, Measure,
Source_Product_Code
    FROM
    (
    SELECT COALESCE(pr.Business_Code, pr.Product_Identifier) AS
Product_Code, attr.Attribute_Status, attr.Attribute_Name,
attr.Attribute_Value, pr.Product_Identifier AS
Source_Product_Code
        FROM Staging_Products pr INNER JOIN Staging_Attributes
attr
            ON pr.Staging_Product_Id = attr.Staging_Product_Id
        INNER JOIN M_Attributes ma
            ON ma.Attribute_Name = attr.Attribute_Name
    WHERE pr.Product_Status = 0 AND ma.Target_Object = 'PRODUCTS'
    AND attr.Attribute_Status IS NOT NULL
    )
    PIVOT
    (
        MAX(Attribute_Value)
        FOR Attribute_Name IN ('TYPE_CODE' AS Type_Code,
        'PRODUCT_NAME' AS Product_Name, 'SUPPLIER_CODE' AS
        Supplier_Code, 'MANUFACTURER_CODE' AS Manufacturer_Code,
        'COLOR' AS Color, 'GENDER' AS Gender, 'MEASURE' AS
        Measure)
    );
-- New Commercial Codes for products Staging view Oracle
version
    CREATE OR REPLACE VIEW Stg_V_New_Commercial_Names
    AS
    SELECT Source_Product_Code, Commercial_Code, Commercial_Name,
Commercial_Manufacturer, Language_Code, Attribute_Link
    FROM
    (
    SELECT attr.Attribute_Name, attr.Attribute_Link,
attr.Attribute_Value, pr.Product_Identifier AS
Source_Product_Code
        FROM Staging_Products pr INNER JOIN Staging_Attributes
attr
        ON pr.Staging_Product_Id = attr.Staging_Product_Id
```

```
    INNER JOIN M_Attributes ma
            ON ma.Attribute_Name = attr.Attribute_Name
    WHERE pr.Product_Status = 1
AND ma.Target_Object = 'COMMERCIAL_NAMES'
)
PIVOT
(
    MAX(Attribute_Value)
FOR Attribute_Name IN ('COMMERCIAL_CODE' AS Commercial_Code,
'COMMERCIAL_NAME' AS Commercial_Name,
 'COMMERCIAL_MANUFACTURER' AS Commercial_Manufacturer,
'LANGUAGE_CODE' AS Language_Code)
);
-- New Commercial Codes for products Staging view Oracle
version
CREATE OR REPLACE VIEW Stg_V_Upd_Commercial_Names
AS
SELECT Source_Product_Code, Commercial_Code, Commercial_Name,
Commercial_Manufacturer, Language_Code, Attribute_Status,
Attribute_Link
FROM
(
SELECT attr.Attribute_Status, attr.Attribute_Link,
attr.Attribute_Name, attr.Attribute_Value, pr.Product_Identifier
AS Source_Product_Code
    FROM Staging_Products pr INNER JOIN Staging_Attributes
attr
            ON pr.Staging_Product_Id = attr.Staging_Product_Id
    INNER JOIN M_Attributes ma
            ON ma.Attribute_Name = attr.Attribute_Name
    WHERE pr.Product_Status = 0
AND ma.Target_Object = 'COMMERCIAL_NAMES'
AND attr.Attribute_Status IS NOT NULL
)
PIVOT
(
    MAX(Attribute_Value)
```

```
FOR Attribute_Name IN ('COMMERCIAL_CODE' AS Commercial_Code,
'COMMERCIAL_NAME' AS Commercial_Name,
 'COMMERCIAL_MANUFACTURER' AS Commercial_Manufacturer,
'LANGUAGE_CODE' AS Language_Code)
 );
```

There are four database views and four tables, one for each SQL view. It could have been just two or even one. There are many options, and I recommend you try to implement them differently. Remember, this is an elementary example. You can see it as a starting point. I would be happy if you would come up with various solutions based on this exercise. All these ideas are, actually, starting points. All you have to do is keep going! And try to find a match between your projects and this exercise, of course.

So, we need to build the latest three tables (materialized views). Let's see them now:

Listing 8-3 Create the middle layer of tables (materialized views)

```
-- Products Staging materialized view (actually simple tables)
for product attributes: the same SQL Server and Oracle script.
CREATE TABLE Stg_Mv_Upd_Products
(
        Product_Code                VARCHAR(20) NOT NULL,
        Type_Code                   VARCHAR(20),
        Product_Name                VARCHAR(255),
        Supplier_Code               VARCHAR(20),
        Manufacturer_Code           VARCHAR(20),
        Color                       VARCHAR(100),
        Gender                      VARCHAR(10),
        Measure                     INT,
        Type_Id                     INT,
        Supplier_Id                 INT,
        Product_Id                  INT,
        Source_Product_Code         VARCHAR(20),
        Attribute_Status            INT
);


CREATE TABLE Stg_Mv_New_Commercial_Names
(
        Commercial_Code             VARCHAR(20) NOT NULL,
```

190

```
        Commercial_Name              VARCHAR(255),
        Commercial_Manufacturer      VARCHAR(20),
        Language_Code                VARCHAR(20),
        Product_Id                   INT,
        Attribute_Link               INT,
        Source_Product_Code          VARCHAR(20)
);
CREATE TABLE Stg_Mv_Upd_Commercial_Names
(
        Commercial_Code              VARCHAR(20) NOT NULL,
        Commercial_Name              VARCHAR(255),
        Commercial_Manufacturer      VARCHAR(20),
        Language_Code                VARCHAR(20),
        Product_Id                   INT,
        Source_Product_Code          VARCHAR(20),
        Attribute_Link               INT,
        Attribute_Status             INT
);
```

The next step is, of course, filling in (temporary) tables based on database views. Here, again, you have all the freedom in the world. First, you can skip the tables entirely if you think you don't need them. Use the database views instead! If you decide to use the tables, you will incur an additional cost. You will need to populate these tables each time before the target system update phase. Let's look at this extra step, the first step in the second phase of development. Let's see what it is about, no big deal, don't worry! Of course, it is better to truncate the tables before.

Listing 8-4 Populate the materialized views, SQL Server, and Oracle

```
-- Same script for both SQL Server and Oracle
-- New products
DELETE Stg_Mv_New_Products;


INSERT INTO Stg_Mv_New_Products (Product_Code, Type_Code,
Product_Name, Supplier_Code, Manufacturer_Code, Color, Gender,
Measure, Type_Id, Supplier_Id, Source_Product_Code)
```

Speedy, a data transfer system. A SQL Exercise

```sql
SELECT p.Product_Code, p.Type_Code, p.Product_Name,
p.Supplier_Code, p.Manufacturer_Code, p.Color, p.Gender,
p.Measure, t.Type_Id, s.Supplier_Id, p.Source_Product_Code
    FROM Stg_V_New_Products p LEFT OUTER JOIN Suppliers s
        ON s.Supplier_Code = p.Supplier_Code
    LEFT OUTER JOIN Product_Types t
        ON p.Type_Code = t.Type_Code;
    -- Products in update
    DELETE Stg_Mv_Upd_Products;
    INSERT INTO Stg_Mv_Upd_Products (Product_Code, Type_Code,
Product_Name, Supplier_Code, Attribute_Status,Manufacturer_Code,
Color, Gender, Measure, Type_Id, Supplier_Id, Product_Id,
Source_Product_Code)
    SELECT p.Product_Code, p.Type_Code, p.Product_Name,
p.Supplier_Code, p.Attribute_Status,p.Manufacturer_Code,
p.Color, p.Gender, p.Measure, t.Type_Id, s.Supplier_Id,
pt.Product_Id, p.Source_Product_Code
    FROM Stg_V_Upd_Products p LEFT OUTER JOIN Products pt
        ON p.Source_Product_Code = pt.Source_Product_Code
    LEFT OUTER JOIN Suppliers s
        ON s.Supplier_Code = p.Supplier_Code
    LEFT OUTER JOIN Product_Types t
            ON p.Type_Code = t.Type_Code;
    -- New products (additional information)
    DELETE Stg_Mv_New_Commercial_Names;
    INSERT INTO Stg_Mv_New_Commercial_Names (Commercial_Code,
Commercial_Name, Commercial_Manufacturer, Language_Code,
Attribute_Link, Source_Product_Code)
    SELECT c.Commercial_Code, c.Commercial_Name,
c.Commercial_Manufacturer, c.Language_Code, C.Attribute_Link,
c.Source_Product_Code
    FROM Stg_V_New_Commercial_Names c;
    -- Products in an update (additional information)
    DELETE Stg_Mv_Upd_Commercial_Names;
    INSERT INTO Stg_Mv_Upd_Commercial_Names (Commercial_Code,
Commercial_Name, Commercial_Manufacturer, Language_Code,
Product_Id, Source_Product_Code, Attribute_Link,
Attribute_Status)
```

```
SELECT c.Commercial_Code, c.Commercial_Name,
c.Commercial_Manufacturer, c.Language_Code, pt.Product_Id,
c.Source_Product_Code, c.Attribute_Link, c.Attribute_Status
   FROM Stg_V_Upd_Commercial_Names c LEFT OUTER JOIN Products pt
      ON c.Source_Product_Code = pt.Source_Product_Code;
```

There is not much to say here. The above logic is a simple copy process; the only new additional information, apart from the database views, is some lookup data. On the other hand, this lookup data can be part of the database view from the beginning. Many options are available in this situation as well. Choose what you think is best, vary, looking for alternative solutions, etc.

Let's see what we have before continuing and starting the final assault. I will make some simple statements selected from the mv tables. Run some queries against the tables, dig into the data and analyze the meanings inside. See the status values because this is the key to understanding, mostly when the products are updated. Things are pretty simple; the status is always 1 for both product and attributes when the pair of shoes comes for the first time through the gate.

Johnny will execute the following queries:

Listing 8-5 Display the materialized views, SQL Server, and Oracle

```
-- Display data from the MV Stg_Mv_New_Products. Same queries
for SQL Server and Oracle.
SELECT Product_Code AS Code, Type_Code AS Type,
Supplier_Code AS Supplier, Manufacturer_Code AS Man, Color,
Gender, Measure, Product_Name AS Name
FROM Stg_Mv_New_Products;


-- Display data from the MV Stg_Mv_Upd_Products
SELECT Product_Code AS Code, Type_Code AS Type,
Supplier_Code AS Supplier, Manufacturer_Code AS Man, Color,
Gender, Measure, Product_Name AS Name
FROM Stg_Mv_Upd_Products;


-- Display data from the Stg_Mv_New_Commercial_Names
SELECT Commercial_Code AS Code, Commercial_Name AS Name,
Commercial_Manufacturer AS Man, Language_Code AS Language,
Product_Id, Attribute_Link AS Link,
Source_Product_Code AS Src_Pr_Code
FROM Stg_Mv_New_Commercial_Names;
```

```
-- Display data from the Stg_Mv_Upd_Commercial_Names
SELECT Commercial_Code AS Code, Commercial_Name AS Name,
Commercial_Manufacturer AS Man, Language_Code AS Language,
Product_Id, Attribute_Link AS Link,
    Source_Product_Code AS Src_Pr_Code, Attribute_Status AS Status
FROM Stg_Mv_Upd_Commercial_Names;
```

He quickly took a look at the staging area, and he was quite happy. The image was what he needed, and it looks exactly like the target. Despite the highly normalized form of the staging, Johnny transformed this picture into the target's free design due to the pivot facility. Let's see the data below, one by one.

Table 8-2 New products attributes (Stg_Mv_New_Products)

Code	Type	Supplier	Man	Color	Gender	Measure	Name
NKS_BB B_138	AS	EN	NULL	Green	Female	NULL	Nike Zoom Vaillant Boom

Table 8-3 Updated products attributes (Stg_Mv_Upd_Products)

Code	Type	Supplier	Man	Color	Gender	Measure	Name
AT12_TS_09 8	NULL	NULL	NULL	White	NULL	NULL	White Adidas Torsion ZX
AT12_TS_09 8	NULL	LS	MLS	NULL	NULL	NULL	NULL

Table 8-4 Commercial names for new products (Stg_Mv_New_Commercial_Names)

Code	Name	Man	Language	Product Id	Link	Src_Pr_Code
NIK_TAU RIEL	Nike golden elves	MLS	EN	NULL	1	NKS_BBB_138

Table 8-5 Commercial names upd products
Stg_Mv_Upd_Commercial_Names

Code	Name	Man	Language	Product Id	Link	Status	Src Pr Code
Miau11	Miau Steffi	FFM	EN	2	1	1	AT12_TS _098
BlueWz 1	The first blue wizard	MLS	EN	2	2	1	AT12_TS _098

Please take a good look at the data as it is essential. Here is the data from the staging area in the target format. Very convenient due to the pivoting facility. I would like to review again:

♣   There are two products and three rows. How is that possible? Sometimes two is three, right? Try to read something about the philosophical ideas behind mathematics. It is incredible and fascinating. Sure! Let's solve this mystery! There is a new product with the code NKS_BBB_138. There is a record for that. The reason is simple; the item is new. Thus, all attributes are brand-new to the staging and target. However, the second footwear article, AT12_TS_098, has two rows. Why this? Well, the reason is the obsessive status. There are two types of attributes for this product in an update: new and editable, and this fact is the key to both records. You can see a row with the attribute status one and another one with the zero value for the attribute status. Attributes with a not null value are either new (1) or in an update (0). For example, the supplier code equal to LS belongs to the row with attribute one; it is a new attribute. Alternatively, the white color belongs to the row with the status of zero. As a result, the color is an attribute in an update. The value will turn white instead of what it was before. The mystery is solved, dear Watson, as Sherlock Holmes might say!

♣   See the Product_Id column, the primary target key for the product table. The shoes with the code AT12_TS_098 have a value of 2 for Product_Id. This product already exists in the target. It was added in the previous execution if you remember. Alternatively, the product with the code NKS_BBB_138 has no value for product_id because it is new, so it does not exist in the target yet.

♣   Otherwise, if you check each attribute, you will see the rest of the values. For example, the LS supplier code with id equal to 2 is an update for AT12_TS_098. The EN provider code with the code identical to one is a new attribute for the new product NKS_BBB_138. Some details are not part of the execution, such as Measure, for example.

Now that we have deeply analyzed the staging, we can move on to the logic and start the target update process.

Final step, start updating the target

The last part of the process, as we already know, is the most important. Finally, we get to the point where Angelique will see everything! In her system, of course. The passion and devotion in John's eyes became visible some time ago, so it's no secret. She considers the opportunity if we can call it that.

I'm from the '70s, married for 30 years with the same woman, and it was love at first sight. I did not overthink, and I love her. We were poor, but it does not matter! I have never felt deprived of my freedom, although I have always been married, and after thirty years, I can say the same thing. Nowadays, our dear millennials and their future generations are very complicated people, and it takes time for them to get engaged. They have their algorithms to measure and measure dozens of times before deciding to start something. The old and endless conflict of generations is always present, as human nature. We will never fully understand our sons and daughters, grandchildren, and great-granddaughters, as they will never fully understand us.

Angelique and Johnny are millennials, so the calculations of reason are still in full swing, despite the clarity in Johnny's eyes. No one knows what will happen; let's wait and see. Please don't ask me to reveal their secret until the end, right here in this book, because I have to respect their privacy! Not even at the end of the book, I don't know if I can do it! Unfortunately, even they do not know what will happen to their relationship!

So it's time to move on! Let's update the target, and I'll start with the Products table, the central table of the manufacturing system. Previously, everything was new. Now, some things are new, while others are present and need updating. As a result, SQL code is more complicated because we have to cover both scenarios. See the logic below for SQL Server.

Listing 8-6 Generate the attributes in the target area (second run) SQL Server

```
-- Generate the products in the target, SQL Server version
DECLARE @v_Max_Product_Id      INT;
SELECT @v_Max_Product_Id = MAX(Product_Id) FROM Products;


-- 01 Add new products
```

```
WITH sr (Code, Name, Type_Id, Supplier_Id, Manufacturer_Code,
Color, Gender, Measure, Source_Product_Code)
AS
(

    SELECT Product_Code AS Code, Product_Name AS Name,
    Type_Id, Supplier_Id, Manufacturer_Code, Color, Gender,
    Measure, Source_Product_Code
    FROM Stg_Mv_New_Products
)
INSERT INTO Products (Product_Id, Code, Name, Type_Id,
Supplier_Id, Manufacturer_Code, Color, Gender, Measure,
Source_Product_Code)
SELECT COALESCE(@v_Max_Product_Id, 0) +
ROW_NUMBER() OVER (ORDER BY sr.Code) AS Product_Id,
sr.Code, sr.Name, sr.Type_Id, sr.Supplier_Id,
sr.Manufacturer_Code, sr.Color, sr.Gender, sr.Measure,
sr.Source_Product_Code
FROM sr
WHERE NOT EXISTS
(

    SELECT 1 FROM Products dest
    WHERE dest.Code = sr.Code
);
-- 02 Update the mv table with the new product identifier
UPDATE Stg_Mv_New_Products
SET Product_Id = sr.Product_Id
FROM Stg_Mv_New_Products dest INNER JOIN Products sr
    ON sr.Code = dest.Product_Code;

-- 03 Update new or existing attributes for products (Name).
WITH sr (Source_Product_Code, Product_Id, Name)
AS
(

    SELECT Source_Product_Code, Product_Id,
    Product_Name AS Name
    FROM Stg_Mv_Upd_Products
    WHERE Attribute_Status IS NOT NULL
```

```
        AND Product_Name IS NOT NULL
)
UPDATE Products
SET Name = sr.Name
FROM Products dest INNER JOIN sr
    ON sr.Source_Product_Code = dest.Source_Product_Code
AND sr.Product_Id = dest.Product_Id ;
-- 04 Update new or existing attributes for products(Type)
WITH sr (Source_Product_Code, Product_Id, Type_Id)
AS
(
    SELECT Source_Product_Code, Product_Id, Type_Id
    FROM Stg_Mv_Upd_Products
    WHERE Attribute_Status IS NOT NULL AND Type_Id IS NOT NULL
)
UPDATE Products
SET Type_Id = sr.Type_Id
FROM Products dest INNER JOIN sr
    ON sr.Source_Product_Code = dest.Source_Product_Code
AND sr.Product_Id = dest.Product_Id ;
-- 05 Update new or existing attributes for products(Supplier)
WITH sr (Source_Product_Code, Product_Id, Supplier_Id)
AS
(
    SELECT Source_Product_Code, Product_Id, Supplier_Id
    FROM Stg_Mv_Upd_Products
    WHERE Attribute_Status IS NOT NULL
    AND Supplier_Id IS NOT NULL
)
UPDATE Products
SET Supplier_Id = sr.Supplier_Id
FROM Products dest INNER JOIN sr
    ON sr.Source_Product_Code = dest.Source_Product_Code
AND sr.Product_Id = dest.Product_Id ;
-- 06 Update new or existing attributes for products(Color)
WITH sr (Source_Product_Code, Product_Id, Color)
```

```
AS
(
    SELECT Source_Product_Code, Product_Id, Color
    FROM Stg_Mv_Upd_Products
    WHERE Attribute_Status IS NOT NULL AND Color IS NOT NULL
)
UPDATE Products
SET Color = sr.Color
FROM Products dest INNER JOIN sr
    ON sr.Source_Product_Code = dest.Source_Product_Code
AND sr.Product_Id = dest.Product_Id ;
-- 07 Update new or existing attributes for products(Measure)
WITH sr (Source_Product_Code, Product_Id, Measure)
AS
(
    SELECT Source_Product_Code, Product_Id, Measure
    FROM Stg_Mv_Upd_Products
    WHERE Attribute_Status IS NOT NULL AND Measure IS NOT NULL
)
UPDATE Products
SET Measure = sr.Measure
FROM Products dest INNER JOIN sr
    ON sr.Source_Product_Code = dest.Source_Product_Code
AND sr.Product_Id = dest.Product_Id ;
-- 08 Update new or existing attributes for products(Gender)
WITH sr (Source_Product_Code, Product_Id, Gender)
AS
(
    SELECT Source_Product_Code, Product_Id, Gender
    FROM Stg_Mv_Upd_Products
    WHERE Attribute_Status IS NOT NULL AND Gender IS NOT NULL

)
UPDATE Products
SET Gender = sr.Gender
FROM Products dest INNER JOIN sr
```

```
      ON sr.Source_Product_Code = dest.Source_Product_Code
 AND sr.Product_Id = dest.Product_Id ;
 GO
```

The logic is composed of two parts. The first part refers to new products and is a SQL insert statement into the Product table. See the first instruction. We have added the additional condition to check if the product code already exists. Usually, this can be verified from the beginning by a consistency rule. There is a unique constraint on product code, but why rely on it when manipulating it in code? How can this be possible? How can we already have the code if it is not part of the accounting? Well, very simple! Maybe the code was already added by Angelique, and Joanna wasn't aware! So perhaps the code exists as a target product in manufacturing. In this case, Joanna and Angelique should talk somehow and see how to solve this coincidence. Sometimes users have to decide; the business always leads the process! Remember that we, the programmers, are somehow servants of the company's business. We are not scientists, and our degree of objectivity is relative and not absolute, if I may say so. We rely on business, and our goal is to try to implement it as well as possible. We are not as free people as scientists!

So let's review in the same way:

♣ The first instruction adds new products. The data source is the Stg_Mv_New_Products object, where new products are stored. We generate a unique primary key for Product_id, and that's it. We are already confident that we have all the elements due to the way we developed the materialized view earlier, adding all the necessary details. Additionally, we add the not exists condition to make sure the code does not exist.

♣ The second statement will update the product identifier for the materialized view table (Stg_Mv_New_Products).

♣ The third instruction is to manage the products in an update. We do this for each attribute. There may be better ways. I have never said, and I will never say, that this model and example is the best. It's a simple exercise, and I think it can serve people who work with SQL and data migration systems or not necessarily. There can be segments of any software system in which we have to manipulate data between two parts, not necessarily between two distinct modules but within one. To come back, see the first update where I want to update the name. The source table is now Stg_Mv_Upd_Products. If you remember, there were two records. We automatically think of the famous Oracle error TOO_MANY_ROWS. Don't worry; there is not much danger for this error. If you recheck the two rows, you will see that each attribute will have precisely one value that is not null because an active product's characteristic is either new (it has the value one) or in an update (with the value zero). Consequently, this condition will always return one value only.

♣   See the following conditions, similar. For each attribute, we check if it exists in the current import and update. You can see that, for example, for Measure, the update will do nothing. The status of the measure attribute is null, so there will be no change for it. Performing multiple updates several times is not very efficient for large imports, and performance may not be the best. If there is a large execution with products in updates, it may take some time to run. There may be better ways. The SQL update statement is sometimes a nightmare; we all know that. If we can find better ways and consider other solutions, please do so! Unfortunately, the update action is one of the most common data manipulation statements, so we have to accept it. The most important thing is to minimize the amount of data to update. It seems trivial, but sometimes trivial answers are not easy to get!

What's next? Of course, check the product table and see the changes.

Listing 8-7 Display the list of products in the target (second run) SQL Server

```
-- Display the list of products in the target
SELECT Code, Type_Id, Supplier_Id, Manufacturer_Code AS Man,
Color, Gender, Measure, Source_Product_Code AS Src_Code
FROM Products ;
```

Angelique will automatically see them once she refreshes her system. Programmers are always more comfortable running a simple select statement than checking the application! Please check each step-by-step attribute, finally move the previous product image to an excel and compare it to the new one. The purpose is simple; check if the changes take place correctly in the products table.

Table 8-6 Target products table (Products)

Code	Type Id	Supplier Id	Man	Color	Gender	Measure	Src Code
AT12_RE _106	2	1	MLS	Black	Unisex	NULL	AT12_R E_106
AT12_TS _098	2	2	NULL	White	Male	NULL	AT12_T S_098
NKS_BKM _135	3	1	FFM	Silver	Male	41	NM92_D D_191

NKS_LRM_093	2	2	NULL	Pink	Female	NULL	NM94_AX_121
ABC	2	2	NULL	Silver	Female	42	NULL
NKS_BBB_138	2	1	NULL	Green	Female	NULL	NKS_BBB_138

Please take a look at each attribute and see the results. For example, now the color is white. The color was previously black and has now turned white, depending on the state of the attribute. In this case, the state is zero, which means the color change. After this first verification, see the manufacturer. Before, there was no manufacturer. The first execution brought nothing. Between the two implementations, Angelique could have added one, but she did not. The second run updates the manufacturer. The new value is MLS. Even if this is still an update statement, the manufacturer is new depending on its condition, from Jean Luc's perspective. Finally, if you look at Measure, you will see the null value as it was in the beginning and is now. The lack of value means that the Measure is a passive attribute; it has never participated in the data migration system until now. Sometimes we programmers add information for the dark days, we think it will become necessary later, and we design it in advance.

Regardless of the data in the "*Shoes are everywhere*" software system, such as the product table, we must be aware that users like Angelique can always update the data. For example, between two runs of such a data migration system, users can update the information, even more, delete it. The data in one target like "*Shoes are everywhere*" can be updated in two ways: from the "*Yellow Panther*" source or by regular users like Angelique. However, the data migration system may or may not recognize user updates. It is not easy to signal these changes. As a result, a data migration system will ignore target user interactions unless there is a way to synchronize and record these changes. In such a scenario, the burden and cost of such a continuous registration process are quite significant. The price is sometimes too high for the benefit. At least, this happens in some scenarios. However, there may be exceptions, and I do not deny the possibility.

Adding commercial names for products

Now I will slightly change the execution order, and I will not continue with the Oracle version immediately. I plan this later. I will continue and add the commercial names and continue to use the SQL Server version. I hope you remember these trade names for products because a shoe item can be presented in different ways, using multiple commercial terms. The purpose of this additional piece of code is to handle these commercial names.

Before moving on to the next phase, logic itself, I suggest reviewing the materialized views tables' data regarding commercial names. There are two tables, the Stg_Mv_New_Commercial_Names table, which store these names for the new products. There is also the Stg_Mv_Upd_Commercial_Names table that stores the trade names of products in an update. See the data above (see Table 8-4 and 8-5).

The first record is the trade name Nike Golden Elves for the product NKS_BBB_138. This product has a product identifier, which is 6, and this 6 is the new identifier generated in the previous logic. There is a row in the Stg_Mv_New_Commercial_Names table, and this is the row in the image above, the first line. Furthermore, there is the trade name Miau Steffi for the product with the code AT12_TS_098. These two trade names are both new because they did not exist before the interface ran. You can see that the second table contains the attribute status column, which means that the status of a commercial name can be one (new) or zero (existing). Both trade names should populate the dedicated target table, Commercial_Names.

Speaking of which, let's look at logic first, SQL Server:

Listing 8-8 Generate commercial names Target (second execution) SQL Server

```
-- Generate Commercial names SQL Server
-- 01 Update the mv table with the new product identifier
UPDATE Stg_Mv_New_Commercial_Names
SET Product_Id = sr.Product_Id
FROM Stg_Mv_New_Commercial_Names dest INNER JOIN Products sr
    ON sr.Code = dest.Source_Product_Code;
-- 02 New commercial names for new products
INSERT INTO Commercial_Names (Commercial_Code, Product_Id,
Commercial_Name, Manufacturer_Code, Language_Code)
SELECT sr.Commercial_Code, sr.Product_Id, sr.Commercial_Name,
sr.Commercial_Manufacturer AS Manufacturer_Code,
sr.Language_Code
FROM Stg_Mv_New_Commercial_Names sr
WHERE NOT EXISTS
(
    SELECT 1 FROM Commercial_Names dest
```

```
      WHERE sr.Commercial_Code = dest.Commercial_Code
);
-- 03 New commercial names for products in an update
INSERT INTO Commercial_Names (Commercial_Code, Product_Id,
Commercial_Name, Manufacturer_Code, Language_Code)
SELECT sr.Commercial_Code, sr.Product_Id, sr.Commercial_Name,
sr.Commercial_Manufacturer AS Manufacturer_Code,
sr.Language_Code
FROM Stg_Mv_Upd_Commercial_Names sr
WHERE sr.Attribute_Status = 1
AND NOT EXISTS
(
    SELECT 1 FROM Commercial_Names dest
    WHERE sr.Commercial_Code = dest.Commercial_Code
);
-- 04 Update commercial names for products in an update, name
UPDATE Commercial_Names
SET Commercial_Name = sr.Commercial_Name
FROM Commercial_Names dest INNER JOIN
Stg_Mv_Upd_Commercial_Names sr
    ON sr.Commercial_Code = dest.Commercial_Code
WHERE sr.Attribute_Status = 0
AND sr.Commercial_Name IS NOT NULL;
-- 05 Update commercial names for products in update
manufacturer
UPDATE Commercial_Names
SET Manufacturer_Code = sr.Commercial_Manufacturer
FROM Commercial_Names dest INNER JOIN
Stg_Mv_Upd_Commercial_Names sr
    ON sr.Commercial_Code = dest.Commercial_Code
WHERE sr.Attribute_Status = 0
AND sr.Commercial_Manufacturer IS NOT NULL;
-- 06 Update commercial names for products in update, language
UPDATE Commercial_Names
SET Language_Code = sr.Language_Code
FROM Commercial_Names dest INNER JOIN
Stg_Mv_Upd_Commercial_Names sr
    ON sr.Commercial_Code = dest.Commercial_Code
```

```
WHERE sr.Attribute_Status = 0
AND sr.Language_Code IS NOT NULL;
GO
```

Oh, we managed to get through this phase as well. What a relief! Now, Angelique has everything she asked from the Panther. She's already talked to Joanna, and they're going to a pub for some cocktails, you know, lady stuff! Like in American movies! I hope they will not drink too much, like in the same films; they have some IT systems to run!

On the other hand, Jean-Luc and Johnny will go too, but they will drink things for men in a different place! Some whisky, eventually root beer, like in Deep Space 9! They have to celebrate, the *"Speedy"* works quite well, and the data moves from here to there, as Angelique requests.

Now, let's describe the logic that populates the commercial names that appear in "*Yellow Panther*." Do not hesitate to appreciate Jean'Luc's effort because he spent a lot of energy creating his logic inside the Panther to populate the source area. His action is also commendable. Even though source tables are so simple, completing them is not always an easy task.

♣ In the first statement, we update the product identifier for the mv table (Stg_Mv_New_Commercial_Names). We need this to update the table with commercial names; this is mandatory.

♣ The second statement uses the Stg_Mv_New_Commercial_Names table. This table contains a list of trade names for new products. I guess you can see that there may be a mistake here. Do you think I should add the "not exists" condition to ensure the code doesn't exist yet? Or maybe the primary key is wrong. Perhaps it would have been better to add a primary key with the combination of business code and product identifier. The question here is: is the business code unique in itself, at the enterprise level, or is the business code unique to each product? Both choices could be right, depending on the business. My choice shows that I have decided to consider a consistency rule in advance. This SQL rule will check any new product with a commercial name, and if there one already, the process will stop, or the duplicates will be isolated and revised later.

♣ The third statement checks the source table with updated products, the Stg_Mv_Upd_Commercial_Names table. A commercial name can be new or editable. You can see the Attribute_Status equal to one condition, which means we manage new trade names for existing products. The logic is similar to the previous one, only that now I decided to use the condition "not exist." See the similarity and differences between the first two instructions. Of course, if there is another rule of consistency in force here, we can skip the "does not exist" condition.

♣ The SQL statements 4, 5, and 6 are similar, and the purpose is to manage existing attributes for existing products. You can see the condition Attribute_Status equal to zero, which means I'm affecting existing commercial names for existing products and update some sub-fields.

Another approach for commercial names

There are several trade names in the current execution, new for the "*Shoes are everywhere*" system. However, some are for new products, such as NIK_TAURIEL for NKS_BBB_138, while others are for existing products, such as Meow11 and BlueWz1. These are commercial names for shoe item AT12_TS_098. The first two instructions in the logic that deals with trade names are for these situations. The latter covers cases where some trade names are in an update.

Now we have to finish this second execution with the Oracle version. However, you can change the logic a bit and use a different approach. Since commercial names are the product's attributes, you can add the SQL logic in one shot and not two. Why add the various shoe items and associated commercial codes in two steps instead of adding everything together? However, I will keep them separately for simplicity! I will add two pieces of logic and update both the products and the trade names in different functionalities.

Secondly, I will think of a setting regarding commercial names so I can follow two alternative approaches. I think you remember the metadata table M_Settings. I will add a new application setting that will handle commercial name updates in two ways. Things are clear if the products are new to the target; the logic is always the same. But if the products are in an update and the trade name already exists, what to do? Well, let's see below the choices!

♣ The first approach is to update existing commercial names. If the commercial name already exists, and some fields are coming from the source as different, the update will solve the problem for Angelique. Joanna changed the name for Miau11, and the name will become Miau dear Steffi instead of Miau Steffi. The update will change the name in the target.

♣ The second solution is different. For some reason, Jean-Luc may not send changed trade names or may not consider it necessary. In Jean-Luc's logic, he will always send all the commercial codes and view them all in the target system. He will prefer to delete the existing commercial names in the target and add everything back from the Panther. This solution has the inconvenience that it might delete commercial names manually added by Angelique. You need to be very careful with this approach.

For this, we need a new setting so that we can use one approach or another. Let's consider the third process setting and call it UPDATE_COMMERCIAL_NAMES. The values will be TOTAL or INCREMENTAL. If the setting value is TOTAL, the logic will delete all existing commercial names in the target and add the new ones from the source. Otherwise, the SQL logic will check each field and update accordingly, only for the commercial names in an update. Here is the new setting.

Listing 8-9 Adding new metadata setting SQL Server and Oracle

```
-- Same script for Oracle and SQL Server. Don't forget to
commit if running on Oracle.
INSERT INTO M_Settings(Setting_Id, Setting_Name,
Setting_Value, Setting_Description)
VALUES (3, 'UPDATE_COMMERCIAL_NAMES', 'TOTAL', 'You can update
commercial names either removing what we have or updating field
by field. Accepted values TOTAL or INCREMENTAL');
```

We now have three settings. In the next chapter, I will show you how to use the other two. Make a selection from the M_Settings metadata table and see the contents inside. We will go further and continue with the last piece of logic, and we will prepare to conclude this chapter.

Listing 8-10 Update products for Oracle

```
-- Generate the products in the target, Oracle version
DECLARE
    v_Max_Product_Id        INT;
    v_Count                 INT;
BEGIN
    -- 01 Store the last product identifier in the target
    SELECT COUNT(*) INTO v_Count FROM Products;
    IF v_Count > 0 THEN
            SELECT MAX(Product_Id)
            INTO v_Max_Product_Id FROM Products;
    ELSE
            v_Max_Product_Id    := 0;
    END IF;
    -- 02 Add new products from the staging to the target
```

Speedy, a data transfer system. A SQL Exercise

```
    INSERT INTO Products (Product_Id, Code, Name, Type_Id,
Supplier_Id, Manufacturer_Code, Color, Gender, Measure,
Source_Product_Code)
    SELECT v_Max_Product_Id + ROW_NUMBER() OVER (ORDER BY p.Code)
AS Product_Id, p.Code, p.Name, p.Type_Id, p.Supplier_Id,
p.Manufacturer_Code, p.Color, p.Gender, p.Measure,
Source_Product_Code
        FROM
        (
    SELECT sr.Product_Code AS Code, sr.Product_Name AS Name,
sr.Type_Id, sr.Supplier_Id, sr.Manufacturer_Code, sr.Color,
sr.Gender, sr.Measure, sr.Source_Product_Code
        FROM Stg_Mv_New_Products sr
        WHERE NOT EXISTS
        (
            SELECT 1 FROM Products dest
            WHERE dest.Code = sr.Product_Code
        )
        ) p;
-- 03 Update the product identifier for the mv new products
        UPDATE Stg_Mv_New_Products dest
        SET Product_Id = (SELECT sr.Product_Id
        FROM Products sr WHERE sr.Code = dest.Product_Code)
        WHERE EXISTS
        (
            SELECT 1 FROM Products sr
            WHERE sr.Code = dest.Product_Code
        );
    -- 04 Update new or existing attributes. Name.
        UPDATE Products dest
        SET Name = (
        WITH sr (Source_Product_Code, Product_Id, Name)
        AS
        (
            SELECT Source_Product_Code, Product_Id,
            Product_Name AS Name
            FROM Stg_Mv_Upd_Products
            WHERE Attribute_Status IS NOT NULL
```

```
        AND Product_Name IS NOT NULL
)
SELECT sr.Name
FROM sr
WHERE sr.Source_Product_Code = dest.Source_Product_Code
AND sr.Product_Id = dest.Product_Id
)
WHERE EXISTS
(
        SELECT 1 FROM Stg_Mv_Upd_Products sr
WHERE sr.Source_Product_Code = dest.Source_Product_Code
        AND sr.Product_Id = dest.Product_Id
        AND sr.Attribute_Status IS NOT NULL
        AND sr.Product_Name IS NOT NULL
);
-- 05 Update new or existing attributes. Type.
UPDATE Products dest
SET Type_Id = (
WITH sr (Source_Product_Code, Product_Id, Type_Id)
AS
(
        SELECT Source_Product_Code, Product_Id, Type_Id
        FROM Stg_Mv_Upd_Products
WHERE Attribute_Status IS NOT NULL AND Type_Id IS NOT NULL
)
SELECT sr.Type_Id
FROM sr
WHERE sr.Source_Product_Code = dest.Source_Product_Code
AND sr.Product_Id = dest.Product_Id
)
WHERE EXISTS
(
        SELECT 1 FROM Stg_Mv_Upd_Products sr
WHERE sr.Source_Product_Code = dest.Source_Product_Code
        AND sr.Product_Id = dest.Product_Id
        AND sr.Attribute_Status IS NOT NULL
```

```
        AND sr.Type_Id IS NOT NULL
);
-- 06 Update new or existing attributes. Supplier.
UPDATE Products dest
SET Supplier_Id = (
WITH sr (Source_Product_Code, Product_Id, Supplier_Id)
AS
(
        SELECT Source_Product_Code, Product_Id, Supplier_Id
        FROM Stg_Mv_Upd_Products
        WHERE Attribute_Status IS NOT NULL
        AND Supplier_Id IS NOT NULL
)
SELECT sr.Supplier_Id
FROM sr
WHERE sr.Source_Product_Code = dest.Source_Product_Code
AND sr.Product_Id = dest.Product_Id
)
WHERE EXISTS
(
        SELECT 1 FROM Stg_Mv_Upd_Products sr
WHERE sr.Source_Product_Code = dest.Source_Product_Code
        AND sr.Product_Id = dest.Product_Id
        AND sr.Attribute_Status IS NOT NULL
        AND sr.Supplier_Id IS NOT NULL
);
-- 07 Update new or existing attributes. Color.
UPDATE Products dest
SET Color = (
WITH sr (Source_Product_Code, Product_Id, Color)
AS
(
        SELECT Source_Product_Code, Product_Id, Color
        FROM Stg_Mv_Upd_Products
        WHERE Attribute_Status IS NOT NULL
        AND Color IS NOT NULL
```

```
        )
        SELECT sr.Color
        FROM sr
WHERE sr.Source_Product_Code = dest.Source_Product_Code
AND sr.Product_Id = dest.Product_Id
)
WHERE EXISTS
(
        SELECT 1 FROM Stg_Mv_Upd_Products sr
WHERE sr.Source_Product_Code = dest.Source_Product_Code
        AND sr.Product_Id = dest.Product_Id
        AND sr.Attribute_Status IS NOT NULL
        AND sr.Color IS NOT NULL
);
-- 08 Update new or existing attributes. Color.
UPDATE Products dest
SET Measure = (
WITH sr (Source_Product_Code, Product_Id, Measure)
AS
(
        SELECT Source_Product_Code, Product_Id, Measure
        FROM Stg_Mv_Upd_Products
        WHERE Attribute_Status IS NOT NULL
        AND Measure IS NOT NULL
)
SELECT sr.Measure FROM sr
WHERE sr.Source_Product_Code = dest.Source_Product_Code
AND sr.Product_Id = dest.Product_Id
)
WHERE EXISTS
(
        SELECT 1 FROM Stg_Mv_Upd_Products sr
WHERE sr.Source_Product_Code = dest.Source_Product_Code
        AND sr.Product_Id = dest.Product_Id
        AND sr.Attribute_Status IS NOT NULL
        AND sr.Measure IS NOT NULL
```

```
);
-- 09 Update new or existing attributes. Color.
UPDATE Products dest
SET Gender = (
WITH sr (Source_Product_Code, Product_Id, Gender)
AS
(
        SELECT Source_Product_Code, Product_Id, Gender
        FROM Stg_Mv_Upd_Products
        WHERE Attribute_Status IS NOT NULL
        AND Gender IS NOT NULL
)
SELECT sr.Gender
FROM sr
WHERE sr.Source_Product_Code = dest.Source_Product_Code
AND sr.Product_Id = dest.Product_Id
)
WHERE EXISTS
(
        SELECT 1 FROM Stg_Mv_Upd_Products sr
WHERE sr.Source_Product_Code = dest.Source_Product_Code
        AND sr.Product_Id = dest.Product_Id
        AND sr.Attribute_Status IS NOT NULL
        AND sr.Gender IS NOT NULL
);
    COMMIT;
END;
/
```

You can see that the logic is very similar to SQL Server. In the first part, I add new products, and in the second part, I update the products by attribute if it comes as in an update from "*Yellow Panther.*" Because the logic is almost the same, there's not much to say, eventually to notice the differences between Oracle and SQL Server. SQL Server can generally adapt to Oracle updates better, I would say. The specific SQL Server syntax in the update is not available in Oracle, and this is one reason for the different syntax between the two.

You can check the products now and see the changes. You will get the same results as in SQL Server, of course. Now comes the last part, updating the commercial names using the Oracle version. Let's see how we use the setting.

Listing 8-11 Update commercial names for Oracle

```
-- Generate the Commercial names in the target, Oracle.
DECLARE
    v_Commercial_Names_Approach        VARCHAR2(255);
    v_Count                            INT;
BEGIN
    SELECT COUNT(*) INTO v_Count FROM M_Settings
    WHERE Setting_Name = 'UPDATE_COMMERCIAL_NAMES'
    AND Setting_Value IN ('TOTAL', 'INCREMENTAL');
    IF v_Count = 1 THEN
    SELECT Setting_Value INTO v_Commercial_Names_Approach
            FROM M_Settings
            WHERE  Setting_Name = 'UPDATE_COMMERCIAL_NAMES';
    ELSE
            -- We Assume that default value is TOTAL
            v_Commercial_Names_Approach := 'TOTAL';
    END IF;
-- 01 Update the product identifier commercial new products
    UPDATE Stg_Mv_New_Commercial_Names dest
    SET Product_Id = (SELECT sr.Product_Id
    FROM Products sr WHERE sr.Code = dest.Source_Product_Code)
    WHERE EXISTS
    (
            SELECT 1 FROM Products sr
            WHERE sr.Code = dest.Source_Product_Code
    );
    -- 02 New commercial names for new products
    INSERT INTO Commercial_Names (Commercial_Code, Product_Id,
Commercial_Name, Manufacturer_Code, Language_Code)
    SELECT sr.Commercial_Code, sr.Product_Id, sr.Commercial_Name,
sr.Commercial_Manufacturer AS Manufacturer_Code,
sr.Language_Code
        FROM Stg_Mv_New_Commercial_Names sr
```

```
WHERE NOT EXISTS
(
        SELECT 1 FROM Commercial_Names dest
        WHERE sr.Commercial_Code = dest.Commercial_Code
);
-- 03 New commercial names for existing products
INSERT INTO Commercial_Names (Commercial_Code, Product_Id,
Commercial_Name, Manufacturer_Code, Language_Code)
SELECT sr.Commercial_Code, sr.Product_Id, sr.Commercial_Name,
sr.Commercial_Manufacturer AS Manufacturer_Code,
sr.Language_Code
    FROM Stg_Mv_Upd_Commercial_Names sr
    WHERE sr.Attribute_Status = 1 AND NOT EXISTS
    (
            SELECT 1 FROM Commercial_Names dest
            WHERE sr.Commercial_Code = dest.Commercial_Code
    );
    IF v_Commercial_Names_Approach = 'TOTAL' THEN
            -- 04 Delete existing names for existing products
            DELETE Commercial_Names dest
            WHERE EXISTS
            (
                    SELECT 1 FROM Stg_Mv_Upd_Commercial_Names sr
                WHERE sr.Commercial_Code = dest.Commercial_Code
                    AND sr.Attribute_Status = 0
            );
            -- 05 Add existing names for existing products
INSERT INTO Commercial_Names (Commercial_Code, Product_Id,
Commercial_Name, Manufacturer_Code, Language_Code)
SELECT sr.Commercial_Code, sr.Product_Id, sr.Commercial_Name,
sr.Commercial_Manufacturer AS Manufacturer_Code,
sr.Language_Code
    FROM Stg_Mv_Upd_Commercial_Names sr
    WHERE sr.Attribute_Status = 0 ;
    ELSE
        -- 06 Update commercial name for existing products
        UPDATE Commercial_Names dest
        SET Commercial_Name = (
```

214

```
        SELECT sr.Commercial_Name
        FROM Stg_Mv_Upd_Commercial_Names sr
        WHERE sr.Commercial_Code = dest.Commercial_Code
        AND sr.Attribute_Status = 0
        AND sr.Commercial_Name IS NOT NULL
                );
    -- 07 Update manufacturer code for existing products
    UPDATE Commercial_Names dest
    SET Manufacturer_Code = (
        SELECT sr.Commercial_Manufacturer
        FROM Stg_Mv_Upd_Commercial_Names sr
        WHERE sr.Commercial_Code = dest.Commercial_Code
        AND sr.Attribute_Status = 0
        AND sr.Commercial_Manufacturer IS NOT NULL
            );
    -- 08 Update language code for existing products
    UPDATE Commercial_Names dest
    SET Language_Code = (
        SELECT sr.Language_Code
        FROM Stg_Mv_Upd_Commercial_Names sr
        WHERE sr.Commercial_Code = dest.Commercial_Code
        AND sr.Attribute_Status = 0
        AND sr.Language_Code IS NOT NULL
        );
    END IF;
    COMMIT;
END;
/
```

Finally, we finished with the second execution, and now we can yet understand the concept of incrementality. Let's quickly look at how we update commercial names. Try to do the same for any other database system, if it's the case.

♣   First, we check the setting to see how we will update existing commercial codes for existing products. There are two acceptable values, total and incremental. If there is no value or anything else, we use the default value of total. If the value is TOTAL, we will remove and replace instead of update.

♣   Second, we update the materialized view table for new commercial names with the product identifier. See instructions 01. We need to do this because there is no product ID yet. Of course, we could fill in this table right now instead of earlier.

♣   After that, we add new commercial names for new products. See the second statement.

♣   Similarly, we add new commercial names for existing products. See statement 03.

♣   Depending on the setting, we choose to remove existing commercial names and replace them with those from the Panther. We do this if the setting's value is TOTAL. Otherwise, we update attribute by attribute as before.

After all this hard work, do a few checks yourself. Check both target tables Products and Commercial_Names, eventually, the materialized views tables. Do some review, look at the staging tables, and understand how this works.

The last step is to finalize the execution and change the status of the imports table. Let's do that again, and we are ok!

Listing 8-12 Complete the second execution

```
-- Complete the implementation, SQL Server version
UPDATE Executions
SET End_Date = GETDATE(), Execution_Status = 'SUCCESS'
WHERE Execution_Status = 'STARTED' ;


-- Complete the import, Oracle version
UPDATE Executions
SET End_Date = SYSDATE, Execution_Status = 'SUCCESS'
WHERE Execution_Status = 'STARTED' ;
```

Now you can query the Executions table and see the two records.

Some conclusions and what's next

We have completed two executions of our data transfer system. Angelique now has a mix of products in her system. Some of them are hers, some shoes she created over time. Joanna and her team create other shoe items, transfer them to manufacturing, and now Joanna can see them both! She can see everything! Of course, Johnny is eager and eager to have his dream dinner! I think it's close.

I think you can see the flexibility of such a system. The example is quite simple, but it can suggest complex projects; it can help programmers use similar approaches to be involved in such projects. I do not hide, and I still promote SQL in such situations as this. The simple purpose is to manipulate data in a classic format, such as relational, and these approaches are very appropriate.

In the following chapters, I want to mention a few things about this exercise and open up more possibilities. Another chapter with some techniques and a final introduction will complete this exercise.

9 Let's play more! Some new features

What about the settings?

I completed the data transfer process, explaining significant features such as incrementality and continuity. I ran the process twice and made the distinction between the first (ever) round, which will always bring new things, and the next, which could get new things, but could update and even delete them. Try to imagine a real-life process with one or more entities and structures both in the source and target ones! The exercise is relatively simple, and the reason is didactic; this is a book and not a project! The book aims to open horizons and ideas and, finally, to help specialists deal with specific projects similar to this one. Moreover, even if you are maybe involved in a regular type of project, the purpose of transferring data is so common everywhere! My goal is to help you and this and, of course, encourage you not to forget about the old SQL language!

The complexity of real projects is always much more significant than any book. Any computer science student, for example, will learn concepts and theories, algorithms and calculations, languages, frameworks, and tools. One will try to recognize everything, depending on the times and places where one lives. However, when that student starts working for a software company, for example, and sees the reasons behind all the theoretical lessons learned in college, someone might often feel overwhelmed. A problem that may seem small and trivial to any end-user could be a severe challenge for the junior programmer and not necessarily junior. Fortunately or not, nowadays, with so many layers within the software company, the programmer doesn't get to talk directly to the end-user, so someone is exempt from explanations and, finally, from some struggles! As with this book and all of this exercise, take it for granted. What you see here is not real life, but it is a pale approximation of it.

Even though I think I've finished presenting the simple data transfer system, I'd like to add a few more exercises to complete my plan. I want to show you some options and techniques that will somehow try to complete the example.

Let's start, though!

Suppliers and Manufacturers, one way or another

Let's take one more look at the M_Settings metadata table. There are three values in this table, and I invite you to review them. For that, I will now query the M_Settings table.

Table 9-1 List of data migration settings

Id	Name	Value
1	ALLOW_NEW_MANUFACTURERS_FROM_SOURCE	YES
2	ALLOW_NEW_SUPPLIERS_FROM_SOURCE	NO
3	UPDATE_COMMERCIAL_NAMES	TOTAL

I want to focus on the two settings that deal with suppliers and manufacturers. These suppliers are present in both "*Yellow Panther*" and "*Shoes are everywhere*" systems. Joanna and Angelique share them very often. However, these two systems are separate, and there is no mechanism to ensure the sharing process. A provider may be present in Panther and not at the destination or vice versa.

You can see the name of the settings as well as the descriptions. It will specify whether one can create a provider in the target system as part of *"Speedy"* or if it must already exist. If the provider must already exist in the target system, then a consistent SQL rule will prevent its use in the process. Otherwise, the process will create the vendor at the destination as part of the process.

Angelique decided that new manufacturers can be created in the target as part of the process while suppliers cannot, and a SQL consistency rule will prevent their usage. She chooses this approach by talking to Joanna, on the one hand, and Johnny and Jean-Luc, on the other.

There is usually an initialization at the beginning of any such project. This configuration data is static, such as lookup, and is Panther's data required in the target system. Among the lists, we can undoubtedly find suppliers and manufacturers. In a kind of initial phase, Joanna will deliver a list of suppliers and manufacturers to Jean-Luc. He will give this List to Johnny. Master Babanus will check with Angelique and eventually add the missing manufacturers or suppliers. Thus, we can consider that, in the initial phase, producers and suppliers are in sync. However, over time, Joanna and her team can add new manufacturers or suppliers to Panther. Now the big question arises: what happens if there is such a new supplier or new manufacturers? And this question can get two answers, depending on the setting values.

To start, let's add these two vendors now, in The Panther, and consider two products using each of them. See the script below:

Listing 9-1 New supplier and manufacturer

```
/*
Both SQL Server and Oracle
    -- We suppose that Joanna added two new providers to the
Panther: one supplier and one manufacturer.
    -- These are not present in the destination system.
    INSERT INTO Suppliers (Supplier_Id, Supplier_Code,
Supplier_Name, Country_Id, City, Address)
    VALUES (4, 'SM1', 'New Shoes From Mexico', 27, 'Mexico',
'Blvd. Adolfo López Mateos 3901');


    INSERT INTO Manufacturers (Manufacturer_Code,
Manufacturer_Name, Country_Id, City, Address)
    VALUES ('MYLS', 'Mary Lu Shoes', 36, 'Dallas', '22, Dallas
101');
*/
DELETE Gate_Details;
DELETE Gate_Header;
-- Product in update
INSERT INTO Gate_Header (Product_Identifier, Business_Code)
VALUES ('AT12_TS_098', 'AT12_TS_098');
-- New product
INSERT INTO Gate_Header (Product_Identifier, Business_Code)
VALUES ('NKS_BBB_139', 'NKS_BBB_139');
INSERT INTO Gate_Details (Gate_Detail_Id, Product_Identifier,
Attribute_Name, Attribute_Value)
VALUES (1, 'AT12_TS_098', 'PRODUCT_NAME', 'White Adidas
Torsion ZX');
INSERT INTO Gate_Details (Gate_Detail_Id, Product_Identifier,
Attribute_Name, Attribute_Value)
VALUES (2, 'AT12_TS_098', 'SUPPLIER_CODE', 'SM1');


INSERT INTO Gate_Details (Gate_Detail_Id, Product_Identifier,
Attribute_Name, Attribute_Value)
```

```
   VALUES (3, 'NKS_BBB_139', 'PRODUCT_NAME', 'Nike Zoom Vaillant
Boom 09');
   INSERT INTO Gate_Details (Gate_Detail_Id, Product_Identifier,
Attribute_Name, Attribute_Value)
   VALUES (4, 'NKS_BBB_139', 'COLOR', 'White');
```

Before running this script, notice that the first SQL insert statement is a comment. This comment will explain that these two vendors are new to "*Yellow Panther*," newly created by Joanna. They do not exist in the "*Shoes are everywhere!*"

Angelique is not aware of this addition. She can add these providers manually, and this is an alternative. Joanna can call Angelique and ask her to add them. But these were the old days, before *"Speedy!"* This direct collaboration was rare because the lookup data is static.

Nevertheless, the need for these calls was unpleasant and inefficient. But now *"Speedy"* is present. Among other consequences, now there is a minimal manual intervention, no phone calls, no conversations between Joanna and Angelique, nothing. *"Speedy"* should work in total silence, and Angelique should be absorbed only by her work in the manufacturing process. At the same time, Joanna only works as an accountant.

I guess you noticed that there is a new gateway coming from "*Yellow Panther*." Moreover, among the attributes, you can see the new supplier (SM1). So, Johnny received the data from Jean-Luc with this new supplier. He realizes that this does not exist in the target.

He checked the value of the setting "ALLOW NEW MANUFACTURERS FROM SOURCE". There are two possible values, either YES or NO. The current value is NO, which means that *"Speedy"* cannot add new suppliers as part of its process.

This supplier is not eligible: use a SQL consistency rule

What do you think is the best way to stop a non-existent target supplier from entering the destination? As the above setting is NO, there should be a kind of policy according to which suppliers should exist in the target system. *"Speedy"* is not responsible for generating static data but only adding dynamic attributes, such as items shoes. So there has to be a way to stop this new supplier (SM1). And what is the best way to do that? You know the answer already. Johnny should create a new SQL consistency rule!

But these rules already exist! Because Johnny's sense of anticipation is excellent! Check the consistency rule This_Suplier_Does_Not_Exists_In_The_Target; is rule number 6. Please review it before running the check process!

Let's check the errors:

Listing 9-2 Check the errors, SQL Server

```sql
-- The process of checking the gate, SQL Server version
DECLARE
    @v_Rule_Id                  INT,
    @v_Rule_SQL                 NVARCHAR(4000),
    @v_Count                    INT,
    @v_The_Gate_Is_Consistent   NVARCHAR(3);


    UPDATE Gate_Details
    SET Error_Id = NULL
    WHERE Error_Id IS NOT NULL;
    UPDATE Gate_Header
    SET Error_Id = NULL
    WHERE Error_Id IS NOT NULL;
    DECLARE C_Consistency_Rules CURSOR FOR
    SELECT Rule_Id, Rule_SQL
    FROM M_Consistency_Rules
    ORDER BY 1;
BEGIN
    OPEN C_Consistency_Rules;
    FETCH NEXT FROM C_Consistency_Rules
    INTO @v_Rule_Id, @v_Rule_SQL;
    WHILE @@FETCH_STATUS = 0
    BEGIN
            EXECUTE sp_executesql @v_Rule_SQL;
            FETCH NEXT FROM C_Consistency_Rules
            INTO @v_Rule_Id, @v_Rule_SQL;
    END;
    CLOSE C_Consistency_Rules;
    DEALLOCATE C_Consistency_Rules;
```

```
SELECT @v_Count = COUNT(*) FROM
        (
        SELECT Error_Id FROM Gate_Header
        WHERE Error_Id IS NOT NULL
        UNION ALL
        SELECT Error_Id FROM Gate_Details
        WHERE Error_Id IS NOT NULL
        ) a;
IF @v_Count > 0
BEGIN
        SET @v_The_Gate_Is_Consistent = 'NO';
        INSERT INTO Gate_Header_Errors
        (Product_Identifier, Error_Id)
        SELECT Product_Identifier, Error_Id
        FROM Gate_Header WHERE Error_Id IS NOT NULL
        UNION
        SELECT Product_Identifier, Error_Id
        FROM Gate_Details WHERE Error_Id IS NOT NULL;

   INSERT INTO Gate_Details_Errors (Gate_Detail_Id,
Product_Identifier, Attribute_Name, Attribute_Value, To_Delete,
Error_Id)
   SELECT Gate_Detail_Id, Product_Identifier, Attribute_Name,
Attribute_Value, To_Delete, Error_Id
        FROM Gate_Details WHERE Error_Id IS NOT NULL
        UNION
   SELECT d.Gate_Detail_Id, d.Product_Identifier,
d.Attribute_Name, d.Attribute_Value, d.To_Delete, h.Error_Id
        FROM Gate_Details d INNER JOIN Gate_Header_Errors h
              ON h.Product_Identifier = d.Product_Identifier
        WHERE h.Error_Id IS NOT NULL ;

        END
        ELSE
              SET @v_The_Gate_Is_Consistent = 'YES';
        PRINT @v_The_Gate_Is_Consistent;
   END;
```

```
GO
```

We are already familiar with this logic. Maybe we'll make a few more remarks about this error checking logic. First, let's look at the error table. You have noticed that the logic output is *NO*, which means that the gate is not clean. So there are errors. We'll run the next query:

Listing 9-3 The List of the errors, SQL Server

```sql
-- List of errors: SQL Server
SELECT h.Product_Identifier AS Product_Id, rh.Rule_Name AS
Error_Name, NULL AS Attribute_Name, NULL AS Attribute_Value
    FROM Gate_Header_Errors h INNER JOIN M_Consistency_Rules rh
        ON rh.Rule_id = h.Error_Id
    WHERE h.Error_Id IS NOT NULL
    UNION
SELECT d.Product_Identifier AS Product_Id, rd.Rule_Name AS
Error_Name, d.Attribute_Name, d.Attribute_Value
    FROM Gate_Details_Errors d INNER JOIN M_Consistency_Rules rd
        ON rd.Rule_id = d.Error_Id
    WHERE d.Error_Id IS NOT NULL;
```

If you have the patience to analyze the data below carefully, you may see some strange results:

Table 9-2 List of errors, the first approach

Product Id	Error Name	Attribute Name	Attribute Value
AT12_TS_098	This Suplier Does Not Exists In The Target	NULL	NULL
AT12_TS_098	This Suplier Does Not Exists In The Target	PRODUCT_NAME	White Adidas Torsion ZX
AT12_TS_098	This Suplier Does Not Exists In The Target	SUPPLIER_CODE	SM1

Now let's also see the data in the gate before continuing the analysis. Please run the query below:

Listing 9-4 The source area, SQL Server

```
-- The data in the gate, first approach SQL Server
SELECT h.Product_Identifier AS Product_Id, d.Attribute_Name,
d.Attribute_Value, d.Error_Id
   FROM Gate_Header h INNER JOIN Gate_Details d
     ON h.Product_Identifier = d.Product_Identifier ;
```

Here is our data after running this query. Execution stops; some data is in the error table, and here is what is in the source area.

Table 9-3 The gate, the first approach, SQL Server

Product Id	Attribute Name	Attribute Value	Error Id
AT12_TS_098	PRODUCT_NAME	White Adidas Torsion ZX	NULL
AT12_TS_098	SUPPLIER_CODE	SM1	6
NKS_BBB_139	PRODUCT_NAME	Nike Zoom Vaillant Boom 09	NULL
NKS_BBB_139	COLOR	White	NULL

There are four rows and one error! Why this? The reason is related to how *"Speedy"* works. There are a few questions to ask. Something may seem a little strange!

♣   What to do with the errors? We can record the error right in the gateway using the error_id column. We can complete the error tables and have a history of unforeseen mistakes in time. Or both, as we do now!

♣   What do we do with the whole process? Is it okay to continue? Is it better to interrupt? If we continue the process, do we need to find a way to isolate the errors and continue without them? How can we do that? In our case, we stopped the process and copied the errors into the error tables. By isolating the shoe items with the mistakes, we can continue with the rest of them, for example.

♣   What kind of information did I transfer to the error tables? As you can see, not only did I copy the error, but also the entire data set for that product! In our case, the material AT12_TS_098 has errors, while the second material is clean. As you can see, the logic copies the entire dataset that contains the data related to that product. The second product is unaffected, so this remains where it is, friendly and safe!

The example above is an approach to error management in such a system. We can argue with certainty, and we can accept that this is not the best approach.

A disadvantage is that the error logic will suspend the entire process every time the gate data break some consistency. This statement is true, but Jean-Luc's team should be aware of all these consistency rules. The logic inside the "*Yellow Panther*" should be to avoid these anticipated mistakes, so it shouldn't happen in the end!

Another disadvantage could be the error tables; why should we copy all the records in a specific shoe item and not just the errors? The reason is that sometimes, in this standardized design, some rows are logically correlated. Joanna and Jean-Luc will continue to investigate the error tables. Consequently, to make sure they have all the details for a correct diagnosis, it may be better to copy everything and not just the errors and copy the entire product.

However, let's look at the other approach. We will use the Oracle version to take care of the handling error system in a different way. Here is the logic: see below.

Listing 9-5 Check the errors, Oracle

```
-- The process of checking the gate, Oracle version
SET SERVEROUTPUT ON
DECLARE
    v_Rule_Id               INT;
    v_Rule_SQL              VARCHAR2(4000);
    v_Count                 INT;
    v_The_Gate_Is_Consistent  VARCHAR2(3);


    CURSOR C_Consistency_Rules IS
    SELECT Rule_Id, Rule_SQL
    FROM M_Consistency_Rules
    ORDER BY 1;
BEGIN
    UPDATE Gate_Details
    SET Error_Id = NULL
    WHERE Error_Id IS NOT NULL;
    UPDATE Gate_Header
    SET Error_Id = NULL
    WHERE Error_Id IS NOT NULL;
```

```
    COMMIT;
    OPEN C_Consistency_Rules;
    LOOP
            FETCH C_Consistency_Rules
            INTO v_Rule_Id, v_Rule_SQL;
            EXIT WHEN C_Consistency_Rules%NOTFOUND;
            EXECUTE IMMEDIATE v_Rule_SQL;

            COMMIT;
    END LOOP;
    CLOSE C_Consistency_Rules;
    SELECT COUNT(*) INTO v_Count FROM
            (
            SELECT Error_Id FROM Gate_Header
            WHERE Error_Id IS NOT NULL
            UNION ALL
            SELECT Error_Id FROM Gate_Details
            WHERE Error_Id IS NOT NULL
            ) a;
    IF v_Count > 0 THEN
    INSERT INTO Gate_Header_Errors
  (Product_Identifier, Error_Id)
    SELECT Product_Identifier, Error_Id
    FROM Gate_Header WHERE Error_Id IS NOT NULL;
  INSERT INTO Gate_Details_Errors (Gate_Detail_Id,
Product_Identifier, Attribute_Name, Attribute_Value, To_Delete,
Error_Id)
  SELECT Gate_Detail_Id, Product_Identifier, Attribute_Name,
Attribute_Value, To_Delete, Error_Id
    FROM Gate_Details
    WHERE Error_Id IS NOT NULL
    UNION
  SELECT d.Gate_Detail_Id, d.Product_Identifier,
d.Attribute_Name, d.Attribute_Value, d.To_Delete, h.Error_Id
  FROM Gate_Details d INNER JOIN Gate_Header_Errors h
    ON h.Product_Identifier = d.Product_Identifier
  WHERE h.Error_Id IS NOT NULL
```

227

```
AND d.Error_Id IS NOT NULL;
-- Clear errors from the header
  DELETE Gate_Details
  WHERE Error_Id IS NOT NULL;
      -- Clear the header if there are errors no details
  DELETE Gate_Header dest
  WHERE Error_Id IS NOT NULL
  AND NOT EXISTS (SELECT 1 FROM Gate_Details sr
  WHERE sr.Product_Identifier = dest.Product_Identifier);
    COMMIT;

          v_The_Gate_Is_Consistent  := 'YES';
    ELSE
          v_The_Gate_Is_Consistent  := 'YES';
    END IF;
    DBMS_OUTPUT.PUT_LINE (v_The_Gate_Is_Consistent);
  END;
  /
```

There is a significant difference between these two approaches, and the aim is to explain a little how easily we can implement the alternative. However, the problem here is not the difficulty of implementation but the implications of any of the two approaches.

I copied the errors in the dedicated tables in the Oracle version and removed them from the gate. In this way, the portal should be clean. Accordingly, I always specify the message that the gateway is consistent. This message means that, in such a scenario, the process can continue. However, it is possible, for example, to have no data at all. Let's say we have a gate full of errors, and nothing is there. Well, in this case, even if the process will start, nothing will happen.

On the other hand, it is easy to add a check with a count and change the message to NO if there is no data in the entrance. More than that, the tricky issue here is that some of the so-called clean records could be in some relation with some of the deleted rows. Jean-Luc needs to check this possibility, eventually ask Joanna for advice.

Let's check the errors table and the gate now and compare them with the previous approach:

Listing 9-6 The List of the errors, Oracle

```
-- List of errors Oracle
SELECT h.Product_Identifier AS Product_Id,
rh.Rule_Name AS Error_Name, NULL AS Attribute_Name,
NULL AS Attribute_Value
FROM Gate_Header_Errors h INNER JOIN M_Consistency_Rules rh
    ON rh.Rule_id = h.Error_Id
WHERE h.Error_Id IS NOT NULL
UNION
SELECT d.Product_Identifier AS Product_Id,
rd.Rule_Name AS Error_Name,
d.Attribute_Name, d.Attribute_Value
FROM Gate_Details_Errors d INNER JOIN M_Consistency_Rules rd
    ON rd.Rule_id = d.Error_Id
WHERE d.Error_Id IS NOT NULL;
```

Now let's see the results:

Table 9-4 List of errors, the first approach

Product Id	Error Name	Attribute Name	Attribute Value
AT12_TS_098	This Suplier Does_ Not Exists In The Target	SUPPLIER_CODE	SM1

You can compare tables 9-2 and 9-4 and see the differences. We save all the entity's details and display the element in our case in the first approach. We do this because we are not sure if isolating some attributes could cause inconsistencies. The gate's design is very standardized, and many areas can be like a family. Or, let's remember the old Alexandre Dumas, like the four musketeers, all for one and one for all!

On the contrary, in the second approach, we copy what is necessary and the errors themselves in the errors tables.

In terms of gate data, let's see the difference. We will interrogate the source area again. Bu source area I mean the gate, obviously. Never forget that the gate is the source area, despite its simplicity.

Listing 9-7 The source area, Oracle

```
-- The data in the gate, Oracle
SELECT h.Product_Identifier, d.Attribute_Name,
d.Attribute_Value, d.Error_Id
   FROM Gate_Header h INNER JOIN Gate_Details d
      ON h.Product_Identifier = d.Product_Identifier ;
```

Here is our data after running the error checking process. The data transfer process can continue; there are no errors, and here is what is in the source area.

Table 9-5 The gate, the first approach, Oracle

Product Id	Attribute Name	Attribute Value	Error Id
AT12_TS_098	PRODUCT_NAME	White Adidas Torsion ZX	NULL
NKS_BBB_139	PRODUCT_NAME	Nike Zoom Vaillant Boom 09	NULL
NKS_BBB_139	COLOR	White	NULL

I'm sure everyone will say that the second approach is much better. Maybe it is, but I can tell you that it is more challenging to implement and riskier. Try to increase the complexity, add more entities and attributes, add everything to such a standardized design and see that the second approach is quite challenging.

A better example to understand the implications is to look at a commercial name. This type of attribute is more complicated. Four fields characterize such a commercial code, a key, and three secondary properties. If any of the four has a problem of any kind and there is a consistency rule that detects this, we can update all the error fields, not just the one with the error.

But we can add a manufacturer

Now let's move on to the second provider, the manufacturer. If you go back to the settings, you'll see that you cannot create new suppliers within the target, but you can create new manufacturers. There are two values of the system setting, and there is a significant difference between the implementations.

However, a manufacturer has many characteristics. In general, if you have a sort of table that required a transfer, either partially or totally, there is a critical property of the columns: nullability. If, for example, someone wants to create a manufacturer in the "*Shoes are everywhere*" software, one needs to specify values for all the mandatory columns unless there are default values.

If you look at the manufacturers and check the definition (Listing 2-1), you can see the following columns:

- ♣ Manufacturer Code (varchar (20)) mandatory PK

- ♣ Manufacturer Name (varchar (255) mandatory

- ♣ Country_Id (Int) fk to countries (varchar(255) mandatory

- ♣ City varchar(255) mandatory

- ♣ Address varchar(255) optional

As you can see, most fields are mandatory. If one can create a manufacturer via *"Speedy,"* then all its attributes should become the system's attributes. Consequently, we need to add new details to the metadata table.

The answer relies on the M_Attributes metadata table. If you want to transfer any entity's attribute via *"Speedy,"* this needs to be part of the metadata table. Thus, we need to create some new properties in the metadata table. Let's define them!

Listing 9-8 New attributes

```
-- The list of new characteristics that define a manufacturer,
any of Oracle or SQL Server
  INSERT INTO M_Attributes (Attribute_Name, Attribute_Type,
Target_Object, Attribute_Usage, Attribute_Length,
Attribute_Data_Type)
  VALUES ('MANUFACTURER_NAME', 'SIMPLE', 'MANUFACTURERS',
'IMPORT', '20', 'STRING');
  INSERT INTO M_Attributes (Attribute_Name, Attribute_Type,
Target_Object, Attribute_Usage, Attribute_Length,
Attribute_Data_Type)
  VALUES ('COUNTRY', 'SIMPLE', 'MANUFACTURERS', 'IMPORT', '255',
'STRING');
  INSERT INTO M_Attributes (Attribute_Name, Attribute_Type,
Target_Object, Attribute_Usage, Attribute_Length,
Attribute_Data_Type)
  VALUES ('CITY', 'SIMPLE', 'MANUFACTURERS', 'IMPORT', '255',
'STRING');
  INSERT INTO M_Attributes (Attribute_Name, Attribute_Type,
Target_Object, Attribute_Usage, Attribute_Length,
Attribute_Data_Type)
```

```
VALUES ('ADDRESS', 'SIMPLE', 'MANUFACTURERS', 'IMPORT', '255',
'STRING');
```

These four attributes are the missing ones that will allow the manufacturer's definition in the destination through the "*Speedy*" system. The information will come from the "*Yellow Panther*" through the gate and eventually reach the manufacturers' table. Of course, not before entering the intermediate area.

Once again, let's examine the new gateway, as now we will have the manufacturer instead of the supplier. For that, we will re-generate the gateway once more. Let's see the new data.

Listing 9-9 New gate (new manufacturers)

```
-- Add new source area, new manufacturer
DELETE Gate_Details;
DELETE Gate_Header;
-- Product in update
INSERT INTO Gate_Header (Product_Identifier, Business_Code)
VALUES ('AT12_TS_098', 'AT12_TS_098');
-- New product
INSERT INTO Gate_Header (Product_Identifier, Business_Code)
VALUES ('NKS_BBB_139', 'NKS_BBB_139');


INSERT INTO Gate_Details (Gate_Detail_Id, Product_Identifier,
Attribute_Name, Attribute_Value)
VALUES (1, 'AT12_TS_098', 'PRODUCT_NAME', 'White Adidas
Torsion ZX');
INSERT INTO Gate_Details (Gate_Detail_Id, Product_Identifier,
Attribute_Name, Attribute_Value)
VALUES (2, 'AT12_TS_098', 'COLOR', 'White');
INSERT INTO Gate_Details (Gate_Detail_Id, Product_Identifier,
Attribute_Name, Attribute_Value)
VALUES (3, 'NKS_BBB_139', 'PRODUCT_NAME', 'Nike Zoom Vaillant
Boom 09');
INSERT INTO Gate_Details (Gate_Detail_Id, Product_Identifier,
Attribute_Name, Attribute_Value)
VALUES (4, 'NKS_BBB_139', 'MANUFACTURER_CODE', 'MYLS');
INSERT INTO Gate_Details (Gate_Detail_Id, Product_Identifier,
Attribute_Name, Attribute_Value)
VALUES (5, 'NKS_BBB_139', 'COLOR', 'White');
```

```
INSERT INTO Gate_Details (Gate_Detail_Id, Product_Identifier,
Attribute_Name, Attribute_Value)
  VALUES (6, 'NKS_BBB_139', 'MANUFACTURER_NAME', 'Mary Lu
Shoes');
  INSERT INTO Gate_Details (Gate_Detail_Id, Product_Identifier,
Attribute_Name, Attribute_Value)
  VALUES (7, 'NKS_BBB_139', 'COUNTRY', 'US');
  INSERT INTO Gate_Details (Gate_Detail_Id, Product_Identifier,
Attribute_Name, Attribute_Value)
  VALUES (8, 'NKS_BBB_139', 'CITY', 'Dallas');
  INSERT INTO Gate_Details (Gate_Detail_Id, Product_Identifier,
Attribute_Name, Attribute_Value)
  VALUES (9, 'NKS_BBB_139', 'ADDRESS', '22, Dallas 101');
```

Let's see the values, execute the query 9-7.

Table 9-6 The gate, the second approach, Oracle or SQL Server

Product Id	Attribute Name	Attribute Value
AT12_TS_098	PRODUCT_NAME	White Adidas Torsion ZX
AT12_TS_098	COLOR	White
NKS_BBB_139	PRODUCT_NAME	Nike Zoom Vaillant Boom 09
NKS_BBB_139	MANUFACTURER_CODE	MYLS
NKS_BBB_139	COLOR	White
NKS_BBB_139	MANUFACTURER_NAME	Mary Lu Shoes
NKS_BBB_139	COUNTRY	US
NKS_BBB_139	CITY	Dallas
NKS_BBB_139	ADDRESS	22, Dallas 101

Here is the new gate or the latest source area. Jean-Luc did his job right, as always! There are no suppliers now, but there is a manufacturer. The manufacturer MYLS exists in the "*Yellow Panther*" but does not exists in the "*Shoes are everywhere.*" Consequently, the situation is similar to the previous one. The big difference is the value of the data migration setting. Before this, if a supplier does not exist in the target system, this is prohibited. The SQL consistency rule will stop this supplier from reaching the target. Users like Angelique will manually create these suppliers on target, and *"Speedy"* will run again later after the suppliers are part of the destination.

However, in this case, there is a different approach. The creation of non-existing manufacturers is allowed. The setting specifies that it is possible to create new manufacturers as part of *"Speedy."* If you check the SQL consistency rule number 7(This_Manufacturer_Does_Not_Exists_In_The_Target), you will see that the gate will pass the check this time. See the rule below.

Listing 9-10 Consistency rule handling manufacturers

```
-- Consistency rule This Manufacturer_Does_Not
Exists_In_The_Target, see the SQL statement.
UPDATE Gate_Details
SET Error_Id = 7 FROM Gate_Details dest
WHERE dest.Attribute_Name = 'MANUFACTURER_CODE' AND
(
    SELECT Setting_Value FROM M_Settings
    WHERE Setting_Name = 'ALLOW_NEW_MANUFACTURERS_FROM_SOURCE'
) = 'NO'
AND NOT EXISTS
(
    SELECT 1 FROM Manufacturers sr
    WHERE UPPER(sr.Manufacturer_Code) =
UPPER(dest.Attribute_Value)
);
```

Because the value for setting *"ALLOW NEW MANUFACTURERS FROM SOURCE* "is YES, the query above will not return anything. Thus, the manufacturer will pass the verification logic. The check will not raise an error and will not stop the process, adequately starting. However, the manufacturer needs to be in the system before the products that are using them. Thus, the *"Speedy"* will create it as part of its logic. That is why we have a new set of attributes (see above). These attributes will specify the details of the brand-new manufacturers as part of the process. You can see the missing manufacturer information in the set of import tables. See the attributes like country, city, and address. All these are for manufacturers. Now let's see the logic. You need to do some steps on your own, in any system you use, before running this part. Here is what you need to do:

♣ Run the check logic. Because the setting allows the manufacturer's creation, the check logic should pass.

♣ Generate an execution identifier.

♣ Run the steps that will create data in the staging area. Check the models in Listings 7-5 and 7-7 if using SQL Server, eventually, 7-6 and 7-8 if you use Oracle. If you use anything else, prepare a similar logic for your database system.

♣ Run the steps 7-6 or 7-8, depending on what system you use. Before anything else, check if the setting allows new manufacturers' creation as part of the logic. If yes, add the manufacturers here from the staging area. You can create some views and eventually materialized views for manufacturer data. Once the manufacturers are in the target, you can add this to the shoe items.

This last part is for you, dear reader. I believe it is right for you to participate with the team, Johnny, Angelique, Joanna and Jean-Luc, and me, and add your contribution to *"Speedy."* The instructions are pretty straightforward, as seen above. I wish you good luck and be ready, and this is the beginning of your contribution. Other tasks might follow. Of course, you are free people, for various reasons you can decline the invitation to work! It is up to you to decide!

Joanna deletes a product. How should Angelique react?

I want to address another topic. I am referring to the situation when certain information disappears from the source. Let's say that, for some reason, Joanna deletes a product from "*Yellow Panther*." The product NM92_DD_191 is an excellent pair of shoes, such as Nike Lance men's cycling shoes 41. There have been some accounting mistakes, and Joanna realizes that this product should never be in the Panther. She decided to take this product out of her system. The product evaporated, spread like ashes in the wind, disappeared into nothingness!

Before having *"Speedy,"* these kinds of actions do not bother anyone. They do not have serious consequences. Double work was part of everyone's life, whenever necessary. Of course, if the shoe item was deeply involved in all kinds of accounting operations, the removal was not quite a piece of cake. But there was a logic inside the "*Yellow Panther*" that was taking care of this. In any case, the delete process was an internal process inside the Panther.

However, now the Panther is not alone anymore. It has a sister. The "*Yellow Panther*" and the "*Shoes are everywhere*" are currently in the fraternity, and things are not the same as before. Consequently, if a product disappears from the source, the target should know. Joanna and Angelique are together now, and Angelique should be aware that one of her shoe items is somehow orphaned!

I know you noticed the column To_Delete in the source area. The purpose of this column, right from the start, is to signal such events and allow the destination to take any actions they might consider.

Hence, what should Angelique do in the target if Joanna deletes some elements from the source? I want to introduce a few options, as is not one single choice. It depends, as always, on the business.

We talked about the source and the "*Yellow Panther*" software system without anticipating too much. This lack of interest is because we considered the gate to reflect the Panther, according to Angelique's needs, and we thought this to be sufficient. However, there is a piece of code inside the Panther that fills the gate, which is essential. Imagine that Jean-Luc knows this part by heart because he is the designer of this logic. Now, trying to anticipate what's inside, shoe items can have a kind of flag that signals their departure to the "*Shoes are everywhere*" app!

There may be many ways to warn about the deletion because that's it, a delete warning. Jean-Luc receives the warning message saying: "Dear Jean-Luc, this article is not in the scope. Therefore, we need to remove it from the system. Please signal your shadow software to take appropriate action!"

Jean-Luc has to prepare a new gate. Suppose there is a new material with the code ABC123, like in Jackson five's famous song. Hence, the gate will contain two products: one new shoe item, ABC123, and a flag for the deletion of a product already present before, NM92_DD_191. Let's see the gate, as generated by the head of the Panther, our dear Jean-Luc.

Listing 9-11 The gate, one new and one deleted material

```
-- Recreate the entrance, same script for Oracle and SQL
Server
DELETE Gate_Details;


DELETE Gate_Header;
-- New product
INSERT INTO Gate_Header (Product_Identifier, Business_Code)
VALUES ('ABC123', 'ABC123');
-- Deleted product
INSERT INTO Gate_Header (Product_Identifier, Business_Code,
To_Delete)
VALUES ('NM92_DD_191', 'NKS_BKM_135', 1);
INSERT INTO Gate_Details (Gate_Detail_Id, Product_Identifier,
Attribute_Name, Attribute_Value)
```

```
VALUES (3, 'ABC123', 'PRODUCT_NAME', 'Adidas Zomba 124');
INSERT INTO Gate_Details (Gate_Detail_Id, Product_Identifier,
Attribute_Name, Attribute_Value)
VALUES (4, 'ABC123', 'MANUFACTURER_CODE', 'MYLS');
INSERT INTO Gate_Details (Gate_Detail_Id, Product_Identifier,
Attribute_Name, Attribute_Value)
VALUES (5, 'ABC123', 'COLOR', 'Red');
```

Before continuing, run a query against the gateway. First of all, if you will query the gate data as it is in Listing 9-7, for example, you will lack two essential things:

♣ The To_Delete attribute is not present, so we need to add it.

♣ The inner join is not enough. We need to use a left outer join to see the data. The reason is quite simple. The material for delete has no details. What details could it have? When someone at the source wants to signal to someone on the target side that one of their objects is no longer present, it is enough to give a signal, like a flag.

Now, let's see the query first so that we can visualize the gate.

Listing 9-12 Query the data in the gate, one new and one deleted material

```
-- The data in the gate, one delete product
SELECT h.Product_Identifier, d.Attribute_Name,
d.Attribute_Value, h.To_Delete
FROM Gate_Header h LEFT OUTER JOIN Gate_Details d
    ON h.Product_Identifier = d.Product_Identifier ;
```

The left outer join will allow us to see the deleted material. Here is the data from the gate:

Table 9-7 The gate, delete, Oracle or SQL Server

Product Id	Attribute Name	Attribute Value	To Delete
ABC123	PRODUCT_NAME	Adidas Zomba 124	NULL
ABC123	MANUFACTURER_CODE	MYLS	NULL
ABC123	COLOR	Red	NULL
NM92_DD_191	NULL	NULL	1

Speedy, a data transfer system. A SQL Exercise

The gate is ready to go; the mighty Jean-Luc did his duty. Now, the first thing before anything else, the check process. If you remember, among the SQL rules, there is one handling these scenarios of deleted shoe items from the Panther. Go back to chapter 4 and review Listing 4-4, explaining rule number 1. Let's see the SQL statement:

Listing 9-13 The SQL consistency rule 1

```
-- The set of consistency rules: SQL Server version
UPDATE Gate_Header SET Error_Id = 1
FROM Gate_Header dest
WHERE dest.To_Delete = 1
AND NOT EXISTS (
    SELECT 1 FROM Staging_Products sr
    WHERE sr.Product_Identifier = dest.Product_Identifier
    ) ;
-- The set of consistency rules: Oracle version
UPDATE Gate_Header dest SET Error_Id = 1
WHERE dest.To_Delete = 1
AND NOT EXISTS (
    SELECT 1 FROM Staging_Products sr
    WHERE sr.Product_Identifier = dest.Product_Identifier
) ;
```

The product identifier NM92_DD_191 is part of the table Staging_Products. Hence, the shoe item is in the destination system, which means that the flag deletion is consistent and the SQL rule will pass.

I leave some of the next steps for you.

♣ Add a new execution identifier. See the Listing 7-4.

♣ Generate the data in the staging area. See the Listing 7-5 (SQL Server) or Listing 7-6 (Oracle).

The question is, what shall we do if a pair of shoes is not in the Panther anymore. What will happen in the destination system?

There are at least 2-3 possible solutions:

♣ You can remove the shoe item from the "*Shoes are everywhere*" system too. This solution might not be convenient, however possible.

♣ You can do nothing. The fact that the products are not in accountancy anymore does not necessarily mean they cannot remain in manufacturing.

238

♣   You can specify a flag for the product to determine that the shoe item is not valid somehow anymore. Not being in accountancy can invalidate somehow the footwear.

You can see Listing 8-5 (SQL Server) or Listing 8-8 (Oracle) and include the logic for material deletion, anyone you consider. Take this as a second piece of homework, after the previous one in this chapter, with manufacturer addition. As you can see, this book has everything, the technical side with a lot of SQL exercises, a fictional side with, I hope, lovely characters like Joanna and Jean-Luc, and even homework for you, dear readers!

10   Other features: how to handle errors and logs

Some additional components

I want to continue the previous chapter and show some more features that a system like *"Speedy"* should have. For example, error handling has been a fairly broad segment in this book. However, what we have not done so far has been to analyze other errors, in addition to the anticipated ones, errors that may occur during the process's execution. Let's say Johnny didn't anticipate a specific error from the beginning. Moreover, in the logic written by his team, some mistakes crept in that, of course, they were not aware. If such a situation happens, and I can assure you it does because, like us humans, our code is not perfect too, there should be a mechanism to store these errors for subsequent analysis.

Hence, what we need and I want to show here is a simple error handling mechanism. You can find this in hundreds of books; It is a classic mechanism, nothing special! In the first instance, we already have the set of SQL consistency rules, which are great and do the most challenging part. The higher the number of anticipated errors, the higher the efficiency of the process and its quality. However, despite these SQL rules, problems can still arise during the transfer process. Hence, we need a mechanism to handle errors, and this is the standard mechanism with a table and dedicated logic. We will do that on the following pages.

Another thing I want to talk about is the log facility. Any such system, clearly delimited by steps and sub-steps, must be eligible for a registration process. Typically, we need to record what we do and save some logging information, which is another topic that wants to present a simple log system. Again, things will be relatively trivial, a log table and an attached logic. They are somehow sister activities, from the implementation point of view.

Nevertheless, the purpose is entirely different. The log will store some necessary information about steps and sub-steps and always keep that (data). On the contrary, the error table will store information related to the errors and will show-up from time to time when there are errors during the execution.

With this occasion, we will reach a new level. As you perhaps noticed, I preferred to avoid using any procedural objects, like stored procedures and functions, etc. As mentioned several times during the book, my purpose was not to promote a language like Transact SQL or PL SQL but to promote an adequate

SQL level. If you ask me, as a personal opinion, of course, I will recommend you to use these languages specific to relational databases. But this was not my intention, but to promote the right level of SQL, no matter where it is used, in Transact SQL or C #, for example. However, in this last chapter, I will make an exception and use some persistent objects like stored procedures to illustrate my purpose. I want to show how we build a simple mechanism of handling errors and a log, so I need a better place for that. My home is the relational database, and the native languages for this are PL SQL, Transact SQL, etc.

Consequently, I will use stored procedures for this chapter. I know some Java developers will not be pleased, so I advise them to transcribe the code below accordingly. If they think it is better to write SQL code in Java, it is their choice. I have no intention of convincing them otherwise. But I want to persuade them to write a better SQL whenever possible because this affects their performance. To conclude, if you're going to try this code anywhere else, please be my guests! In the end, you will reach the same SQL!

Errors: expected or unexpected

We started working on the error handling system from the moment we decided to create these SQL gate consistency rules. To be more precise, Johnny did everything! The set of SQL statements is a step for a clean gate. If Johnny's logic is accurate, things will go as well as possible. Nevertheless, problems can occur at every stage and sub-step. If this is the case, they should be marked so that, later, Johnny can investigate the reasons for the error and correct it.

If the gate is inconsistent according to any SQL rule, the unreliable data migrates to these sets of tables (Gate_Header_Errors and Gate_Details_Errors). This copy process allows for further analysis to see what happens when these gate records are inaccurate. Standard and expected errors should not arrive, so the issue is on Jean-Luc's side.

The set of SQL consistency rules is not constant. It has an initial value and then increases as the application starts working. This evolution means that, initially, people like Johnny and Jean-Luc discover some of the possible inconsistencies. Later, as the system works, new ones appear, and their number increases. After a while, the anticipated errors become optimal, and further inconsistencies appear less and less.

However, there will always be a place for the unforeseen. Therefore, even if the check process passes and the process is in progress, errors may occur during it. These are unexpected errors. Usually, a number and a message identify these errors. We all know the famous ORA errors, for example. Saving these errors in a specific table is very important. This object is the error table, and some information should generally be available in it. See some examples below:

♣ The error identifier. Each database system has an error number that identifies the error. For example, if the data violates a unique constraint somewhere in the logic, a specific number identifies this error. This number exists in any database system, either Oracle, SQL Server, DB2, etc. Generally, a variable will store this identifier and then move it to the error table.

♣ The error message. The above number always has a meaning given by a description. This message is predefined and explains the error. For example, for Oracle, the specific message is "Unique Constraint Violated." For SQL Server, the associated message is "Violation of PRIMARY KEY constraint '[CONSTRAINT].' Cannot insert duplicate key in object '[TABLE].' The duplicate key value is ([VALUE])."

♣ Some common examples break a specific constraint, conversion errors, exceeding the maximum length, missing values for required fields, etc. Apart from the error definition, other indicators are useful. When does the error occur? Time information. Consequently, a timestamp or date is always present in such an error table. It is essential to know when the error occurs!

♣ Another question is: in which part of the logic does the error occur? For example, can the error occur when transferring data from the gateway to the intermediate zone? Or maybe the error occurs in the second part of the process, updating the target area. Usually, any sub-step is a function or a procedure, etc. The name of this logic is also part of the table error. If the error occurs in a Transact SQL or PL SQL stored procedure, this object name will be part of the error table.

♣ There can be many SQL statements inside the object that defined the sub-step. We can use a variable to label each relevant SQL statement to store relevant information about the sub-step point. This way, when the error occurs, the **last** value of the label will be present in the error table.

♣ Another useful piece of information could be when the error occurs in an object, such as a function or procedure, if applicable. Sometimes it is possible to know precisely where the error occurs. If so, it is worth saving this information.

♣ Type of error. For example, if we anticipate the mistake through the verification system, the error type will be equal to zero. Otherwise, if the error is unexpected, this will be one. Of course, by increasing the complexity, this classification can go further.

♣ In this way, we can store the most relevant information in the error table that will allow us to investigate later. Trying to see what is happening is not always an easy task. Sometimes you have to be like Sherlock Holmes, and it can take a long time to realize what happened. Saving all this information will allow us to find out what is happening, when, and where. These are the three elements that help us solve the mysteries of errors.

Let's create this table following the instructions above:

Listing 10-1 Create errors table

```
-- Create the errors table SQL Server
CREATE TABLE Errors
(
    Id              INT IDENTITY(1, 1) PRIMARY KEY NOT NULL,
    Execution_Id    INT,
    Error_Id        INT NOT NULL,
    Error_Message   NVARCHAR(4000) NOT NULL,
    Object_Name     NVARCHAR(30) NOT NULL,
    Error_Date      SMALLDATETIME DEFAULT (GETDATE()),
    Error_Line      INT,
    Error_Type      INT,
    SQL_Id          NVARCHAR(4000)
);
-- Create the errors table Oracle
CREATE SEQUENCE Seq_Errors;
CREATE TABLE Errors
(
    Id              INT PRIMARY KEY NOT NULL,
    Execution_Id    INT,
    Error_Id        INT NOT NULL,
    Error_Message   VARCHAR2(4000) NOT NULL,
    Object_Name     VARCHAR2(30) NOT NULL,
    Error_Date      DATE DEFAULT (SYSDATE),
    Error_Line      INT,
    Error_Type      INT,
    SQL_Id          VARCHAR2(4000)
);
```

After building this table, we need to create a function or procedure to manage it correctly. Any process of this kind, in which the goal is to transfer data from different points to others, has numerous sub-steps, and these are units of code. Each of these units will call this specific error function and store the relevant information in case of errors. This approach is classic. There is no mystery here, of course!

Depending on the technology, a function or procedure will have this task to manage the error table and record anticipated errors if they occur during data processing. Each sub-stage of the process will call this function. This procedure will write the error information into the dedicated table whenever something happens, and the process crashes.

As mentioned, I will change the paradigm and use some procedural objects, such as stored procedures. However, the workplace is not necessarily my main concern. Since we are talking about manipulating data without too much user interference, it seems the right approach that the dedicated languages are PLSQL and Transact SQL, and specialized people are database developers. But this is not relevant in the matter, anyway.

So, let's create a stored procedure that handles errors, a simple one. We will start with Transact SQL and SQL Server, as usual.

Listing 10-2 Handle errors logic SQL Server

```
-- Error handling logic, SQL Server version
IF OBJECT_ID('Handle_Errors') IS NOT NULL
    DROP PROCEDURE Handle_Errors
GO
CREATE PROCEDURE Handle_Errors
(
    @p_Execution_Id     INT = NULL,
    @p_Error_Id         INT,
    @p_Error_Message    NVARCHAR(4000),
    @p_Object_Name      NVARCHAR(30),
    @p_Error_Line       INT = NULL,
    @p_Error_Type       INT,
    @p_Sql_Id           NVARCHAR(4000)
)
AS
DECLARE
    @v_Error_Date       DATETIME,
    @v_Execution_Id     INT,
    @v_Count            INT;
BEGIN
    SET @v_Error_Date = GETDATE();
```

```
    SELECT @v_Execution_Id = CASE WHEN @p_Error_Type = 0
THEN NULL ELSE @p_Execution_Id END;
    INSERT INTO Errors (Execution_Id, Error_Id, Error_Message,
Object_Name, Error_Date, Error_Type, Error_Line, Sql_Id)
    VALUES   (@v_Execution_Id,   @p_Error_Id,   @p_Error_Message,
@p_Object_Name,  @v_Error_Date,  @p_Error_Type,  @p_Error_Line,
@p_Sql_Id);
    SELECT @v_Count  = COUNT(*) FROM Executions
    WHERE Execution_Id = @v_Execution_Id;
    IF @v_Count = 1
            UPDATE Executions
            SET Execution_Status = 'FAILURE'
            WHERE Execution_Id = @v_Execution_Id;
END;
GO
```

Here's the logic behind using the SQL Server database to manage errors. Two main things should be part of this logic. First, this procedure will record the information that will identify a specific database error. As you can see, we have classified the types of errors according to expectations. If the error is one that we expect, then the error type is zero as a SQL consistency error. In this case, the process starts or not, depending on the implementation.

If not, there is no execution identifier at all because the error stops the process. I assume this scenario here that the process will stop if there is an anticipated error. But it is also possible to isolate database errors and continue execution.

The logic is quite simple. Let's describe it quickly:

♣ Check the nullability of the parameters. Show a lot about them. Always look carefully at this feature of a parameter. For example, the fact that the execution parameter is optional explains the characteristic of anticipated rules. If an error occurs due to a consistency rule violation, the data migration process might stop. Thus, there will be no execution identifier because the process will not start.

♣ Consequently, this execution identifier is optional. The record line parameter is optional too. See how the nullability of the parameter and the error type works together. If the error type is zero, so we expect the error, there is no import. We expect the standard errors from the beginning, and the process will not start in this case. See the variable v_Execution_Id.

♣ Suppose there is an error either in the set of consistency rules or during the process. In this case, this procedure will take the information that defines the error, the place where the error occurs, and the error's time and the date and store it into the dedicated error table.

♣ The last step of the logic is to update the executions table and set the appropriate flag to failure.

Let's look at the Oracle version of this logic before continuing and see how to use this logic during the data migration process:

Listing 10-3 Handle errors logic Oracle

```
-- Error handling logic, Oracle version
CREATE OR REPLACE PROCEDURE Handle_Errors
(
        p_Execution_Id              INT := NULL,
        p_Error_Id                  INT,
        p_Error_Message             VARCHAR2,
        p_Object_Name               VARCHAR2,
        p_Error_Line                INT := NULL,
        p_Error_Type                INT,
        p_Sql_Id                    VARCHAR2
)
AS
        v_Next_Id                   INT;
        v_Error_Date                DATE;
        v_Execution_Id              INT;
        v_Count                     INT;
BEGIN
        v_Error_Date        := SYSDATE;
        v_Next_Id           := Seq_Errors.NEXTVAL;
        v_Execution_Id      := CASE WHEN p_Error_Type = 0
THEN NULL ELSE p_Execution_Id END;
    INSERT INTO Errors (Id, Execution_Id, Error_Id, Error_Message,
Object_Name, Error_Date, Error_Type, Error_Line, Sql_Id)
    VALUES (v_Next_Id, v_Execution_Id, p_Error_Id,
p_Error_Message, p_Object_Name, v_Error_Date, p_Error_Type,
p_Error_Line, p_Sql_Id);

        SELECT COUNT(*) INTO v_Count FROM Executions
        WHERE Execution_Id = v_Execution_Id;
```

```
IF v_Count = 1 THEN
        UPDATE Executions
        SET Execution_Status = 'FAILURE'
        WHERE Execution_Id = v_Execution_Id;
    END IF;
    COMMIT;
END;
/
```

The above is the error handling logic. It is widespread, nothing special, and you can find it in almost any manual. Add the errors information, location information, and time information, mostly. What else to be said? Of course, we need to analyze the function call. Usually, each step will call this procedure to store the information in case of error. Even if the goal is to anticipate everything using SQL consistency rules, we will never be sure and leave a place for the surprise. If there is one rule in life, it is this: unexpected things must always happen, and you never know what you might find in the next corner of your life. And programming is an excellent example of our real life. Errors are the perfect scenario, and any programmer knows that no matter how many precautions he takes, an error can occur at any time.

Let me tell you a story! Since there was a guru in an ideal and perfect world, he wrote the SQL data transfer system. The logic was brilliant, and that guru could anticipate any inconsistency. He skipped this error handling procedure. Only that that guru never existed! And now I ask you, with your hand on your heart, can someone say that we have reached perfection and that nothing can happen? I think the answer is no, so this procedure is always necessary.

The next question is, how do we call this logic, and where? We need to imagine *"Speedy,"* an entire data transfer system, and use PLSQL or Transact SQL. We will choose one part of the flow and see how to use this logic consistently. You have the freedom to use what you want; if your SQL is better in Java, please use Java!

It's time to see the error handling functionality!

Let's see the logic that makes the verification and turn it into a stored procedure. As an exercise of imagination, or as a work for improvement, you can try to transform the previous chapters' logic into a persistent system, using anything you want. You can use a layer of stored procedures within SQL Server or Oracle, or you can try to do the same thing in Java or C#, you decide!

Listing 10-4 Check gate consistency logic Oracle

```
-- The process of checking the gate, Oracle version
CREATE OR REPLACE PROCEDURE Check_Consistency
(
    p_The_Gate_Is_Consistent            OUT VARCHAR2
)
AS
    v_Rule_Id                   INT;
    v_Rule_SQL                  VARCHAR2(4000);
    v_Count                     INT;
    v_Error_Id                  VARCHAR2(3);
    v_Error_Message             VARCHAR2(4000);
    v_Object_Name               VARCHAR2(30);
    v_Error_Type                INT;
    v_Sql_Id                    VARCHAR2(4000);
    CURSOR C_Consistency_Rules IS
    SELECT Rule_Id, Rule_SQL
    FROM M_Consistency_Rules
    ORDER BY 1;
BEGIN
    UPDATE Gate_Details
    SET Error_Id = NULL
    WHERE Error_Id IS NOT NULL;

    UPDATE Gate_Header
    SET Error_Id = NULL
    WHERE Error_Id IS NOT NULL;
    COMMIT;
    OPEN C_Consistency_Rules;
    LOOP
            FETCH C_Consistency_Rules
            INTO v_Rule_Id, v_Rule_SQL;
            EXIT WHEN C_Consistency_Rules%NOTFOUND;
            EXECUTE IMMEDIATE v_Rule_SQL;
```

```
        COMMIT;
    END LOOP;
    CLOSE C_Consistency_Rules;
    SELECT COUNT(*) INTO v_Count FROM
        (
        SELECT Error_Id FROM Gate_Header
        WHERE Error_Id IS NOT NULL
        UNION ALL
        SELECT Error_Id FROM Gate_Details
        WHERE Error_Id IS NOT NULL
        ) a;
    IF v_Count > 0 THEN
        SELECT MIN(err.Error_Id) INTO v_Error_Id
        FROM
        (
                SELECT Error_Id FROM Gate_Header
                WHERE Error_Id IS NOT NULL
                UNION
                SELECT Error_Id FROM Gate_Details
                WHERE Error_Id IS NOT NULL
        ) err;
        SELECT Rule_Name INTO v_Error_Message
        FROM M_Consistency_Rules
        WHERE Rule_Id = v_Error_Id;

    Handle_Errors (NULL, v_Error_Id, v_Error_Message,
    'Check_Consistency', NULL, 0, 'Check_Consistency');
        p_The_Gate_Is_Consistent   := 'NO';
    ELSE
        p_The_Gate_Is_Consistent   := 'YES';
    END IF;
  END;
  /
```

Now compare this stored procedure with the code in Chapter 4, Listing 4-15. The logic is similar, and the big difference is that now the consistency error check takes place in a persistent form, like a stored procedure. Moreover, there is an output parameter with YES or NO values, explaining whether the gate is consistent or not. Besides, we performed the error handling procedure. If there is a violation of the consistency rule, the rule identifier becomes an error. The error itself is in the error table. This way, the system will have all the errors in one place, including those specified by the SQL consistency rules. This logic takes place before the process, so there is no execution identifier. As an alternative to this, we can isolate the errors so that the operation can continue, and the error table will also contain this information.

You can see the flow; let's review:

♣   Reset the flag to null in the source area, the gate. In this way, we start with no errors, as we should.

♣   Check all SQL consistency rules and update the flag whenever an SQL statement returns any rows. In this way, after digging into all the rules, some gate lines may record a flag value. That value represents the rule identifier.

♣   Check the gate for errors. If so, get the minimum value and record it in the error table and the rest of the information. Specify the value Yes for the output parameter, which means that, indeed, the gate is inconsistent. Otherwise, if there are no flags set, the entrance is consistent, and there is no error in the errors table.

Now that we have seen the logic of consistency in a persistent form and with a complete handling error mechanism, let's continue with the SQL Server version. But this time, I will not merely translate the same logic into SQL Server, but I will try to use the error management logic in another place of the process, in the first big step, when we move the data from the gate to the Staging area.

For that, we will take the logic in Staging, moving products from Source to Staging. We will transform this SQL script into an object in the same approach, like a stored procedure. Let's see how it works.

Listing 10-5 Generate the products in Staging SQL Server

```sql
-- Transfer products to the staging area, SQL Server version
IF OBJECT_ID('Transfer_Products_Staging') IS NOT NULL
    DROP PROCEDURE Transfer_Products_Staging
GO
CREATE PROCEDURE Transfer_Products_Staging
AS
BEGIN
    DECLARE @v_Current_Execution_Id        INT;
    DECLARE @v_New                         INT;
    DECLARE @v_Existing                     INT;
    DECLARE @v_Error_Id                     INT;
```

```
DECLARE @v_Error_Message                 NVARCHAR(4000);
DECLARE @v_Error_Line                    INT;
DECLARE @v_Sql_Id                        NVARCHAR(4000);
SET @v_New               = 1;
SET @v_Existing          = 0;
BEGIN
BEGIN TRY
        BEGIN TRANSACTION T_Transfer_Products;
        SET @v_Sql_Id = '01 Set current import';
        SELECT @v_Current_Execution_Id = Execution_Id
        FROM Executions WHERE Execution_Status = 'STARTED';

    SET @v_Sql_Id = '02 Reset Status Staging products';
    UPDATE Staging_Products
    SET Product_Status = NULL
    WHERE Product_Status IS NOT NULL;
    SET @v_Sql_Id = '03 New product Staging_Products';
INSERT INTO Staging_Products (Product_Identifier,
Business_Code, Execution_Id, Product_Status)
    SELECT sr.Product_Identifier, sr.Business_Code,
@v_Current_Execution_Id AS Execution_Id, @v_New AS
Product_Status
    FROM Gate_Header sr
    WHERE NOT EXISTS
    (
            SELECT 1 FROM Staging_Products dest
    WHERE sr.Product_Identifier = dest.Product_Identifier
    );
    SET @v_Sql_Id= '04 update Staging products';
    UPDATE Staging_Products
    SET Product_Status = @v_Existing,
Execution_Id = @v_Current_Execution_Id,
Business_Code = sr.Business_Code, To_Delete = sr.To_Delete
    FROM Staging_Products dest INNER JOIN Gate_Header sr
            ON sr.Product_Identifier = dest.Product_Identifier
    WHERE Product_Status IS NULL;
    COMMIT TRANSACTION T_Transfer_Products;
```

```
END TRY
BEGIN CATCH
        IF (XACT_STATE()) = -1
        BEGIN
                ROLLBACK TRANSACTION T_Transfer_Products;
        END
        IF (XACT_STATE()) = 1
        BEGIN
                COMMIT TRANSACTION T_Transfer_Products;
        END
        SELECT  @v_Error_Id = ERROR_NUMBER(),
        @v_Error_Message = ERROR_MESSAGE(),
        @v_Error_Line = ERROR_LINE ();
    EXECUTE Handle_Errors @v_Current_Execution_Id, @v_Error_Id,
@v_Error_Message, 'Transfer_Products_Staging', @v_Error_Line, 1,
@v_Sql_Id;
        END CATCH
        END
    END
    GO
```

Now, the error handling procedure works differently than before. In verification logic, the goal is to execute a set of SQL statements, and if any of them return data, they are errors. In this context, if the SQL consistency rules return any row, the rule identifier becomes an error and updates the error table by dedicated logic.

In this scenario, as in all others, we do not expect mistakes. The data transfer process works in steps and sub-steps and, in each of them, executes various pieces of SQL code. Suppose that, for one reason or another, something happens during these steps, such as some constraint violations, conversion errors, or any other database errors. In this case, the dedicated error handling logic will capture the information that will identify the error.

You can see the try-catch block and how we can store valuable information that captures the error, such as the error ID, associated message, and line. These three parameters identify what is happening. The import identifier, current date, and object name (Step) determine when the error occurs and what part of the flow. All this information will allow Jean-Luc to diagnose what happened and try to take action. The failure can come from his logic; maybe he wrongly generates some data from the Panther. If it is not the case, Jean-Luc will pass the information to Johnny, and he will investigate the logic. Maybe there are some errors in the

"*Speedy*" logic itself. One way or another, having this error information is the starting point of the investigation.

In this way, we can be precisely at the time of the error with the same data. I assumed the use of the same gate. The golden rule of fixing a mistake of any kind is that of the possibility of reproducing the error.

Take a look at the SQL ID. This string is a simple feature that can be very useful if used consistently. This string is simply a tag that identifies the following SQL statement. This way, when there is an error of any kind, the last value will be moved nicely to the error table by the error handling logic. Hence, you can go straight to the dirty place and get to the crime scene immediately. It is a great advantage, and the method is so simple! The only thing is that you always need to remember to add this label before every SQL statement.

The transaction policy is specific to each system, and there are too many things to discuss. Note that in this scenario, the capture block will rollback the transaction and handle error logic. These are not necessarily related, but if we want to have coherent things, at least at the current stage, this is the recommended approach. Recording the error in its place and restoring the transaction are two actions that generally work hand in hand.

The Oracle block will be similar; check on this one:

Listing 10-6 Generate the products in Staging Oracle

```
-- Transfer products to the staging area, Oracle version
CREATE OR REPLACE PROCEDURE Transfer_Products_Staging
AS
      v_Current_Execution_Id          INT;
      v_New                           INT;
      v_Existing                      INT;
      v_Error_Id                      INT;
      v_Error_Message                 VARCHAR2(4000);
      v_Error_Line                    INT;
      v_Sql_Id                        VARCHAR2(4000);
BEGIN
      v_New             := 1;
      v_Existing        := 0;
      v_Sql_Id          := '01 Set current import';
      SELECT Execution_Id INTO v_Current_Execution_Id
      FROM Executions WHERE Execution_Status = 'STARTED';
      v_Sql_Id     := '02 Reset Status for Staging products';
```

```
UPDATE Staging_Products
SET Product_Status = NULL
WHERE Product_Status IS NOT NULL;
v_Sql_Id      := '03 new products Staging_Products ';
INSERT INTO Staging_Products (Staging_Product_Id,
Product_Identifier, Business_Code, Execution_Id, Product_Status)
SELECT Seq_Staging_Products.NEXTVAL AS Staging_Product_Id,
sr.Product_Identifier, sr.Business_Code, sr.Execution_Id,
sr.Product_Status
    FROM
    (
            SELECT sr.Product_Identifier,
    v_Current_Execution_Id AS Execution_Id,
    v_New AS Product_Status, sr.Business_Code
        FROM Gate_Header sr
        WHERE NOT EXISTS
        (
            SELECT 1 FROM Staging_Products dest
        WHERE sr.Product_Identifier = dest.Product_Identifier
        )
    ) sr;
    v_Sql_Id      := '04 update table Staging_Products';
    UPDATE Staging_Products dest
    SET Product_Status = v_Existing,
    Execution_Id = v_Current_Execution_Id,
        Business_Code = (SELECT sr.Business_Code FROM Gate_Header
sr WHERE sr.Product_Identifier = dest.Product_Identifier),
        To_Delete = (SELECT sr.To_Delete FROM Gate_Header sr WHERE
sr.Product_Identifier = dest.Product_Identifier)
    WHERE Product_Status IS NULL AND EXISTS
    (
            SELECT 1 FROM Gate_Header sr
        WHERE sr.Product_Identifier = dest.Product_Identifier
    );
    COMMIT;
EXCEPTION WHEN OTHERS THEN
    v_Error_Id := SQLCODE;
```

```
    v_Error_Message := SQLERRM;
  Handle_Errors (v_Current_Execution_Id, v_Error_Id,
v_Error_Message, 'Transfer_Products_Staging', v_Error_Line, 1,
v_Sql_Id);
  END;
  /
```

To continue, I want to illustrate another useful feature in a data transfer system like this. We just saw how to handle errors, if any. Another administrative layer is the process log.

Sometimes we have to record the steps and finally the sub-steps for various reasons. One of them is to measure performance. If you have performance issues and want to improve, you should know where the problem is. To see this, you should be able to measure the timings step by step, for example. And here is our next topic.

The data transfer log

The error table is fundamental. Any system like *"Speedy"* needs an efficient way of accounting for errors. There have been several occasions in this book when we have discussed errors, and I think we have approached this part quite well. However, in addition to errors, taking into account the particularity of the *"Speedy"* system, it is also necessary and merely possible to record events in a kind of process log. It was mainly considering the lack of interactions in such back-end processes. This lack is one nice thing that characterizes such a system. There is no user interaction or feedback; the operation is as quiet as a fish. If you remember the movie "Arizona Dream" and the great poem about the fish:

"The fish doesn't think.

The fish is mute.

Expressionless.

The fish doesn't think,

Because the fish knows

Everything."

This poem is part of the song "This is a film" from the soundtrack of "Arizona Dream" (Emir Kusturica / Goran Bregovic). Like the fish, the data transfer system or process is mute and expressionless. From the moment Angelique presses the button labeled sync until she sees the data in her system, the process takes place in complete silence. Suddenly, Angelique sees new shoe items in the window, sees changes in existing products without doing anything! It is a real miracle, this process.

The *"Speedy"* system knows everything and transfers information from the *"Yellow Panther"* to *"Shoes are everywhere"* in an instance. As in the famous song performed by Goran Bregovic.

If the error table stores information about possible errors during the process, another table could be handy in certain situations. I mean a log table. This kind of table is not related to errors that may occur but to the course of events and recording these events.

Any process like *"Speedy"* is a set of steps and sub-steps. Each step is programmatically defined in one way or another, depending on the language and technology used. In our particular case, we are talking about functions, procedures, packages, etc.

The log table records the steps during the process. It has many purposes, among which we remember the descriptions of the flow divided into small pieces, the so-called steps. If the process is more complex, the steps can divide into sub-steps, and the log will store some information about the execution. This information will per cycle, process step, or sub-step, possibly the programmatic object's name, function, or procedure. Furthermore, data such as lists of sources and target objects could part of this log table. For example, we could insert data from 1-2 tables into others 1-2 tables in one specific step. This information is descriptive and describes one particular step's primary goal, transfer data from individual sources to specific targets.

In addition to the descriptive role, the log can play a significant role in measuring execution times. As always, database performance is a critical factor in any success, and in this perspective, we may want to measure timing in stages and sub-stages. For that, a date and time information is necessary. First of all, the best programmers manage to obtain optimal performance in what they achieve. Another category is those specialized in detecting performance problems and finding various ways to improve. But no matter what field someone is in, they need to measure performance to do something. And this is another essential utility of a log.

These are just a few critical points of a log table in such a process. More could be useful, for sure. However, I would say that it can be a starting point for a real project of this type in a whole enterprise that uses many software systems that have to collaborate in one way or another and exchange data.

Now, let's design our example of a log table:

Listing 10-7 Create the log table

```
-- Create the log table SQL Server
CREATE TABLE Log
(
```

```
    Id                   INT IDENTITY(1, 1) PRIMARY KEY NOT NULL,
    Step                 INT,
    Execution_Id         INT,
    Object_Name          NVARCHAR(30) NOT NULL,
    Sources              NVARCHAR(255),
    Targets              NVARCHAR(255),
    Log_Date             SMALLDATETIME DEFAULT (GETDATE()),
    Exec_Phase           INT
);
-- Create the log table Oracle
CREATE SEQUENCE Seq_Log;
CREATE TABLE Log
(
    Id                   INT PRIMARY KEY NOT NULL,
    Step                 INT,
    Execution_Id         INT,
    Object_Name          VARCHAR2(30) NOT NULL,
    Sources              VARCHAR2(255),
    Targets              VARCHAR2(255),
    Log_Date             DATE DEFAULT (SYSDATE),
    Exec_Phase           INT
);
```

This new table has the following columns:

♣ The step. We did not speak too much about this, although this is an essential part of the system. "*Speedy*" is a set of steps, possibly sub-steps, and a metadata table with steps is, for sure, necessary. I leave it to you to define it yourself later.

♣ Execution identifier. Everything is associated with an execution. Consequently, whenever we record something, this is part of a specific implementation.

♣ Object name. Any part of the process appears in a particular programming object, such as the function or procedure, the package, etc. This information is part of the log because we need to know where and where the code the event described is.

♣ Sources. The source object's chain, such as the set of tables, views, or inline functions, or anything else of any kind, is the source of step information. Maybe not all steps have this, but most for sure.

♣ Targets. The set of target objects, tables, etc. Similarly, this information stores the target objects. These two columns are descriptive but show the purpose step. In most cases, the purpose of a stage is to transfer data from different sources to different targets.

♣ Log date. The data of the event is one of the essential elements of a log. Sometimes a timestamp is even better than a date.

♣ Log Phase. This field, combined with the log data, allows us to measure the range of any step. I propose to call a log function that will populate this table twice, at the beginning and end of each step. In this way, we can always measure the time for each step. This pair of fields is a good achievement, as you will soon see.

The complexity of such a process is relatively low, starting from its purpose. This logging procedure only stores some step information periodically. Therefore, there is no logic of any kind within it. Instead, the error handling procedure is subject to increasing complexity, depending on the implementation. But there is not so much in the log events procedure.

Hence, let's build the mechanism that will populate the log. Let's see and start with a SQL Server version of it.

Listing 10-8 Handling the log table SQL Server

```
-- Create the logging procedure SQL Server
IF OBJECT_ID('Handle_Log') IS NOT NULL
    DROP PROCEDURE Handle_Log
GO
CREATE PROCEDURE Handle_Log
(
    @p_Execution_Id             INT,
    @p_Step                     INT,
    @p_Object_Name              NVARCHAR(30),
    @p_Sources                  NVARCHAR(255) = NULL,
    @p_Targets                  NVARCHAR(255) = NULL,
    @p_Exec_Phase               INT
)
AS
DECLARE
    @v_Log_Date                 DATETIME,
    @v_Count                    INT;
BEGIN
```

258

```
    SET @v_Log_Date = GETDATE();


    INSERT INTO Log (Execution_Id, Step, Object_Name, Sources,
Targets, Log_Date, Exec_Phase)
    VALUES (@p_Execution_Id, @p_Step, @p_Object_Name, @p_Sources,
@p_Targets, @v_Log_Date, @p_Exec_Phase);
    END;
    GO
```

See the parameter that manages the phase. The majority's meaning is evident; there are parameters associated with the log columns, as in any classical insertion logic. Let's linger a bit on the execution phase parameter. It refers to the moment of execution within the calling procedure. It can be zero or one. If it is zero, the log procedure runs at the beginning of the calling process, and if it is one at the end. We can decide intermediate phases, such as two or three, if specific steps can be more complex and split into several execution sequences. This division may occur from time to time, but the beginning and end should generally be sufficient. However, it depends on the implementation.

What is the purpose of this execution phase? Which other than the measurement of execution times, so important for any process. Time is money, and you know the proverb. Practically, performance means, first and foremost, time. Especially from the database perspective, we can measure relatively easily. Thus, every time executes the log procedure, Johnny store the execution date at that time. Because Johnny ran the login procedure at the beginning and end of each step, he precisely knows each step or sub-step duration. This facility is so crucial for someone who wants to have the possibility to measure and improve performance!

We are done with this too. I advise you to practice and add more complexity to the logging functionality, then see more scenarios depending on the business you have in mind.

Before we continue, let's give a little space to those who work exclusively in Oracle. Paradoxically, although it is relatively affordable for an SQL programmer to run on any database system, many database programmers have worked solely on Oracle all their lives. However, projects drive our path, and there were always Oracle projects on the market! For these dedicated guys from the Oracle database, let's see their version.

Listing 10-9 Handling the log table Oracle

```
-- Create the logging procedure Oracle
CREATE OR REPLACE PROCEDURE Handle_Log
(
    p_Execution_Id              INT,
    p_Step                      INT,
    p_Object_Name               VARCHAR2,
    p_Sources                   VARCHAR2 := NULL,
    p_Targets                   VARCHAR2 := NULL,
    p_Exec_Phase                INT
)
AS
    v_Log_Date                  DATE;
    v_Count                     INT;
BEGIN
    v_Log_Date          := SYSDATE;
    INSERT INTO Log (Execution_Id, Step, Object_Name, Sources,
Targets, Log_Date, Exec_Phase)
    VALUES (p_Execution_Id, p_Step, p_Object_Name, p_Sources,
p_Targets, v_Log_Date, p_Exec_Phase);
    END;
    /
```

Now let's add the log segment somewhere in one of the pieces of code. I suggest you go to the target now and choose some of the logic from the target. For example, we will select Listing 8-5. We will turn it into a stored procedure and add both functionality and error management, and logging. Let's look at the SQL Server version first.

Listing 10-10 Add products in the target SQL Server

```
-- Transfer product to the target area, SQL Server
IF OBJECT_ID('Transfer_Products_Target') IS NOT NULL
    DROP PROCEDURE Transfer_Products_Target
GO
CREATE PROCEDURE Transfer_Products_Target
AS
    -- Error variables
    DECLARE @v_Error_Id             INT;
```

```
    DECLARE @v_Error_Message        NVARCHAR(4000);
    DECLARE @v_Error_Line           INT;
    DECLARE @v_Sql_Id               NVARCHAR(4000);

    DECLARE @v_Step                 INT;
    DECLARE @v_Sources              NVARCHAR(255);
    DECLARE @v_Targets              NVARCHAR(255);
    DECLARE @v_Start                INT;
    DECLARE @v_End                  INT;

    DECLARE @v_Count_New            INT;
    DECLARE @v_Count_Upd            INT;
    DECLARE @v_Current_Execution_Id INT;
BEGIN
    SET NOCOUNT ON
    SET XACT_ABORT ON
    SET @v_Start                = 0;
    SET @v_End                  = 1;

SET @v_Sources = ' Stg_Mv_New_Products; Stg_Mv_Upd_Products ';
    SET @v_Targets          = ' Products';

    SET @v_Step             = 15;
    SET @v_Count_New =
(SELECT COUNT(*) FROM Stg_Mv_New_Products);
    SET @v_Count_Upd =
(SELECT COUNT(*) FROM Stg_Mv_Upd_Products);
    SELECT @v_Current_Execution_Id = Execution_Id
FROM Executions WHERE Execution_Status = 'STARTED';
EXECUTE Handle_Log @v_Current_Execution_Id, @v_Step,
'Transfer_Products_Target', @v_Sources, @v_Targets, @v_Start;

    IF @v_Count_New + @v_Count_Upd > 0
    BEGIN
    BEGIN TRY
            BEGIN TRANSACTION T_Transfer_Products_Tgt;
```

261

Speedy, a data transfer system. A SQL Exercise

```
-- Generate the products in the target, SQL Server
        DECLARE @v_Max_Product_Id INT;
        SET @v_Sql_Id= '02 Set max product';
SELECT @v_Max_Product_Id = MAX(Product_Id)
FROM Products;
    SET @v_Sql_Id = '03 new shoes, Stg_Mv_New_Products';


WITH sr (Code, Name, Type_Id, Supplier_Id, Manufacturer_Code,
Color, Gender, Measure, Source_Product_Code)
    AS
    (
SELECT Product_Code AS Code, Product_Name AS Name, Type_Id,
Supplier_Id, Manufacturer_Code, Color, Gender, Measure,
Source_Product_Code
    FROM Stg_Mv_New_Products
    )
INSERT INTO Products (Product_Id, Code, Name, Type_Id,
Supplier_Id, Manufacturer_Code, Color, Gender, Measure,
Source_Product_Code)
SELECT COALESCE(@v_Max_Product_Id, 0) + ROW_NUMBER() OVER
(ORDER BY sr.Code) AS Product_Id, sr.Code, sr.Name, sr.Type_Id,
sr.Supplier_Id, sr.Manufacturer_Code, sr.Color, sr.Gender,
sr.Measure, sr.Source_Product_Code
FROM sr
WHERE NOT EXISTS
    (
        SELECT 1 FROM Products dest
        WHERE dest.Code = sr.Code
    );
SET @v_Sql_Id= '04 Update Stg_Mv_New_Products';
UPDATE Stg_Mv_New_Products
SET Product_Id = sr.Product_Id
FROM Stg_Mv_New_Products dest INNER JOIN Products sr
        ON sr.Code = dest.Product_Code;
SET @v_Sql_Id = '05 Update Products, change Name';
WITH sr (Source_Product_Code, Product_Id, Name)
AS
(
```

262

```
SELECT Source_Product_Code, Product_Id, Product_Name AS Name
    FROM Stg_Mv_Upd_Products
    WHERE Attribute_Status IS NOT NULL
    AND Product_Name IS NOT NULL
    )
    UPDATE Products
    SET Name = sr.Name
    FROM Products dest INNER JOIN sr
ON sr.Source_Product_Code = dest.Source_Product_Code
AND sr.Product_Id = dest.Product_Id ;
    SET @v_Sql_Id= '06 Update Products change Type';
    WITH sr (Source_Product_Code, Product_Id, Type_Id)
    AS
    (
        SELECT Source_Product_Code, Product_Id, Type_Id
        FROM Stg_Mv_Upd_Products
        WHERE Attribute_Status IS NOT NULL
        AND Type_Id IS NOT NULL
    )
    UPDATE Products
    SET Type_Id = sr.Type_Id
    FROM Products dest INNER JOIN sr
ON sr.Source_Product_Code = dest.Source_Product_Code
AND sr.Product_Id = dest.Product_Id ;

    SET @v_Sql_Id = '07 Update Products change Supplier';

    WITH sr (Source_Product_Code, Product_Id, Supplier_Id)
    AS
    (
        SELECT Source_Product_Code, Product_Id, Supplier_Id
        FROM Stg_Mv_Upd_Products
        WHERE Attribute_Status IS NOT NULL
        AND Supplier_Id IS NOT NULL
    )
    UPDATE Products
```

```
    SET Supplier_Id = sr.Supplier_Id
    FROM Products dest INNER JOIN sr
ON sr.Source_Product_Code = dest.Source_Product_Code
AND sr.Product_Id = dest.Product_Id ;
    SET @v_Sql_Id = '08 Update Products change Color';
    WITH sr (Source_Product_Code, Product_Id, Color)
    AS
    (
         SELECT Source_Product_Code, Product_Id, Color
         FROM Stg_Mv_Upd_Products
         WHERE Attribute_Status IS NOT NULL
         AND Color IS NOT NULL
    )
    UPDATE Products
    SET Color = sr.Color
    FROM Products dest INNER JOIN sr
ON sr.Source_Product_Code = dest.Source_Product_Code
AND sr.Product_Id = dest.Product_Id ;

    SET @v_Sql_Id = '09 Update Products change Measure';
    WITH sr (Source_Product_Code, Product_Id, Measure)
    AS
    (
         SELECT Source_Product_Code, Product_Id, Measure
         FROM Stg_Mv_Upd_Products
         WHERE Attribute_Status IS NOT NULL
         AND Measure IS NOT NULL
    )
    UPDATE Products
    SET Measure = sr.Measure
    FROM Products dest INNER JOIN sr
ON sr.Source_Product_Code = dest.Source_Product_Code
AND sr.Product_Id = dest.Product_Id ;

    SET @v_Sql_Id = '10 Update Products change Gender';
    WITH sr (Source_Product_Code, Product_Id, Gender)
```

```
AS
(
        SELECT Source_Product_Code, Product_Id, Gender
        FROM Stg_Mv_Upd_Products
        WHERE Attribute_Status IS NOT NULL
        AND Gender IS NOT NULL
)
UPDATE Products
SET Gender = sr.Gender
FROM Products dest INNER JOIN sr
ON sr.Source_Product_Code = dest.Source_Product_Code
AND sr.Product_Id = dest.Product_Id ;

COMMIT TRANSACTION T_Transfer_Products_Tgt;
END TRY
BEGIN CATCH
        IF (XACT_STATE()) = -1
        BEGIN
                ROLLBACK TRANSACTION T_Transfer_Products_Tgt;
        END
        IF (XACT_STATE()) = 1
        BEGIN
                COMMIT TRANSACTION T_Transfer_Products_Tgt;
        END

SELECT  @v_Error_Id = ERROR_NUMBER(),
@v_Error_Message = ERROR_MESSAGE(),
@v_Error_Line = ERROR_LINE ();

EXECUTE Handle_Errors @v_Current_Execution_Id, @v_Error_Id,
@v_Error_Message, 'Transfer_Products_Target', @v_Error_Line, 1,
@v_Sql_Id;
        END CATCH
        END

EXECUTE Handle_Log @v_Current_Execution_Id, @v_Step,
'Transfer_Products_Target', @v_Sources, @v_Targets, @v_End;
```

```
END
GO
```

This code above is a serious matter, and we seem to be getting closer to real life! Well, I can say that this is almost a complete step without being a problematic scenario. As you can see, there are both errors and logs, and basically, this step of managing products covers everything, the basics at least. If there is an error, the error table will record all the necessary information that will explain it. Second, the logic will document every step like this and, in addition to the descriptive information, timings may be present, allowing performance measurements.

When we talk about performance, we come to the most challenging segment of any system. In programming, there are no simple things, or everything we do is a simple matter. We can consider this as a paradox. To not be accused of arrogating knowledge about the entire programming area, I will specify that I refer to relational databases' programming, mostly SQL programming.

We can talk for days and weeks about optimizer, indexes and materialized views, various techniques. These are essential things, and a performance specialist knows them and has spent a lot of time trying to understand and use these facilities. Before anything else, in any system, including a system like this, measuring times is essential. We need to measure the calendars first.

One of the most unpleasant problems for any user using any system is poor performance. No user likes to stay and wait for any window to open. In the process of data transfer, when trying to improve performance, someone needs to measure each step and sub-step so that they can track and dissect the steps with inappropriate timings. After that, one will analyze the SQL statements, rewrite some of them, check the indexes, read the execution plans, see what happens, etc. There are so many things on the agenda when we look at the steps. The opportunity to measure for performance is the first reason for a log like this!

I will also show the Oracle version of this logic, and with that, we prepare to conclude direct SQL code presentations.

Listing 10-11 Add products in the target Oracle

```
-- Transfer product to the target area, Oracle
CREATE OR REPLACE PROCEDURE Transfer_Products_Target
AS
    v_Error_Id              INT;
    v_Error_Message         VARCHAR2(4000);
    v_Error_Line            INT;
    v_Sql_Id                VARCHAR2(4000);
    v_Step                  INT;
```

```
        v_Sources                   VARCHAR2(255);
        v_Targets                   VARCHAR2(255);
        v_Start                     INT;
        v_End                       INT;
        v_Count                     INT;
        v_Object_Name               VARCHAR2(30);
        v_Current_Execution_Id      INT;
        v_Max_Product_Id            INT;
        v_Count_New                 INT;
        v_Count_Upd                 INT;
    BEGIN
        v_Start                     := 0;
        v_End                       := 1;
        v_Sources                   := 'Stg_Mv_New_Products';
        v_Targets                   := 'Products';
        v_Step                      := 15;
        v_Object_Name               := 'Transfer_Products_Target';

        SELECT COUNT(*) INTO v_Count_New FROM Stg_Mv_New_Products;
        SELECT COUNT(*) INTO v_Count_Upd FROM Stg_Mv_Upd_Products;

        SELECT COUNT(*) INTO v_Count FROM Executions
        WHERE Execution_Status = 'STARTED';
        IF v_Count = 1 THEN
                SELECT Execution_Id INTO v_Current_Execution_Id
                FROM Executions WHERE Execution_Status = 'STARTED';
        END IF;
    Handle_Log (v_Current_Execution_Id, v_Step, v_Object_Name,
v_Sources, v_Targets, v_Start);

        IF v_Count_New + v_Count_Upd > 0 THEN
                v_Sql_Id            := '02 Set max product';

                SELECT COUNT(*) INTO v_Count FROM Products;

                IF v_Count > 0 THEN
```

```
SELECT MAX(Product_Id) INTO v_Max_Product_Id FROM Products;
        ELSE
                v_Max_Product_Id    := 0;
        END IF;


            v_Sql_Id := '03 add new products';
    INSERT INTO Products (Product_Id, Code, Name, Type_Id,
Supplier_Id, Manufacturer_Code, Color, Gender, Measure,
Source_Product_Code)
    SELECT v_Max_Product_Id + ROW_NUMBER() OVER (ORDER BY p.Code)
AS Product_Id, p.Code, p.Name, p.Type_Id, p.Supplier_Id,
p.Manufacturer_Code, p.Color, p.Gender, p.Measure,
Source_Product_Code
    FROM
    (
    SELECT sr.Product_Code AS Code, sr.Product_Name AS Name,
sr.Type_Id, sr.Supplier_Id, sr.Manufacturer_Code, sr.Color,
        sr.Gender, sr.Measure, sr.Source_Product_Code
        FROM Stg_Mv_New_Products sr
        WHERE NOT EXISTS
        (
                SELECT 1 FROM Products dest
                WHERE dest.Code = sr.Product_Code
        )
    ) p;


    v_Sql_Id   := '04 Update Stg_Mv_New_Products id';
        UPDATE Stg_Mv_New_Products dest
        SET Product_Id = (SELECT sr.Product_Id FROM Products sr
    WHERE sr.Code = dest.Product_Code)
        WHERE EXISTS
        (
                SELECT 1 FROM Products sr
                WHERE sr.Code = dest.Product_Code
        );


        v_Sql_Id    := '05 Update Products change Name';
        UPDATE Products dest
```

```
SET Name = (
WITH sr (Source_Product_Code, Product_Id, Name)
AS
(
   SELECT Source_Product_Code, Product_Id,
   Product_Name AS Name
   FROM Stg_Mv_Upd_Products
   WHERE Attribute_Status IS NOT NULL
   AND Product_Name IS NOT NULL
)
SELECT sr.Name
FROM sr
WHERE sr.Source_Product_Code = dest.Source_Product_Code
AND sr.Product_Id = dest.Product_Id
     )
WHERE EXISTS
(
     SELECT 1 FROM Stg_Mv_Upd_Products sr
WHERE sr.Source_Product_Code = dest.Source_Product_Code
AND sr.Product_Id = dest.Product_Id
AND sr.Attribute_Status IS NOT NULL
AND sr.Product_Name IS NOT NULL
     );
v_Sql_Id     := '06 Update Products change Type_Id';
UPDATE Products dest
SET Type_Id = (
WITH sr (Source_Product_Code, Product_Id, Type_Id)
AS
(
     SELECT Source_Product_Code, Product_Id, Type_Id
     FROM Stg_Mv_Upd_Products
     WHERE Attribute_Status IS NOT NULL
     AND Type_Id IS NOT NULL
     )
     SELECT sr.Type_Id
     FROM sr
```

```
WHERE sr.Source_Product_Code = dest.Source_Product_Code
AND sr.Product_Id = dest.Product_Id
        )
        WHERE EXISTS
        (
        SELECT 1 FROM Stg_Mv_Upd_Products sr
WHERE sr.Source_Product_Code = dest.Source_Product_Code
AND sr.Product_Id = dest.Product_Id
AND sr.Attribute_Status IS NOT NULL
AND sr.Type_Id IS NOT NULL
        );
v_Sql_Id      := '07 Update Products change Supplier';

UPDATE Products dest
SET Supplier_Id = (
WITH sr (Source_Product_Code, Product_Id, Supplier_Id)
AS
(
        SELECT Source_Product_Code, Product_Id, Supplier_Id
        FROM Stg_Mv_Upd_Products
        WHERE Attribute_Status IS NOT NULL
        AND Supplier_Id IS NOT NULL
)
SELECT sr.Supplier_Id
FROM sr
WHERE sr.Source_Product_Code = dest.Source_Product_Code
AND sr.Product_Id = dest.Product_Id
)
WHERE EXISTS
(
        SELECT 1 FROM Stg_Mv_Upd_Products sr
WHERE sr.Source_Product_Code = dest.Source_Product_Code
AND sr.Product_Id = dest.Product_Id
AND sr.Attribute_Status IS NOT NULL
AND sr.Supplier_Id IS NOT NULL
        );
```

```
v_Sql_Id      := '08 Update Products change Color';

UPDATE Products dest
SET Color = (
WITH sr (Source_Product_Code, Product_Id, Color)
AS
(
        SELECT Source_Product_Code, Product_Id, Color
        FROM Stg_Mv_Upd_Products
        WHERE Attribute_Status IS NOT NULL
        AND Color IS NOT NULL
)
SELECT sr.Color
FROM sr
WHERE sr.Source_Product_Code = dest.Source_Product_Code
AND sr.Product_Id = dest.Product_Id
        )
WHERE EXISTS
(
        SELECT 1 FROM Stg_Mv_Upd_Products sr
WHERE sr.Source_Product_Code = dest.Source_Product_Code
AND sr.Product_Id = dest.Product_Id
AND sr.Attribute_Status IS NOT NULL
AND sr.Color IS NOT NULL
        );
v_Sql_Id      := '09 Update Products change Measure';

UPDATE Products dest
SET Measure = (
WITH sr (Source_Product_Code, Product_Id, Measure)
AS
(
        SELECT Source_Product_Code, Product_Id, Measure
        FROM Stg_Mv_Upd_Products
        WHERE Attribute_Status IS NOT NULL
        AND Measure IS NOT NULL
```

```
)
SELECT sr.Measure
FROM sr
WHERE sr.Source_Product_Code = dest.Source_Product_Code
AND sr.Product_Id = dest.Product_Id
)
WHERE EXISTS
(
        SELECT 1 FROM Stg_Mv_Upd_Products sr
WHERE sr.Source_Product_Code = dest.Source_Product_Code
AND sr.Product_Id = dest.Product_Id
AND sr.Attribute_Status IS NOT NULL
AND sr.Measure IS NOT NULL
);
v_Sql_Id        := '10 Update Products change Gender';

UPDATE Products dest
SET Gender = (
WITH sr (Source_Product_Code, Product_Id, Gender)
AS
(
        SELECT Source_Product_Code, Product_Id, Gender
        FROM Stg_Mv_Upd_Products
        WHERE Attribute_Status IS NOT NULL
        AND Gender IS NOT NULL
)
SELECT sr.Gender
FROM sr
WHERE sr.Source_Product_Code = dest.Source_Product_Code
AND sr.Product_Id = dest.Product_Id
)
WHERE EXISTS
(
        SELECT 1 FROM Stg_Mv_Upd_Products sr
WHERE sr.Source_Product_Code = dest.Source_Product_Code
AND sr.Product_Id = dest.Product_Id
```

```
    AND sr.Attribute_Status IS NOT NULL
    AND sr.Gender IS NOT NULL
          );


          COMMIT;
    END IF;


  Handle_Log (v_Current_Execution_Id, v_Step, v_Object_Name,
v_Sources, v_Targets, v_End);


  EXCEPTION WHEN OTHERS THEN
      v_Error_Id          := SQLCODE;
      v_Error_message     := SQLERRM;


  Handle_Errors (v_Current_Execution_Id, v_Error_Id,
v_Error_Message, v_Object_Name, NULL, 1, v_Sql_Id);
    END;
    /
```

Finally, the last thing I want to do to end this topic is creating a view that displays the measurements. This database view will help the performance specialist, if there is such a thing in the project, to see each step's duration. Because we called the log procedure twice in each process step and sub-step and measured the time at the beginning and end of the phase, a simple database view with a difference between the two timers will show exactly how long each step lasts. We can use a classic database view but not necessarily!

Let's use a different object type and use an inline function instead of a database view for the SQL Server version. Considering that the measure is per execution, we can consider the execution_id execution_id as a parameter. In this case, the measurement report will be per process run. Here is the query below:

Listing 10-12 Add measurement query using an inline function, SQL Server

```
-- Measure execution times SQL Server
IF OBJECT_ID (N'Log_V_Measure', N'IF') IS NOT NULL
    DROP FUNCTION Log_V_Measure;
GO
CREATE FUNCTION Log_V_Measure (@p_Execution_Id INT)
RETURNS TABLE AS
```

```
RETURN
(
    WITH start_log (Step, Object_Name, Sources, Targets,
Start_Date)
    AS
    (
    SELECT Step, Object_Name, Sources, Targets,
    Log_Date AS Start_Date
    FROM Log
    WHERE Execution_Id = @p_Execution_Id AND Exec_Phase = 0
    ),
    end_log (Step, Object_Name, Sources, Targets, End_Date)
    AS
    (
    SELECT Step, Object_Name, Sources, Targets,
    Log_Date AS End_Date
    FROM Log
    WHERE Execution_Id = @p_Execution_Id AND Exec_Phase = 1
    )
  SELECT e.Step, e.Object_Name, e.Sources, e.Targets,
@p_Execution_Id AS Execution_Id,
    CAST(e.End_Date - s.Start_Date AS TIME) AS step_time
    FROM end_log e INNER JOIN start_log s
        ON e.Step = s.Step
)
GO
```

Try to create a complete set of objects and transfer several products. Among other things, you can see how to use the log and check the timings. Create a similar database object for Oracle, eventually a view, with the same purpose. You will see how every step is present in the table and see what happened during the process.

From the database performance point of view, if you can generate from somewhere some test data and create some hundreds of shoes with their properties, you will have some timings to measure. Here you can try to rewrite some logic and decrease the timings. Try to follow the application developers' path, replace the set-based SQL code with the procedural, atomic style so appreciated by them, and recheck the timings. You will better understand why I promote the set-based approach, specific to database developers, and why I consider the inappropriate programming style causing problems in our databases.

11   It's time for some improvements

A mixture of things, this book

We are nearing the end. I hope it will be a happy ending, at least for some of you. In these pages, I wanted to illustrate a specific SQL system. As mentioned in the introduction, I am a SQL programmer, and I am doing SQL for many years. I love this simple model with rows and columns, and I enjoy the simplicity of SQL language. This paper's first goal is to promote my preferred technology as a database developer and not a product specialist. I consider this work as a continuation of my previous one, and in the end, the reasons are similar. There are still many SQL requests because the relational database remains there, used by so many enterprises. With this, the SQL language is so present, even if it is an additional skill near other technologies like Java, C#, Python, etc. Unfortunately, many of us programmers either consider SQL as a piece of cake or eventually a depreciated technology. Of course, it depends on our projects; sometimes it is not too much, sometimes not.

The goal is to show how to write SQL accurately and encourage IT technicians to use SQL whenever needed and use it properly. If, in the previous book, I tried to show how one must write SQL correctly and use a set-based and holistic approach instead of the atomic and procedural approach so close to what they usually write at the application level. The current book assumes the holistic approach and explains a system that intensively uses SQL, a data transfer between two systems, a source, and a target. There is still so much SQL at the back-end level and, apart from new features, improvements, and syntaxes, the first is a matter of style.

On the other hand, the source of my book is my experience. I have been experimenting with such kinds of projects for a long time. I had the chance to design and develop such systems, and now I decided to share a few thoughts with you. As a former teacher and a trainer, I'm the kind of person who loves to share his experiences with others as a programmer. I want to encourage everyone and offer a model, an opening. There are still projects SQL-oriented. Data transfer at the relational level continues to be such a common task. There are so many projects where the primary goal is the same, data transfer and manipulation to exasperation! Honestly, I am desperate when I often see projects where SQL is the best choice, but, for often subjective reasons, technologies that are not native

276

to this back-end purpose, such as data transfer, are preferred. These decisions mainly happen because some markets and people do not consider SQL as a skill in itself but an additional one to something else. John Doe is not a SQL programmer but a Java programmer that sometimes needs to know some SQL. Sometimes it works, but sometimes not. The tricky part is that when one realizes that the complexity of the data manipulation in the relational database is beyond a certain level, it is maybe too late. It would be best to rewrite it because these developers who know some SQL use it unproperly, and the damages in performance are quite considerable. For example, even for a project like *"Speedy,"* a team of developers may choose to do this SQL under Java or C#, etc. And this happens quite often.

There are two aspects to the problem: a project and technology. Moreover, given my penchant for writing and probably not having a very technical style par excellence, I decided to give my book a narrative format. In this way, my book is also a life story. The book's technical component wrapped in scripts and SQL exercises coexisted with the adventures of imaginary characters of users and programmers, such as Johnny, Jean-Luc, Angelique, or Joanna.

Funny but real characters who work in imaginary companies and use fictional software systems such as "*Yellow Panther*" and "*Shoes are everywhere*" make this book somewhat unique and unusual. Even though it is a SQL book that describes a data transfer system, I wanted to address other categories of readers, not necessarily those specializing in programming and SQL. In a software company or any enterprise that develops its software systems, apart from programmers, other categories of professionals, such as analysts, testers, application users, project managers, etc., use more or less SQL. This book is for them too.

This book is at the intersection of technical and social, in one way or another. I set out to describe some hypothetical scenarios and capture certain aspects of companies' social lives. This style of writing a SQL book does not even oppose this programming language. Probably few programming languages are as human as SQL. One of the standard features of the SQL language is "English like." This feature demonstrates the language itself tries to simulate English natural language and succeeds to some extent. When someone programs in SQL, it's almost as if they speak English. This language is, in fact, unique in a way.

This book is in harmony with this SQL feature, being such a practical language, almost like a natural one. Consequently, you can consider this book a book about SQL, a book about a specific type of project, data migration or data transfer, a book about IT social life, and a fiction book with some characters who live close to SQL and IT.

Now, here in the last chapter, I intend to end each topic with a few final considerations and possibly some personal opinions, when appropriate. All aspects of my book listed in the previous subchapter will receive the last cartridge before launch! When I was in the army, I remember how we, the soldiers, counted the days left until the release! The fewer days left, the greater the emotions and the more challenging the wait. The feeling of liberation from the army was indescribable. Of course, this was happening during the years of communism, in Romania dominated by Ceausescu! Now we have reached the end of the book. I hope that this feeling of liberation that everyone has when they finish a book will have, this time, only a positive connotation. I hope that the book's completion will have a success status and not a failure and that feeling of satisfaction when someone adds a new book to the list.

The last step, but maybe the most important

"Speedy" is a simple exercise that describes one common type of project. Doing SQL all my life, at least for the last 20 years, I have always done the same thing, I look at the data, I change the data, I move the data, I play with the data, I transfer the data by changing different parts of it, etc. This data transfer system describes a common situation that is still present in many places, the situation in which many systems live together and sometimes try to collaborate without being fully integrated. Such an approach will help in this task and allow different software products to live in peace and harmony!

The imaginary characters in the book try to give a little real-life to our IT applications. I imagined a real company that uses various systems and needs such data transfer software to integrate them better. In this way, a system like *"Speedy"* becomes part of the lives of people like Johnny, Angelique, Joanna, or Jean-Luc. The book is mainly technical but not the style! I tried to write a book that would also offer moments of non-technical satisfaction and bring some social elements to our lives as a programmer, analyst, tester, or project manager within the companies in which we operate. I know I took a risk, and I also know that my book will receive all sorts of appreciations, some negative ones. Maybe it should have stayed at the technical segment in a proportion of 100%! Perhaps once I will try to do that, but not this time!

However, I sincerely hope that some people will appreciate the book's non-technical component, but that still gives color and human warmth to our computer applications. It is not for nothing that the SQL language is probably the most humane programming language, with chosen keywords as simple as everyday life, such as selecting, adding something, modifying or deleting something from a notebook, etc.

The book is for all types of readers; it is not a book for anyone in particular. I think everyone can read it, a beginner in programming, maybe a data analyst or a project manager or tester. But the book can be read, I think, by more experienced people who are involved in similar projects. It is somewhat accessible even to people who want to change and switch to programming. Today, there are so many people heading to the IT sector who come from other fields.

The last part of the book is to get readers to work. If the first ten chapters were mine and I could try how well I could explain how a distinct type of project works, the last one is for you. I want to suggest a few improvements so that you can benefit more from this experience. I think this is a shortcoming in many books of this type. Readers want to improve something, and they want to understand how they can do this and see some explanations on different topics, etc. After that, they move on.

Where is your effort? Of course, some experienced readers understand some ideas and apply them in their daily activities. Maybe some IT specialists of any kind will use some of these tips in the book in their projects; this would be a remarkable achievement for me! Moreover, perhaps some of them will realize that they can do many things using the old traditional SQL language instead of any sophisticated tools or inappropriate languages; this would be an even more remarkable accomplishment. These are indirect satisfactions, and it is okay because this is the primary purpose of all IT books to help people improve their current and future projects.

But I want to propose a direct achievement this time, and that is to ask you to try to continue my work here.

For this, I want to suggest you improve *"Speedy,"* making some recommendations. Following them will allow you to achieve some worthy goals, such as:

♣ Increasing the level of complexity will allow you to understand the value of such a system better. In this way, in similar projects, you can effectively use some of the knowledge gained here. Add more entities, start with one, imagine some attributes and extend *"Speedy!"* This book might even be a good start for a SQL diploma in a university, for example!

♣ Exercising with such a system will allow you to improve your SQL level if you decide to use the SQL language. Whether you are a Java or Python developer, you may still be involved in relational database projects. It doesn't hurt to practice the correct use of this simple language, SQL. Moreover, it may be beneficial for you, as an application developer, to understand that, in certain situations, using SQL may be more appropriate.

♣ For junior programmers, computer science students, or business people considering switching to technology, completing this scenario and adding more features will help in the future.

♣ Therefore, I strongly advise you to try to do all the exercises in the book and try to add more features, following my recommendations and even better, try to come up with something new and improve the script in the book. The significant advantage will be in your future projects.

Now, I will prepare a list of recommendations, and if any of you are willing to put the bone to work and work extra, I can only be happy. It depends on everyone's time, everyone's level of experience, everyone's abilities, etc. I firmly believe that for some of you, this extra work can help you.

On the other hand, I did not pretend to present complicated things. An experienced database programmer cannot be surprised at all; most concepts are quite common. Such projects are not exotic at all, and many of you have faced them. The purpose of the book is didactic; it is also a book written by a former teacher! Therefore, we can start!

Let's enhance "Speedy"

As mentioned earlier, I will make several suggestions to improve this system. If you want and have time to continue and add more features to this system, decide what to do. I will only propose and, like any recommendation, you can accept or not. You have full freedom to choose!

Define the steps

We have discussed so many times about steps and sub-steps! However, I did not have the time to organize them properly. In a well-organized system of such kind, the steps must take place in a dedicated metadata table. More than that, many metadata tables are missing, I just added some basic ones, and the step table is only one of them.

Consequently, the first task I want to address is the correct organization of steps and sub-steps. For this, I suggest the following:

♣ Create a metadata table for storing system steps and sub-steps.

♣ Some suggested fields in this metadata table are a unique *step identifier*, possibly a numeric, and *step name*. These are the only mandatory fields, in my opinion.

♣ Now, depending on the nature of the steps, I would recommend other features. In most cases, the purpose of a process step is to transfer data. Thus, I recommend the two columns' *sources* and *targets* specify the set of source tables and target tables as part of the step. You can consider a kind of *parent step* if there is a chain of process steps and sub-steps. A *description* of the process step in which you can describe the purpose and implementation is useful because everyone will understand in a few words what is with this step.

♣ In a SQL data transfer system, the steps' logic is in with some objects, such as procedures or functions. The *object name* is part of the step definition.

♣ Try to imagine other features of a step in such a process and add them to the metadata table. In most cases, metadata tables are descriptive and passive as they describe various objects and methods or flows within systems. However, sometimes, metadata objects can be functional and active, as they can effectively trigger different actions between objects in the sources and targets, for example. So, imagining other elements to describe the metadata is can be beneficial.

Once you have correctly designed the step-by-step metadata table, try to use it properly in the process. For example, as part of logic, instead of assigning values to sources, targets, or object names for each step, you can take this information based on the step identifier. For example, in Listing 10-10, you have an arbitrary value step equal to 15. Imagine that this value 15 corresponds to a step named TRANSFER_PRODUCT_TO_TARGET. Based on them, you can quickly fill in all the variables that describe the process step.

Moreover, because almost everything in such a process is part of the step, I suggest you include the step identifier in the log table and the error table. When we measure performance, an internal connection between the log and process step will reveal other useful step-related information. In this way, we improve the significance of the specific measurements in the log.

The error table and error handling procedure should also contain the step, as almost all errors are related to these.

Increase the target's complexity

Think of other data elements and other data structures that will increase the complexity of the target. By other data elements, we could mean other attributes of the product, for example. You can search the internet or go to a shoe store or use common sense to detect other footwear characteristics. Increasing the variety of attributes will automatically increase the logic's complexity and bring it closer to what a real-life project means!

Moreover, you can think of other entities apart from shoes. Adding one more principal entity to the project with all its attributes will dramatically increase its complexity. Any new entity or attribute may require the associated implementation, so a lot of additional work. For example, if you are a student and want to learn how to use SQL correctly, this starting point allows you to create your SQL project. Afterward, you will be able to use this knowledge to implement similar projects in your future career. Keep in mind that my book offers a starting point, and it is up to you to continue or not. If you have the time and the energy to move forward and continue the work in this book, you can create an excellent SQL data migration product!

If you want to create a simple system, you cannot use SQL disparate blocks using PLSQL or Transact SQL code. Suppose you decide to use the database facility, using SQL Server, Oracle, SQL Postgre, or anything else. In this case, you can use the associated language to implement the data transfer process. So use Transact SQL or PL SQL, for example. The bottom line is that you could use packages to analyze Oracle or stored procedures and functions, using SQL Server, to take these two examples.

In such a case, I advise you to create a complete data transfer system using disparate pieces of code from my book and finally improve them as much as you can. For example, you can use a stored procedure for each step. In each stored procedure, you will implement the desired logic. You can decide to divide the business logic into two or more significant segments; for example, the first segment could be checking the set of consistency rules, so checking the source area using a gate. The second segment could be the population of the distribution area in the staging area. The third segment could be the filling of the target area in the distribution area. Finally, you can create a main procedure that will handle the parts.

On the other hand, if you prefer to do the exercise in Java, C # or Python, or whatever, you are free to choose any environment you consider. Using the relational database as sources and targets, you will eventually reach the SQL language. If you think it's more convenient to migrate data using C # than Transact SQL, do it! In the end, this is secondary, and my goal is not to convince anyone of anything. Being a SQL specialist, I consider SQL as the first option. Specifically, I think SQL by using SQL!

In conclusion, I believe that gathering all the code snippets into a real project could benefit some readers.

Archiving the gate

When talking about the gate, the mirror of the source system, one thing might be necessary. Before starting the process, after the checking process, and before starting the flow, it is a good idea to archive the gate. This operation is a simple sub-step or step. There are few things you should do, such as:

♣   Create a table almost identical to the gate. Moreover, I recommend adding the execution identifier to know what gate is associated with what execution.

♣ Build a step for this operation, which means add a row in the metadata table with steps and specify the details of this simple step.

♣ Create a logic to implement this archiving process. The goal is straightforward, copy the gate to this archive table.

In this way, you can always go back to the origins and check whenever there are specific problems. Sometimes, maybe Jean-Luc did something wrong, or the data from Panther was incorrect, and no one realized that in time and the data is already in Angelique's hands. Angelique and Johnny can check the gate for that specific import and can identify the issue. On the contrary, they can deny this assumption if the data is okay and look elsewhere.

The operation of gate archiving is useful, and you can implement it very quickly. Of course, don't forget to add the error handling and logging functionality to the archiving step.

Generate a new execution identifier

I will consider separating this simple logic and creating a separate step for this task, creating a new execution identifier. I continue to advise you on a few simple ones. Some of them are simpler, and others are very complex; some may be relatively trivial, and others may be real challenges. However, it is essential to make sure you try to separate every distinct step based on the goal and implementation, but especially on purpose. If the process step goal is specific, create a separate one, even if the development is trivial.

Consequently, even if this task is so simple, building a new execution identifier, the goal is distinct. As such, it is better to create a new step for this. So what do you have to do?

♣ Define a new step for this purpose, give it a name and an id, describe it in the steps table.

♣ Create a stored procedure, for example, and create a new row in the dedicated table with executions (imports). I guess you could eventually store the unique execution identifier in an output variable. However, there are other ways here.

♣ Call this in the main and take the new execution identifier and add it as a parameter for most of the steps. Alternatively, you can check by status and rely on the fact that you can have one execution in progress at a time. I assumed linearity and sequentiality here; it's a more straightforward scenario. However, in a more complex data migration system, you can consider parallelism, but this will be quite tricky and increase complexity.

Add a completion step

I would recommend a completion stage that will complete the process. You can imagine all sorts of things as part of this process. What came to my mind was the change of status in the execution table. If the execution is successful, the execution state will turn into a success. If the process is a failure and there is an error somewhere, the execution state will somehow signal this through a suitable signal.

However, there may be other things besides this update, and I advise you to try to imagine different points that may be part of the completion process.

What about Johnny and the rest?

I didn't want to create a purely technical book. As you already know, if you reach the end of it, you can see that this is a combination of technique and fiction. The fictional part of the book brings a color specific to the technical aspect. At least that's what I want to believe, as an author! I know that not everyone will agree with this approach, and I am sorry for my disappointed readers. There is also a solution for them. They can move quickly beyond the imaginary part and can go exclusively to the technical part.

When I program and look for specific technical solutions, particularly SQL syntaxes, I look at the variety that google offers. I come across particular articles and often avoid too many explanations and go straight to the syntax. I can't deny this because almost any programmer does this. We struggle in the whirlwind of our work and, most of the time, and we look for punctual solutions that will help us overcome the impasse.

On the other hand, a book does not necessarily have to be like technical documentation. It may be, and many are, but I don't believe it is a must. I wanted this SQL book to look a little different, not like an exclusively technical book. Therefore, I decided to wrap *"Speedy"* in a social uniform! Given the project's specifics, I imagined this shoe company and these picturesque characters like Angelique or Joanna.

I also wanted to present something of such a project's social dimension, and I used a satirical form so that the book would be a pleasant read. Very often, to understand a specific software product of any kind, you also need to understand the users. Over the years in the IT industry, I have had the chance to go directly to various clients in different business areas, meet users, talk to them and understand their activity areas from the most official source. If someone wants to understand, for example, the activity of shoe production, it is best to go directly to the factory! I know this is not a reasonable choice nowadays!

The little story with the two business users, Angelique and Joanna, who work on the two software systems designed as a source and target, gives life to the software systems. Consider the *"Yellow Panther"* and imagine Joanna at the computer doing accounting. Alternatively, what would *"Shoes are everywhere"* be without Angelique? She is the heart of the software application, makes the system alive! On the other hand, the technical guys represent us, programmers and business analysts, and the entire IT infrastructure. What is the *"Yellow Panther"* without Jean-Luc? He is the person who cares about the source; he is the Black Panther of the system, with his supernatural force allows him to fill the gate and handle it whenever there are issues. And the last piece of the puzzle, the brave Johnny, the *"Speedy's"* architect, the brain of such a system.

I hope that people like Johnny and Jean-Luc will read this book despite the imaginary part's unusual appearance and the book's narrative style. On the other hand, I hope this book can be accessible even to people like Joanna and Angelique. More and more people are trying to convert from various fields to IT. Maybe tomorrow, Joanna or Angelique will decide to switch to IT, which is common nowadays. Compared to other programming languages, SQL is accessible and intuitive, and business-experienced users can slowly begin to change to, why not, maybe SQL! But I'm sure other categories of people in an IT company, such as testers, business analysts, or even project managers, can read this book and gain knowledge. This target variety was a reason for this narrative style because I wanted to give accessibility to a smaller category of readers and not just programmers!

Finally, I want to end by quoting the real and famous Speedy Gonzales, *"Ándale Arriba,"* Now is your time to get to work!

12 SQL Annexa. You can always restart!

The first annexa is a SQL script that will drop all the objects from the database. If you execute this file, you will clear everything. After that, you can start everything from scratch, the exercises from the beginning. See below:

Listing 12-1 Drop all objects SQL Server / Oracle

```
-- Same script for Oracle and SQL Server.
DROP TABLE Commercial_Names;
DROP TABLE Products;
DROP TABLE Product_Types;
DROP TABLE Manufacturers;
DROP TABLE Suppliers;
DROP TABLE Languages;
DROP TABLE Countries;
DROP TABLE Gate_Details;
DROP TABLE Gate_Header;
DROP TABLE M_Settings;
DROP TABLE M_Consistency_Rules;
DROP TABLE Staging_Attributes;
DROP TABLE Staging_Products;
DROP TABLE Executions;
DROP TABLE Gate_Details_Errors;
DROP TABLE Gate_Header_Errors;
DROP TABLE M_Attributes;
DROP TABLE Stg_Mv_New_Products;
DROP TABLE Stg_Mv_Upd_Products;
DROP TABLE Stg_Mv_New_Commercial_Names ;
DROP TABLE Stg_Mv_Upd_Commercial_Names ;
DROP TABLE Errors;
DROP TABLE Log;
DROP VIEW Stg_V_New_Products;
DROP VIEW Stg_V_Upd_Products;
```

```
DROP VIEW Stg_V_New_Commercial_Names;
DROP VIEW Stg_V_Upd_Commercial_Names;

DROP PROCEDURE Handle_Errors;
DROP PROCEDURE Handle_Log;
DROP PROCEDURE Transfer_Products_Target;
DROP PROCEDURE Transfer_Products_Staging;

-- Specific Oracle objects
DROP SEQUENCE Seq_Executions;
DROP SEQUENCE Seq_Staging_Products;
DROP SEQUENCE Seq_Staging_Attributes;
DROP SEQUENCE Seq_Errors;
DROP SEQUENCE Seq_Log;
DROP PROCEDURE Check_Consistency;

-- Specific SQL Server
DROP FUNCTION Log_V_Measure ;
```